DESIRÉE WITKOWSKI, D.T.R.

The Passionate Palate

RECIPES FOR
COOKING UP A DELICIOUS LIFE

1999
Llewellyn Publications
St. Paul, Minnesota 55164-0383, U.S.A.

FIRST EDITION
First Printing, 1999

Book design and editing by Rebecca Zins
Cover art by Shelly Bartek
Cover design by Anne Marie Garrison

Library of Congress Cataloging-in-Publication Data
Witkowski, Desirée.
     The passionate palate: recipes for cooking up a delicious life / Desirée Witkowski. —1st ed.
        p.   cm.
        Includes index.
        ISBN 1-56718-824-9
        1. Women—Psychology.   2. Women—Health and hygiene.
     3. Women—Conduct of life.   4. Cookery.   5. Food—Psychological
     aspects.
I. Title.
HQ1206.W78   1999
646.7'0082—dc21

99-35769
CIP

Llewellyn Worldwide does not participate in, endorse, or have any authority or responsibility concerning private business transactions between our authors and the public.
     All mail addressed to the author is forwarded but the publisher cannot, unless specifically instructed by the author, give out an address or phone number.

Llewellyn Publications
A Division of Llewellyn Worldwide, Inc.
P.O. Box 64383, Dept. K824-9
St. Paul, MN 55164-0383, U.S.A.
www.llewellyn.com

Printed on recycled paper in the United States of America

Lead a Luscious Life

*G*o ahead—spoil yourself. Pamper your inner princess. Paint the town red, take a refreshing nap, go outside and play. Yes, play. Go on, no one's looking. You'll feel much happier if you have some fun—and so will everyone around you.

Your first step to a more delicious, delightful life is to open this book. *The Passionate Palate* is full of ideas for living well, seasoned with old-fashioned recipes and new-fashioned ways to pamper your psyche. Indulge your bodily senses—nurture your sense of daring, romance, and humor—and learn how to start living with the passion and joy you crave.

Imagine this . . . if you chose to favor fun over "sense" for just one hour a day, you could:

Laze in a shady summer hammock.

Bake peanut butter cookies with a friend.

Test-drive a car you would like to own.

Have your hair done in French braids, or another hairstyle that makes you feel beautiful.

Plant flowering sweet peas.

Buy a blouse that makes you feel valuable.

Pack up some homemade lemonade and sugar cookies and go on a picnic.

Take a moonlit walk on a beach.

Make an "inspiration book" of your goals and dreams.

Do you feel a little excited? Good. You're ready to make passion a priority. This is your invitation to eat, drink, play, relax—and begin the first day of the rest of your delightful, delicious life.

~

About the Author

$\mathcal{D}$esirée Witkowski is a Registered Dietetic Technician (DTR) with the American Dietetic Association, personal chef, food writer, and nutrition counselor. She is a graduate of the Academy of Culinary Arts in Cerritos, California, and the author of *Skinny Sandwiches* (Surrey Books, 1995), a compilation of over 130 lowfat sandwich creations. A professional astrologer for twenty years, she is an avid student of psychology, metaphysics, and the spiritual realm, fascinated by how the unseen affects our physical lives and dedicated to learning and applying life's spiritual laws.

To Write to the Author

$\mathcal{I}$f you wish to contact the author or would like more information about this book, please write to the author in care of Llewellyn Worldwide and we will forward your request. Both the author and publisher appreciate hearing from you and learning of your enjoyment of this book and how it has helped you. Llewellyn Worldwide cannot guarantee that every letter written to the author can be answered, but all will be forwarded. Please write to:

Desirée Witkowski
‰ Llewellyn Worldwide
P.O. Box 64383, Dept. K824-9
St. Paul, MN 55164-0383, U.S.A.

Please enclose a self-addressed, stamped envelope for reply, or $1.00 to cover costs.
If outside U.S.A., enclose international postal reply coupon.

*T*his book is dedicated to the women who do too much;
to those who postpone present pleasures thinking
they will enjoy themselves later.

~

What would you like your eulogy to say:
"She did her dishes well"? "She made lots of money"?
Accomplishing may pay the bills, but it's relationships and how
we've loved that we are going to think about on our deathbed.
Find your way to do both. We only become harried and lose
our center when we believe that external stuff is more important
than internal stuff. And you know—it'll all come out in
the wash. Do it now because "later" rarely comes.

~

Hold your life intentionally, as if it were
the most scrumptious chocolate eclair.

~

Live on purpose.
Live deliciously.

Contents

*For women who wish to feed their soul,
their mind, and their family.*

Introduction: Why Women, Especially, Require Pleasure   1

When things are right inside, they will go well outside.

👤 Women need to feel good as our modus operandi, yet it is against the system. When we do learn to give our feelings priority, we keep alive our spirit and passion. It is then we can be fully alive with lots of love to give— or we can continue on the downward burnout spiral by giving too much and allowing others to determine our value. Based on Jungian psychology.

Chapter 1: The Power of Food: Physiological and Psychological   11

Our eating habits have the power to energize.

👤 Food is basic to life. It is health, security, nostalgia, pleasure, comfort, and entertainment all rolled into one. What makes a food comforting begins with memories of past eating experiences. Eating to improve your mood and energy; foods that energize: protein and carbohydrates; what to eat when you are stressed out; follow your carbohydrate cravings to lessen PMS; how fat affects moods; guidelines for maintaining health under stress.

Comforts to soothe everyday stress.

🐚 Foods, tips, and philosophy to console a woman's body, soul, and spirit after a long, grueling day. Creating energy; how to take naps. Loving your body; creating a healing environment. De-stressing your chores. Your secret friends: The Crock-Pot, microwave, and restaurants; transition time; soul-nourishing and countrified meals your mother used to make: delicious meatloaves, superlative mashed potatoes, creamy scalloped potatoes, home-made pizza, Grandma's chopped liver, vegetarian lasagna, chicken in a popover, spicy oven-fried chicken, my mother's goulash, buttermilk chicken and biscuits, roasted chicken à la Crock-Pot, Sunday pot roast and gravy, pork chops and sauerkraut, old-fashioned southern banana pudding, perfect pie crusts, Aunt Lucille's best cookies, double chocolate pie, famous oatmeal cookies, Rosalie's chocolate chip sandies, pineapple upside-down cake, baked apples, design your own bread pudding, and more.

Start the day as you want it to go.

🐚 Nutritious breakfasts—a smart investment in your mood and productivity and other reasons to get out of bed: French toast drizzled with Grand Marnier, baked bananas, 7UP pancakes, scones, Auntie's potato pancakes, country egg and green onion sandwich, butter streusel coffee cake, breakfast cheese pie, farmer's breakfast, favorite blueberry muffins, best sausage and biscuits with milk gravy, a Southern-style breakfast: black ham and grits, sweet potato biscuits, sweet apple pancakes. Morning rituals, making childhood memories, investing in friendship, breakfast "feel goods."

Chapter 4: Food for Love   109

Comforts to ease frustrations over relationships.

ঌ Chocolates and carbohydrates: The perfect answer to a lonely Saturday night and other partnership-related frustrations; choosing food (particularly chocolate) and drink to elevate the mood and soothe oneself while under the strain of conflicts with self, family, and significant others: sensuous soups, strengthening cheesecakes, chocolaty desserts, crunchy lowfat snacks. Chocolate kiss cookies, strawberry soup, no-bake chocolate fudge cookies, chocolate cherry bread, five-minute California cheesecake, great-with-everything raspberry sauce, Hillary's cookie recipe, chocolate chip cookie cake, spicy beef and tomatoes, chocolate cream cheese sandwich (and a skinny version), stay-in-bed fruit and wine omelet, hot fudge sundae cake, strawberry-rose cheesecake, and more! Therapeutic suggestions for walking through the emotion: Exercise, good soul music, and friends. Get a pet. Spoil yourself. Take yourself out on a date, enjoy a glass of good wine or beer. Menu for a night of reconciliation; breakup helps.

Chapter 5: Spring and Summer Comforts   141

Creative ways to hurry up spring and ooze into summer.

ঌ Remembering how to enjoy summer as intensely as you did as a little girl: Grow something; tips for a stress-free picnic; how to be a little girl again, and more. Foods you've always loved can now help you get into your swimsuit (several are low in fat): Corn on the cob; corn dogs, corn fritters, create-your-own egg salad, wild woman wilted salad, Sloppy Joes, the perfect summer pasta salad, mediterranean pasta, fruity zucchini bread, Indian fried bread (sweet and savory), salad Niçoise, ratatouille, fluffy fruit salad, my best potato salad, green beans and ham, Auntie's sugar cookies, cinnamon cookies, quick lemon meringue pie, homemade lemonade, piña colada sundae, White Russian parfait cake, luscious lemon-lime poke cake, upside-down apple gingerbread, flower cake, soused strawberries on a

Chapter 6: Cold Weather Comforts   201

Chapter 7: Making Yourself at Home at Work 271

Put passion into your work day.

🐾 Tips for getting comfortable at work: Surround yourself with things you love, such as photographs, books, personal decorating touches, and a mug from home. Getting ready for work; commuting tips; break away at noon; build a support system at work; take full advantage of your breaks. Ways to have fun in a few minutes; lunchtime escapes: Picnics, go to the gym, go swimming, visit parks with ponds and dangle your feet in the water! Dressing for work; boosting efficiency and productivity; you're the boss. Mental vacations. How to do nothing. Snacks to keep at work and foods to brown bag. New-fashioned sandwich fillings: Fifties' cream cheese sandwich, peanut butter chow chow, Elaine's creamed tuna with noodles, all-week pasta salad, and more. Transition time; stress relievers; maximizing your weekends. Feeling at home when you travel: Suggestions for being at home in a hotel room; homey places to visit on the road; how to pick a restaurant; getting your exercise on the road.

Chapter 8: Getting Back Control 311

To alleviate stress, get back in control.

🐾 Our thoughts determine our feelings; hidden sources of stress; determining your idea of success.

Acknowledgments

I am eternally grateful when I think of the friends and family who have contributed to me and therefore to this book.

To my sisters: Eve Boston, Carol Hulka, Tina Martin, and especially Rosie Rouwhurst, who would provide me with countless variations of any recipe I needed at a moment's notice. Thank you from the bottom of my heart for your love and support, recipes, and expertise.

To my mother, Helen Witkowski, Auntie Eve Bennett, Rose Zornes, and to Aunt Lucille Parcheta for the solid, nourishing memories and recipes.

Finally, to Guy Marshall, whose humor and support inspired me with every conversation; and Donna Anderson, whose enthusiasm and recipes carried me. Sharon Dawson and Patrice Herb were a wellspring of ideas and joy. Thanks to Elaine Harvey for her friendship and support, and to Tom Schmidt for his love and computer expertise.

What a wonderful life I've had! I only wish I'd realized it sooner.

—COLLETTE

❦

Have as much fun as you possibly can.

—FROM A LETTER MY DAD WROTE TWO DAYS BEFORE HE DIED

Being a woman is delicious

Why Women, Especially, Require Pleasure

When things are right inside, they will go well outside

Being a woman is delicious. Yet making a living all too often leaves little or no room for frills. And without frills—or pleasure, or joy—we truly miss the point. Being a woman is putting your feelings first, for feelings make up our feminine side: our instinctual nature, the language of the soul. Feelings are our only reliable source of what is true for us. They are our built-in guidance system. Being in tune with our feelings connects us with spirit, our higher power, the universal flow of energy, or whatever words you use to describe God. You know you're there when it feels good. Creating ourselves moment-to-moment through our own centeredness, or what feels right and good for us, is what we're here for—what gives meaning to our lives. Most people live lives of quiet desperation, reflecting unresolved spiritual needs. Being quiet enough to hear our feelings can unify ourselves to embrace this need. Not paying attention to these basic needs can make or break all our other efforts as well, because they are related to the deepest and most fundamental roots of our existence. If we are weak

If men had hot flashes, there would be estrogen in the water.

I

here, there will be weakness everywhere, however much we try to ignore it. But if things are right inside, they will go well outside.

Physiologically, we can thank the hormone estrogen for being feeling-centered creatures. In order to be of value to ourselves, then to others, we must take good care of ourselves to operate as women. Women actually require a minimum of one hour every day to do something that feels good, tastes good, touches or smells good, to maintain emotional health. Both men and women need time out but a woman actually needs it more to revive her sense of self and soul. Our daily pleasures, our self-gratification, are just other words for self-love and self-respect.

I'm sure you've noticed that it's not always easy. Actually it tends to be against the system for us to anchor ourselves in the feminine realm in our efficient life and work environments. In a society where almost everything is affected by business and how much money is in it for us, our world values women who go, go, go. Americans have become so concentrated on work and success that they have lost the ability to relax and have fun. This is because the business world is molded by men who, on the other hand, generally need to produce before they feel good (according to *Knowing Woman: A Feminine Psychology* by Irene Claremont de Castillejo; New York: G. P. Putnam's Sons, 1973). Women are judged as acceptable according to what they do and are rewarded for outward accomplishment. "Be-ing" rather than "do-ing" isn't recognized as desirable, let alone necessary, because it does not directly make money.

Our Puritan heritage reaffirms the same prevailing attitude: work is nobler than play, pain more respectable than pleasure. A woman's power—the instinctive knowing that comes from being in touch with her feelings—according to Clarissa Pinkola Estes, Ph.D. in *Women Who Run with the Wolves* (New York: Ballantine Books, 1992), "is lost in as many ways as there are women: by becoming too involved with ego, by being too exacting, perfectionistic, or unnecessarily martyred, or driven by a blind ambition, or by being dissatisfied—about self, family, community, culture, world—and not saying or doing anything about it, or by pretending we are an unending source for others, or by not doing all we can to help ourselves."

In America, we use sex for everything except pleasure. We talk about it all the time and we eat all the time. But we care more about cholesterol than pleasure! We are the only culture that uses terms like "quickie" and "snack" to describe sex.

—ISABEL ALLENDE, "APHRODITE"

As Carl Jung, the Swiss psychologist, has pointed out,

> We are so busy doing and achieving that we have lost touch with our inner life, that life which gives meaning to symbols and conversely, the symbols which give meaning to the outer life. No other era has so totally divorced outer reality from inner reality. Never before have we been so cut off from the wisdom of nature and the wisdom of our own instincts.

Men and women often lose their sense of self through their own lack of awareness that it is happening. The problem shows up when she works hard, mentally and physically, to produce and bring home the paycheck, day and night, continually negating her body and soul's needs, or when she works in an environment that is aesthetically displeasing to her. It takes courage to announce you're taking the evening off, or to find a more suitable job that pays less, or to say "no" when you don't want to do something and it is expected of you. When a woman's feelings are not given priority, it is she who must give it to herself; otherwise her feeling-centered nature, if abandoned long enough, turns toward burnout: she becomes listless, pale, often has a faraway look in her eye, or she may start becoming angry at the world (and her PMS may reflect this), or get sick just to get some rest.

> When the culture, the society, or the psyche does not support this cycle to return home, many women learn to leap over the gate or dig under the fence anyway. They become chronically ill and purloin reading time in bed. They smile that fangy smile as if all is well and go on a subtle work slowdown for the duration (Estes, *Women Who Run with the Wolves*).

It is then that a woman must realize she needs to anchor herself once more in the pleasures that ground her in whatever way is required by her: By taking a walk, going to the gym, dancing, and so on. Many times I push myself to complete a project and I wake up the next morning exhausted. It is then I best work by putzing around the house, playing computer games, or calling a friend. This is when staring out the window is actually more productive than working.

It is every woman's responsibility to find the time to increase her sense of peace, and to have a ritual or process that helps her "come home" to herself. First make life balanced and beautiful, then concentrate on your works.

First make life balanced and beautiful, then concentrate on your works.

Your Need for Validation and Approval Can Come From Yourself!

It's natural for women to give. Giving is synonymous with having children, as they need care to survive. But we don't seem to know when to stop. We go on pleasing others more than ourselves, denying our wants and needs and satisfying others' needs first because we fear disapproval, or are afraid of appearing selfish. It's as though we're ATM machines, always available for others to draw from. Many of us are so work-oriented that we run our personal life like a business—yet giving away the store isn't good business! So we become workaholics. We get so busy that we don't know what to do with ourselves if we're not. Some of us have so many unfinished projects and so many things to be done that we become easily distracted. (Do you clean your bathroom as you get yourself ready? Or pick up the house before you get yourself dressed? Can you even imagine a man doing this?) Is it any wonder we see ourselves as incompetent if we never feel completion from one job, as the men in our lives normally do?

And have you compared yourself to other women lately—whether they be in the news, on CNN, or in bathing suit ads? They tell us to be a size 6. Because we are not a size 6 (the average American woman wears a size 14, mind you), or are not paragons of perfection as is Martha Stewart, our guilt compels us to work harder still to prove that we are good and desirable. I was at the Maverick the other night (the only dance hall in town), and two friends were envying another woman because she had what they considered the perfect figure. To me these women were missing the point. The woman who said this had the most beautiful eyes I've ever seen and was so slender she probably never dieted in her life—yet she felt she wasn't enough until she had a bigger bust. To me, it was as if all her beauty was abandoned—unclaimed, unseen, unappreciated—by the one who mattered most: Herself.

Always, always be good to yourself. Never, never beat yourself up for not being enough or doing enough. It takes away from your life force.

$\sim$

If we are going to be here to enjoy the families that we nurture,
we had better take care of ourselves,
both physically and emotionally.

$\sim$

Most of us are working two full-time jobs—in the workplace, and then at home—more than women have ever done in history. Research by the United Nations from 1875–1985 found women around the world do two-thirds the world's work and own one-hundredth of the world's wealth while making approximately one-tenth of the world's income. Arlie Hochschild says in her book *The Second Shift* (Avon, 1997) that American women, on average, work around fifteen hours per week longer than men. If anyone needs a break, it's us!

The truth is, we are already wonderful. We need not prove it to anyone. We just need to know this for ourselves and to be a model for our children, so that they don't make the same destructive sacrifices that we have when they are grown. When we choose to validate ourselves—to reclaim and retreat the quiet times (or hell-raising times) and activities that we need—those around us will also learn to value them.

In order to feel good we need to do good, by and for ourselves. And we do that with action. People who tell you that positive thinking is the way to become more successful are accurate, but one of the best ways to think positive is to draw on one's past behavior. Because thoughts are also generated by your actions in the past, a natural way to change your state of mind is to change your behavior. Go ahead and make a reservation for that seminar. Buy yourself a bottle of great perfume or a beautiful briefcase. Stretch a little. The money always comes. It certainly does for your obligations. Have you noticed?

A mark
of a true workaholic
is cleaning house
in your underwear.
—COLLETTE

～

*Giving yourself what you need
helps to eliminate bad habits.*

～

It is no secret that many of us overeat to not feel uncomfortable emotions. I used to defer loneliness and disappointment to food to the point where I had to be eating almost all the time. I was running from acknowledging an unhappy marriage and, later, from the agony of finding love again. What a life, to continually appease a pain when my "cure" caused more stress than facing the feelings! The more we face what we feel, the easier it is to deal with and then to get what we need. Today I can have a chocolate cake on the countertop for days. If I find myself overeating, I know that I'm missing something else I need. Today, I give myself what I need. Do you?

*There is no duty
we so much underrate
as the duty
of being happy.*
—ROBERT LOUIS
STEVENSON

&

When we wholeheartedly treat ourselves well, leaving no room for guilt, we eliminate the need to comfort ourselves with less-than-healthy avenues such as too much food, work, alcohol, drugs, cigarettes, television, and so on.

Being inner-directed lessens stress. Being in tune with yourself is being in tune with God. When we ask ourselves what to do and are quiet long enough to hear the answer, it's like having a hot line to God, like having a partner and consultant built-in. We make better choices. And the more we make our way back to our inner self, the easier it is to get there, and the clearer the answers—life becomes easier, less stressed.

Feeling Good Is the Healthiest Thing You Can Do

One hundred laughs a day provides a cardiovascular workout equivalent to ten minutes of rowing (according to William Fry, M.D., professor emeritus in psychiatry at Stanford University)! And surely you've noticed that you rarely feel fatigued when you're having a good time. Happy people produce more endorphins and enkephalins, brain chemicals that improve T-cell production and strengthen immunity against illness. Happiness, or what happens when we are in tune with our core energy, tends to propagate more happiness as we naturally realign ourselves with feeling good. Joy is a natural energizer!

On the other hand, if you don't acknowledge the stress in your life and find ways to reduce it, your body will respond automatically: think exhaustion, burnout, depression, flu, ulcers, backaches, as well as triggering heart disease, strokes, not to mention turning hair gray. Even everyday emotions like tension and sadness can trigger ischemia—a drop in the heart's blood supply that is often a precursor to a heart attack. In a study published in *The Journal of the American Medical Association,* negative emotions were found to more than double the risk of ischemia.

I am not advocating deliberate search for happiness for its own sake, but as a need, a prerequisite, to be in touch with God, with your soul. And it requires that we take charge of our own lives, our own bodies, and our own minds. Even if the pills, stimulants, or depressants you may take to tranquilize yourself work temporarily, they contribute nothing to your mastery of yourself, which I believe is the purpose for your being here in the first place. You soul learns nothing from a pill. Today is the only moment we have. Take it. Use it. It is your life.

Go for it!
♥

⁓

Without passion and spirit,
we are just a shell.

⁓

Keep yourself alive by honoring your personal needs because you're not really living if you don't. Detach from painful relationships, jobs, and lifestyles. Indulge in delights large and small, from balloon rides to fresh green grass, and don't be surprised to find yourself thinking about yourself. Go for it. Cherish what you're not doing and what you want to do. Only you can ground yourself in the physical world in love, in spirit.

How Can You Create a Delicious Life?

Know that you can have anything you desire, but you have to desire it more than anything. Keep your attention on the kinds of feelings you want to have by putting your attention on the people, things, conditions, and feelings you love and would like to have. We do get what we put our attention on, whether it be problems (hence we get more problems) or their solutions. Likewise, the more activities we engage in that bring us pleasure, the more will come to us. We build our life moment by moment—so start doing something good for yourself, this moment.

My Food Philosophy

Being physical beings, we need nutritious food for the maintenance and growth of our body. We are also spiritual beings, thus we need the joy that comes from treating ourselves and from the memories of the food our mother would make for us. With a little discipline and imagination, we can have a delicious healthy diet, meeting both needs.

Eat sensibly eighty percent of the time.

～

First, have a little discipline: learn the calories and fat contents of foods and it will help you to choose well. Then you'll know the nutrient difference between salad and pie. Next, have the discipline to choose the salad, then, if you're still hungry, have the piece of pie. Eat lowfat foods today, such as skipping the butter on your bread, and reward yourself with an ice cream cone tonight. Or acquaint your taste buds to foods that are a little less rich, such as Breakfast Cheese Pie (page 94) using low or nonfat cream cheese, and you will feel better with less fat and begin to prefer it.

My Life Philosophy

I believe the same balance is needed in life. We need joy as much as we need to do our daily duties. Joy gives life and meaning to our work, easing our load. Note this quote from the Bible, Luke 10: 38-41:

> On their journey Jesus entered a village where a woman named Martha welcomed him to her home. She had a sister named Mary who seated herself at the Lord's feet and listened to his words. Martha, who was busy with all the details of hospitality, came to him and said, "Lord, are you not concerned

that my sister has left me to do the household tasks all alone? Tell her to help me." The Lord in reply said to her, "Martha, Martha you are anxious and upset about many things. One thing only is required. Mary has chosen the better portion and she shall not be deprived of it."

How many times have you chosen to stay in the kitchen and work? (No one will tap you on the shoulder and tell you to start enjoying life.) We each must do it for ourselves.

Why I Wrote This Book

A few years ago I drove to my girlfriend's home in Phoenix, Arizona. She was at work, so I let myself in and I saw a note sitting on the table. She wrote, "make yourself comfortable—make yourself a cup of hot tea, take a bubble bath"—a simple, sweet note that had tremendous impact on me. I had just turned forty and realized I had not paid attention to these most basic nurturing rituals at all in my life—difficult to believe, but true. It wasn't long after that I decided to make a journal of all the nice things I could do for myself. The journaling became a book idea. The book grew and I sent it to my agent. She suggested I add recipes. Of course! What a natural combination. Five years later—here it is.

How to Make Your Palate Passionate

Embrace the people and things that you love and give them your all. After God, we are each others' highest priority. Make them more important than groups and organizations—which includes your job. Love yourself more so that you may come from love more than from duty.

If I were you, I would grab every idea in this book that I like and make it my own. Take it to bed. Take it to the dentist's office, peruse it over coffee. Write in it—add your own ideas, highlight the recipes you want to make. Execute just one of these delicious ideas and you will have paid for the book. Use two or more, and you will be on your way to making your own life delicious.

∼

Chapter 1

Food is life. Food is pleasure. Therefore, all foods are healthy!

❧

The Power of Food: Physiological and Psychological

Our eating habits have the power to energize

Too much of a good thing is wonderful.

—MAE WEST

❧

Life is best lived with undue worry or anxiety, don't you agree? Most of us tend to worry and stress constantly about what we are eating. We make a God out of food. I was on a diet since the age of ten and for thirty years I've used up more time figuring out how to eat less calories than how to be close to someone. A few years ago, I quit my obsession. A man became my obsession instead and I attached my identity to him. When he finally left, I went through the most difficult time of my life. When I thought I hit bottom, I kept on going—and lost fifteen pounds. I faced my emptiness instead of substituting yet another addiction (work, alcohol, drugs) for him. Now when I feel if I am hungry, I don't usually yearn for a man instead (well, let's say eighty percent of the time—I'm still human!) Facing my greatest fear set me free. I've kept my weight loss and haven't worried about calories or fat grams since. Now I have so much more time! I don't stress over that pint of Häagen-Dazs (I prefer light rocky road) or the extra large bag of M&Ms because they *can* fit into a lowfat diet. And if I want it, somehow I need it. When I've eaten enough, my body lets me

II

know. I swear I'll never waste another minute worrying about the fat or the calories in food. It took way too much time out of my life. Does it yours?

The nutrients in food are averaged out over the course of a day or over several days. Thus, high-fat foods—those higher than thirty percent fat— do not necessarily break your diet. The key is balance, and listening to your feelings and learning to use them as a gauge for hunger instead of your emotions. And by the way, it's perfectly natural to crave three more cookies or a dish of ice cream after a disagreement with someone. When we're stressed, we automatically crave foods that will calm us down. If you find yourself adding too many calories, short-circuit tension with quick complex carbohydrate snacks such as popcorn, fresh fruit, fig bars, lowfat cheese, and crackers.

Comfort foods are typically the carbohydrates we tend to reach for to enhance our moods— a quick fix to soothe our emotions. And for good reason: Grains, cereals, and fruits are calming.

～

Eating without knowing what nutrients are in food is like going on a blind date: You trust. Trust? Trust how you feel and how healthy you are blindly? Knowledge is power—at the office and, even more importantly, when it comes to you personally. Knowing what you are eating makes you streetwise, in control. In fact the only real power, the only real control we have, is over ourselves. Knowing the basics of nutrition is the bottom line of developing a way of eating that will keep you healthy throughout life. Besides being healthy, food affects how you feel and how sharp your mind is. That makes it too important not to grab just anything!

The Physiological Power of Food
Eating to improve your mood and energy

It will do you well to remember what you ate a few moments ago. Now, how do you feel? Whatever you eat—tuna, carrots, or a Twinkie—has the power to determine your physical and mental prowess. What you choose to eat can invigorate you or send you shuffling toward the nearest couch, according to pioneering nutrition research at the Massachusetts Institute of Technology.

Foods That Energize: Protein

Eat a lowfat protein breakfast. Your mother was right: If you don't eat a satisfying breakfast, your blood sugar drops and you'll reach for a dough-nut. This is very short-term planning because simple sugars such as doughnuts, pancakes with syrup, pastries, and most muffins shoot instant energy into the bloodstream, producing a sugar high. Insulin takes up the extra sugar, resulting in a sudden drop of energy, and we tend to become hungry, anxious, and moody by midmorning. But there's much more to protein than this . . .

Proteins help to stabilize blood sugar and provide even, steady energy. Therefore, it's appropriate to think of protein also as an energy food because it will help you to feel physically and mentally good, even stronger, not only for ten minutes, but for hours.

Protein is literally brain food. All lowfat protein foods produce quick mood-modifying and energy-boosting results. It is needed to manufacture brain tissue, enzymes, neurotransmitters, and myriad other brain chemicals. Eating protein alone or with a small amount of carbohydrates actually energizes the mind, promoting improved attention, motivation, and reaction time. That's because the presence of protein produces two neurotransmitters, dopamine and norepinephrine, which impart an "IRS brain," as I like to call it. Protein can be used as a tool to meet a mental challenge: Staying up late to study, asking for a raise, or balancing the books. Eating an omelet or lean steak, therefore, will make you more mentally "up" than muffins or oatmeal.

It follows, then, that a tuna sandwich for lunch will more likely keep you on top of things throughout the afternoon than potato soup, in which case you may not make it till afternoon break. For most people, three to four ounces of a protein food such as shellfish, fish, chicken (without the skin), veal, extra-lean beef, beans and legumes, lowfat cottage cheese, yogurt, milk, or tofu will stimulate an alertness response.

Protein is a natural antidote to mental fatigue.

Your Friend Carbohydrates

Carbohydrates boost a brain chemical called serotonin, an antidepressant depleted by fatigue, PMS, stress, and anger. Carbohydrates induce a feeling of calm and relaxation—and can make us feel more in control. When we're nervous and need to calm down and be productive, we automatically reach for a cookie or piece of candy because our body instinctively knows it will act as a mild sedative. Snacking on crackers, popcorn, or lowfat cookies on afternoon break will allow you to calmly focus and finish up the day on a productive note. If you are feeling insecure or anxious about some person, place, or thing, have a bagel, pasta, or a soft drink (not diet) beforehand and you'll not only have more pleasure per calorie, but feel more centered too.

Eat a dinner of pasta or a stuffed potato if you need to let go of anxiety or to simply rest (in other words, not the kind of dinner you would want to make for a hot date). We naturally reach for carbohydrate snacks after a long hard day when we need to unwind. Your body knows that as little as twenty to thirty grams of carbohydrates (a half bagel or a few crackers or cookies) will increase the manufacture of serotonin. You may need up to twice that amount, however, if you are twenty percent or more over your ideal weight, in the days prior to menstruation, or to ease nervousness.

Fruit alone does not set this mood response into motion as quickly as do bread products because fructose (the sugar in fruit) takes longer to digest, and therefore fails to promote serotonin production. Fruit eaten in combination with other carbohydrates such as cereal or in a cobbler, for example, will trigger a relaxation response.

Examples of Carbohydrate-Rich Foods That Are Low in Fat

Whole grain breads, rolls, cereals, and most crackers.

Corn tortillas, waffles.

Oatmeal, grits.

Lowfat cookies such as vanilla wafers, graham crackers, fig bars, and gingersnaps.

Lowfat pastries, pies, and cakes.

Pasta, rice.

Fruit.

Fat-free milk, yogurt, frozen yogurt, ice milk, popsicles, fudgsicles.

Popcorn, carmel corn, rice cakes.

Gelatin, pudding made from nonfat or lowfat milk.

Vegetables.

Jelly beans, licorice, hard candy.

IN CASE OF STRESS, TAKE . . .

1-ounce stick string cheese

½ cup baby carrots

½ cup veggies with salsa

¼ cup dried apricots

½ bagel with lowfat cream cheese

3 rice cakes with a smear of peanut butter

1 flour tortilla

～

Follow Your Carbohydrate Cravings to Lessen PMS

After ovulation, during the last two weeks of the menstrual cycle, the brain's serotonin level drops, causing a drop in mood and energy. Women crave sugar more often as a natural way to boost serotonin levels and produce calmness and mood stability. Therefore, following your natural food cravings may help mood swings and make you a nicer person to be around.

How Fat Affects Moods

A small amount of fat is satisfying. Too much fatty foods dull the mind by diverting blood away from the brain. Foods high in fat also cause serotonin to be stored rather than sent to the brain. When this occurs, the neurotransmitters cannot reach the brain and instead of calm we may feel like a lead balloon.

The weight-producing drawbacks of fat are well known. Adding more than twice the calories of protein or carbohydrates, fat is twice as likely to make you fat, which certainly is not comforting! Excess saturated fat leads to heart disease, strokes, and certain kinds of cancer. And if that's not enough, too much fat makes you sluggish. However, you do need fat, so don't sell yourself short. Your complexion needs essential fatty acids to keep skin moist and wrinkle-resistant. A fat-free diet leads to dry, red skin.

So it is all a balancing act: Up to thirty percent of our diet should be composed of fat and saturated fat to less than ten percent of calories. Therefore, indulging in desserts and high-fat snacks in moderation (only when your body craves it) and splurging on high-carbohydrate goodies the rest of the time seems the obvious answer.

Everyone is slightly different and for some people, specific foods can trigger certain moods. The key always is to understand how your food choices affect how you feel.

How to Keep Blood Sugar Levels Constant, or How to Feel Good Longer

Our body's primary source of energy is glucose. Every cell in the body requires a supply of glucose to some degree, and the brain and central nervous system depend exclusively on glucose to fuel their various processes.

This concentration of glucose in the bloodstream is called your blood sugar level. When that level drops below a certain point, the brain signals for more fuel and we reach for a sweet something to satisfy the craving.

Keeping blood sugar levels constant is the key to weight loss by eliminating hunger pangs and stabilizing emotions so that we feel better and are able to act, not react. We can do this by:

Eating several small meals throughout the day instead of two to three larger ones.

Eating balanced meals.

Eating protein with carbohydrates.

Eating complex carbohydrates (foods high in fiber) rather than simple carbohydrates (foods high in sugar), particularly raw fruits and vegetables.

Eating foods high in fructose.

Drinking more water.

Guidelines for Maintaining Health Under Stress

Eat frequently. Eat four to six small meals evenly throughout the day to keep your blood sugar levels stable (and reduce the chance of eating the bulk of your calories after 5 P.M.). A dip in blood sugar can cause irritability and fatigue. And don't go more than five hours without food. Keep snacks with you, in your purse or in your car. Plan ahead or you will very likely substitute a less nourishing food, such as a candy bar out of the vending machine.

Plan tomorrow's food today. Plan meals in advance to assure good nutrition. Pack your breakfast, lunch, and snacks the night before. Take a few minutes on the weekend to shop for at least three quick and easy midweek dinners.

Avoid caffeine (found in chocolate, coffee, tea, and cola) and refined sugar. Drink decaf for your second cup of coffee, or herbal tea (and select a helping of cottage cheese with your Danish).

Take a vitamin/mineral supplement. Take a multivitamin with close to 100% of the DV (daily value) for most vitamins and minerals. Exception: Men and postmenopausal women should look for a multivitamin with less iron (0 to 50% of the DV). A good multivitamin will help you not notice the side effects of changing hormones, as well as help the body deal with everyday stress.

Stress increases nutrient needs by as much as thirty-three percent, particularly magnesium; antioxidants E, C, and beta-carotene; the B vitamins; and iron, according to a study by the U.S. Department of Agriculture. B vitamins also enhance brain power, according to another study. People with higher levels of vitamins B6, B12, and folic acid scored the best on tests for memory, reasoning, and perception.

Working women need to pay special attention to two nutrients that are especially important to women's health that are difficult to obtain in adequate amounts from food—iron and calcium. Women have a higher need for iron because of monthly blood loss through menstruation and many women don't get enough iron from their diets. Ditto for calcium: It's easy to forget about the importance of calcium-rich foods—it is so much easier to open a can of soda rather than pour a glass of skim milk. A calcium supplement may be needed unless you get three to four servings of calcium-rich foods every day (each serving providing at least 300 milligrams of calcium). Check your vitamin label—1,000 milligrams of elemental calcium is recommended and if the only calcium you get is a glass of milk a day, a supplement with 500 milligrams should meet your needs.

Watch the alcohol. Sure, it may seem like a stress reliever (with very short-term results, as you know), but alcohol can actually add stress and contains empty calories. Try other forms of release, as suggested in this book, like eating a good meal and getting some sleep.

Watch the fat. High fat intake is linked to ovarian cancer, breast cancer, and fibroid tumors, not to mention weight gain. Cut your fat intake down by simply eating less butter, salad dressing, fatty meats, croissants, and the like. Eating more fruits and vegetables, drinking more water and lowfat or nonfat milk, and trying the new low and nonfat products filling the grocery shelves is your best option.

Give and receive hugs. We need touch as much—or more—than we need vitamin C. Without touch, babies fail to thrive and even die. Adults develop "a type of emotional scurvy, although we call it by different terms: depression, stress, anxiety, aggression, and midlife crisis . . . and treat it with drugs that don't work," according to Theresa Crenshaw, M.D., in *The Alchemy of Love and Lust* (Pocket Books, 1996).

If You Are Chronically Tired . . .

You could be iron deficient or something else may be wrong. A blood test will correctly diagnose your problem. Either way, iron losses are much greater in women who menstruate. A marginal iron deficiency reduces oxygen supply to the tissues and the brain. Oxygen-starved tissues leave you feeling tired, irritable, and unable to concentrate. The typical American diet provides only about five to six milligrams of iron in each 1,000 calories—and we need eighteen milligrams! How else besides supplements to get it? Using the old-fashioned cast-iron skillet significantly ups the iron content delivered by the diet. The iron content of 100 grams of spaghetti sauce simmered in a glass dish is three milligrams, but it's eighty-seven milligrams when the sauce is cooked in an enameled iron skillet!

To add to the complexity, iron from plants (non-heme iron) is less likely to be absorbed by the body. Heme iron, the iron present in meat, fish, and poultry, is twenty-three percent more absorbable. Eating vitamin C increases iron absorption, while antacids, tea, coffee, soy protein, wheat bran, and fiber decreases it. Therefore, eat foods that contain vitamin C at every meal and choose a variety of iron-rich foods: Clams, oysters, meat, poultry, shrimp, sardines, tofu, legumes, eggs, fish, dried fruit, molasses, whole grains, cereal, nuts, dark leafy vegetables, and brewer's yeast.

I finally figured out the only reason to be alive is to enjoy it.
—Rita Mae Brown

Never underestimate the power of home cooking

Taste Memories

Nostalgia plays a big role in food passion. Enjoying foods that brought us comfort as kids can make us feel at home, can soothe us with their familiarity, and comfort us by our knowing they will remind us of happy times. I remember Sunday dinner and the omnipresent crispy fried chicken with mashed potatoes and bowls of creamed corn. Just the thought of it, the smell and sizzle of the grease, takes me back to being a kid again. It was consistent. I could count on it every Sunday. And when I make it from time to time, I pretend, just for while, that I'm ten years old again.

Did you steal chocolate chip cookies from the clanky cookie jar after school? Or know the pleasures of licking the bowl clean? The thoughts themselves are pure comfort, and by eating these foods again we can relive the same good feelings—and they may even help us rise joyfully above a blue day.

We know that food physiologically affects us, therefore, we can largely control how we feel by choosing particular foods when we want to feel more relaxed, centered, or be more mentally aware. Why not use these old-fashioned comfort foods and their associating memories (like we used to use our teddy bears) to sink back into ourselves, to draw on the good from the past and make it yours now? It's legal, fashionable, healthy, and free!

Overeating

As we well know, eating can be a substitute for sex and love—an addiction, a driving compulsion to satisfy ourselves and make us feel whole. There are several books that address this issue, such as *Why Weigh? A Guide to Ending Compulsive Eating* by Geneen Roth and *Overcoming Overeating* by Jane R. Hirschman and Carol H. Munter.

Eating only to feel good (emotional eating) is a very common phenomenon. What is important is how we respond to it, taking care not to throw guilt upon guilt. Instead, it is more helpful to understand what is eating us. Before you turn to food for comfort, ask yourself if you're really hungry. If not, figure out what's behind your feelings. Are you feeling lonely? Ask

Eating only to feel good (emotional eating) is a very common phenomenon. What is important is how we respond to it, taking care not to throw guilt upon guilt. Instead, it is more helpful to understand what is eating us. Before you turn to food for comfort, ask yourself if you're really hungry. If not, figure out what's behind your feelings.

∼

directly for affection or companionship. Simply say, "I want some attention!" (This is preferable to not knowing what to say and saying nothing.) If you run to the refrigerator after a spat with someone important in your life, think instead of how you could build a better relationship. Is your job frustrating you? Determine whether the cure is something you can control or not. Take control and make necessary changes. Take your frustrations out in other ways, such as talking to a friend, through exercise, rigorous sports like kayaking, sex, screaming, dancing, painting, writing, or through some good emotion-wrenching music!

∽

Chapter 2

Every single day is a special occasion

❧

The Importance of Finding Pleasure

Comforts to soothe everyday stress

When was the last time you lit a few candles, placed them around the bathtub, then slipped into the warm water under a white blanket of bubbles? When did you last pour a glass of cool champagne to sip with that bubble bath—or have some just because you were in the mood? When was even your last bubble bath? If these images are more like a scene in a movie than your life, I invite you to look at whether or not you are giving yourself what you need to feel safe, valued, and vital each day. It need not be only the bathtub, yet that is a practical way to keep in touch with your female self! I keep candles around my bathtub, a rubber ducky in the corner (I love to play), and lots of creams, oils, and bath scrubs within my reach. I cannot work unless I occasionally do these little things that feel luxurious and fun. What about you? Next time, if you can do so without shocking your system, allow yourself to do what you would like to do. This is not self-indulgence, as we may have been taught. This is self-respect.

Perhaps you, like myself, were raised in the Midwest or with an "all work, no play" life and work ethic. Your parents or religion may have discouraged you from feeling your way through life, expecting you to accomplish and be proved worthwhile. Perhaps your mother never showed you, by her own example, to fulfill yourself first so that you may have more to

And what would you do," the Master said unto the multitude, "if God spoke directly to your face and said, 'I command that you be happy in the world as long as you live.' What would you do then?"

—Richard Bach, "Illusions"

❧

give others fully, in a way that is not resentful nor mechanical. If this scenario strikes a resonant chord in you, you're in good company.

The truth is we really haven't a choice. When it all sifts down, wellness demands a balance between our feelings and reason. We need to indulge because we'll lose that sparkle in our eye—because we'll look to others to fill the need if we don't (then we'll resent and try to control them and they still won't do it anyway)! We need to baby ourselves because it's our birthright. It's our modus operandi, and we cannot work well unless we do. It takes some time to form new habits, so begin slowly. Start with saying "yes" to pleasures that are cheap, abundant, and healthy, such as spending time with good friends, allowing yourself to take naps when you feel tired (if only for fifteen minutes), diving into a romantic novel, or treating yourself to a night at the theater. Start by giving yourself permission to bask, expand, let go. For at least one hour each and every day, favor sensuality over sense. Eliminate words like goal, results, and practical.

When you begin to get used to honoring yourself and your needs, there may well come a time for those "wicked" indulgences. You know what I mean—when you're wanting to be "bad," when you feel like painting the town red, buying a sequined party dress, then dancing on tables (where no one knows you, of course). Go ahead, there are days when you should stay home all day from work with a stack of movies and a giant bowl of Häagen-Dazs. These "mental health days" will become daydreams you'll think back on to relive again and again. (You may not even have to do it again!) You'll tell your kids. You'll tell your grandkids. But more importantly, you'll respect yourself for having the courage to give yourself the crazy escape you need.

You may be wondering, just where does one draw the line? You're quite safe as long as you don't turn your indulgence into a habit that hurts you. And you're probably a long, long ways from there, so keep going. Indulge all five senses, then go on to your sense of daring, your sense of romance, and your sense of humor. By the way, where's your sense of self-honor?

Little by little, slow down and notice what it is that fills and thrills you. What is it you need? Most of us want and need more quality time, good food, rewards, and plain old fun. Allow yourself to give your attention to your joy and your contentment will be an inspiration to others.

Give yourself abundant pleasure and you will have abundant pleasure to give others.
—NEALE DONALD WALSCH, "CONVERSATIONS WITH GOD, BOOK 2"

I know that I intend to feel good about how I've designed my days when I'm looking back from my rocking chair. Be the wise architect of your own life so that you may know the real meaning of success.

~

Correct any attitude you may have that it is expected by a significant other, your mother, or yourself that you are to behave in any particular way in or out of the kitchen.

~

How To Correct a Possible Slave Mentality
How not to be a slave of the kitchen

Never, under any circumstances, admit you like to cook.

Eat out or share with friends as much as possible. Choose frozen and microwavable meals. Or keep shelves well stocked with canned, frozen, dehydrated, and refrigerator foods or you will find yourself cooking the time-consuming old-fashioned way (which may be what you want). Choose!

Learn to measure by eye instead of using measuring cups and spoons.

Cook two casseroles, meatloaves, or a big pot of soup and pack in individual-serving size containers that can go straight from the freezer to the microwave or oven.

Thou wilt show me the path of life: in thy presence is fullness of joy; at thy right hand there are pleasures forevermore.
—PSALM 16:11

Absolute Must-Haves To Streamline Your Valuable Time

Microwaves, dishwashers, and garbage disposals speak for themselves, unless you've been on Mars the past twenty years. (Personally, I like to avoid high-tech devices that only add to your feeling of being rushed and out-of-control, such as a cell phone, a beeper, a fax, or a cappuccino machine.)

Crock-Pot or slow cooker: Crock-Pots will assist you in having dinner and all its accompanying aromas ready for you as you sink into the sofa.

Cordless phones: Indispensable! They give you freedom while allowing you to double up on what you're doing. You may take it to bed and talk to your honey or call a friend while taking a bubble bath, feeding your child or the cat, scrubbing cabinets, planting flowers, cooking, or pacing the floor.

Learn to love your own personal marks of time: Interesting wrinkles; a softer physique; a warmer, more serene heart; and knowing what is really important.

～

Don't be a slave to your phone or to people you would rather not talk to. Tell people that you are available only during certain hours of the day. Invest in an answering machine. You wouldn't let a strange man come into your bedroom, would you? You don't have to talk to them there either. Use it to save time by dodging calls from his ex-girlfriends, your ex-husband and/or ex-boyfriends. Choose a machine with special features, such as one that records conversations (can come in very handy with prank calls), a machine that plays messages back through the receiver (so that no one else can hear any of your phone messages), or a machine that makes it possible for you to leave a personal message for another by having them dial in a code. These features give me a feeling of control. By the way, don't live for your fax machines, e-mail, voice mail, and pagers. They're not what ultimately gives you what you really need. Use them only when absolutely necessary if you want to nourish your emotional and spiritual life. Then there are special telephone features such as call waiting and call return, which can be worth their weight in gold. Through them, you have the capability of automatically calling back your caller, which can reveal where they are calling from!

Garage-door opener: Especially important in the snowy states, these help you stay dry and warm and also makes your home safe and secure.

～

Homemade Bread and Butter

For many, bread is the heart of both breakfast and lunch. It's the one food that goes with, around, and underneath other foods and is a meal in itself. Since it's so elemental, let's buy the best or certainly our favorite. I know that everything is going to be all right when I bite into a piece of buttery toast. And if I should get tired of toast (never have yet!), there is all the variety in the world in choosing a topping—from my mother's blackberry preserves and chunky peanut butter to whipped cream cheese with lox, curried egg salad, or caviar. The simplest is usually the most overlooked and definitely the best.

How To Get Good Bread

Quick bread mix: For that yeast-like texture, try adding club soda or beer to a package of mix, stir it up, and let it sit ten minutes in a loaf pan before baking.

Frozen bread dough (white or whole wheat) in the freezer (also great for a quick homemade pizza). Buy or borrow a bread machine.

Stop by the bakery in larger grocery stores and buy a fresh loaf of the bread they're known for.

Butter your bread with love using sweet butter.

When unexpected joy comes into your life, don't hesitate—feast wholeheartedly!

Sweet Butters

To make the following sweet butters, use a rotary beater or a wooden spoon to cream ½ cup soft butter, then fold in the following ingredient(s). Refrigerate or freeze; serve at room temperature.

Honey Butter: Add ½ cup honey.

Strawberry Butter: Add 1 cup fresh strawberries and ½ cup confectioners' sugar.

Almond Joy Butter: Add ½ cup coconut, 1 tablespoon unsweetened cocoa powder, 2 tablespoons sifted confectioners' sugar, and 1 tablespoon chopped blanched almonds. This is almost too good (although we all know there is no such thing)!

Creating Energy
Or how to get more out of life

Tonight you're going to Las Vegas—so are you tired today? Heck no! Having something to look forward to creates energy. The more interest or energy we give to something, the more energy we receive from it. That's how mental energy works and that's how we get more life (and meaning) from our life. Instead of letting actions, events, or people come and go, focus on them, give them special attention, invest energy in them—and they will create more interest and energy for you.

Plan a few activities that'll really spice up your life over the next few weeks or months. Write a list and make them important to you by thinking about them and making detailed plans.

Some Things to Look Forward to:

Plan a vacation in _____.

Spend a day at a mineral spa, the beach, or a health club.

Take a class with nothing whatsoever to do with work.

Plant flowers.

Call your old friend _____(insert their name here).

Spend an afternoon in a meadow or around a pool with a sketch pad and colored pencils, a journal, a camera, or a good book.

Buy a new computer program you've wanted forever.

Enter a competition in an area where you excel.

Plan a party or a picnic.

Share a good bottle of champagne with a V.S.P. (very special person).

～

Sleep Therapy

It's one of life's pleasures, promotes a healthy body and mind, improves how you look and feel, and can even be a healthy escape! True, sleeping won't allow you to work, but it will allow you to work better when you do it. And sleeping allows the subconscious to work out our problems for us (it helps to ask it, too) and allows for deep psychological healing as well. Even though sleeping is beneficial for just about every problem, it was against my grain to take the time. Finally I learned from a self-employed boyfriend to take naps—even if it is the middle of the morning.

How to Take a Nap

Find a semidark, cozy room with shades or a nice, warm, firm blanket (so that you can pull it over your head) that you designate as a nap blanket. Every time you get under this blanket you will sleep. (It's good for the blanket to know this.) You must be warm, have a content tummy, and be in need of sleep. My boyfriend would have a shot of rum when he was serious about getting some sleep, but hot herbal tea or hot milk works just as well. If you are worried about oversleeping, set the alarm. Now pull the covers over your naked or seminaked body and close your eyes, without worry as to whether you will sleep or not. Rest is almost as good, and it almost always becomes sleep, so just rest . . .

To Help You Sleep . . .

Try reading the dictionary, or try Edgar Allan Poe's system of writing down everything that bothered him before he went to sleep.

Try it for yourself, but go one step further. Write down your worries on one sheet of paper. Then make two columns on another sheet, one labeled "Worries I can do something about" and the other "Worries I can't do anything about." This may help you to accept those things you cannot change. And the act of writing your unsettled problems actually solves the problem to a degree because it gives our subconscious something to work with, including a feeling of certainty that we know what we want instead of worrying about it.

❧

Freezer Sandwiches

To make mornings less hectic, make your lunches the night before or, for extra efficiency, certain sandwiches can be frozen a week ahead.

Prepare a supply of sandwiches at one time and freeze ahead for the whole week. Throw them in the lunchbox early in the morning and presto—they'll thaw in three to four hours, just in time for lunch.

Not all sandwiches freeze well. Do not use mayonnaise, salad dressing, yogurt, sour cream, cottage cheese, or cream cheese as they will separate or change their textures. Do not freeze egg whites, fruits such as oranges and tomatoes, vegetables (including lettuce), and very moist fillings.

To prepare a sandwich for freezing, spread a light coating of diet margarine on both slices of the bread. Other spreads that freeze well are mustard, ketchup, relishes and chutneys, chili sauce, and peanut butter. Cooked meats and hard cheeses may be frozen. Although the cheese may become crumbly, the taste is the same. Label and freeze up to one week.

God's answer to tomorrow's lunch
Meatloaf

Too much food for you? Naw. Freeze half for another time. Meatloaf can also be baked in the oven in muffin tins, (use cupcake wrappers) for individual portions.

Traditional, simple, and therapeutic when you take your tensions out by working your hands into the cool ground meat, meatloaf doesn't take long to put together, although meat departments now sell meatloaf mix ready-made. It takes its time in the oven and I love the smell as much as the taste. It's even better reheated the next day, and the leftovers also make wonderful sandwiches.

Meatloaf can even be cooked in a Crock-Pot or microwave!

Just because it's fast, it doesn't mean you can't put your heart into it. Whatever you make or buy to eat, whenever possible, make love the main ingredient, and you will be nourished on a deeper level.

—ROLANDO MARTINEZ

Crock-Pot instructions: Form meatloaf mixture over the bottom of Crock-Pot; cover and cook on low for 8 to 10 hours (High: 4 to 5 hours).

Microwave instructions: Shape one pound meatloaf mixture into 5 logs (smaller loaves cook more evenly in the microwave oven than does a single, larger loaf). Arrange logs on microwave-safe meat rack. Cover with waxed paper. Microwave on full power for 6 to 7 minutes, rotating dish once. Spoon any sauce or catsup over, then microwave, uncovered, on full power 1 to 2 minutes or until meat is at desired doneness.

How To Dress Up A Meatloaf

Meatloaf Wellington: Form meatloaf mixture into a loaf and place on a baking sheet. Open a container of refrigerated crescent dough and press perforated edges together to form one piece. Wrap around loaf. Bake as recipe directs.

Meatloaf in Round Bread: Cut thin slice from 1 round loaf of French bread and save. Scoop out the inside of the loaf. Add some of the bread crumbs to meatloaf mixture. Make meatloaf and fill bread case with it. Put the top slice back in place. Bake as recipe directs. Serve with hot tomato sauce or salsa.

Being a woman takes more time than being a man. Women need a feeling of space and breath, a chance to sink into herself. Take the time every morning to meet yourself through time alone spent in your own special way (meditation, lighting a candle, reading, walking, or standing on your head— it's different for every woman) so your life remains your life.

—JUDITH DUERK, "CIRCLE OF STONES: WOMAN'S JOURNEY TO HERSELF"

Experiment with a combination of ground meats, vegetables, herbs, filler and flavorings until you derive your own personal recipe—you just can't screw up meatloaf! This cheesy version literally oozes with cheese and makes fabulous sandwiches.

Really good meatloaf mixture can be bought from the meat counter, saving time and money too. Remember that you can use this mixture as a filling to stuff peppers, stuff cabbage, or even stuff tomatoes and zucchini for that matter. The same meatloaf mix will make excellent meatballs by adding ½ cup of gravy and pouring it over the meatballs, then baking them, covered, in a 350-degree oven for 1 hour. You can even shape them into patties, maybe add a few more herbs if you like (there is no wrong herb to use, they are all good—experiment!) and then cook them into breakfast sausage.

Our Favorite Meatloaf
with cheese and mushrooms

1 pound lean ground beef, turkey, or chicken
½ cup chopped onion
¼ cup chopped green pepper
½ cup tomato sauce
1 beaten egg (or 2 whites)
1 cup chopped mushrooms
4 ounces (1 cup) processed lowfat cheddar cheese, diced, such as Velveeta
2 slices of bread, torn into small pieces
½ teaspoon chili powder
⅓ cup chili sauce

Combine all ingredients except chili sauce and shape into loaf in baking dish. Spoon chili sauce over loaf and bake at 350 degrees for 1 hour. Makes 4 servings.

Per serving: 210 calories; 20 grams protein; 16 grams carbohydrate; 8 grams fat; 3 grams saturated fat; 80 mg cholesterol; 558 mg sodium; 1.94 grams fiber.

I used to think of meatloaf as boring until I separated from the standard recipes. Meatloaf is a wonderful medium for experimentation. If you really like pizza, for instance, make this taste even more like one, adding pepperoni, chopped green pepper, and onions. This is my sister Eve's best meatloaf recipe. It rather tastes like pizza.

Eve's Italian Meatloaf

¾ pound lean ground beef
½ pound seasoned pork sausage
½ medium onion, finely chopped
½ cup parmesan cheese
1 tablespoon fresh parsley
½ teaspoon each dried oregano and basil
⅛ teaspoon black pepper
¼ teaspoon each thyme, sage, and fennel seeds
¾ teaspoon garlic salt or powder
1 egg, beaten
1 cup spaghetti sauce, canned
½ cup sliced black olives, optional
1 cup mozzarella, shredded

Put on your favorite music and feel your way into making meatloaf. Combine all ingredients in a large bowl, except mozzarella, using your hands. Divide in half and transfer to an 8-inch glass pie plate. Sprinkle with mozzarella. Cover with the rest of the meat mixture. Pat into a loaf. Bake for 45 minutes at 350 degrees. Makes 8 servings.

Per slice: 452 calories; 33 grams protein; 4 grams carbohydrate; 33 grams fat; 13 grams saturated fat; 141 mg cholesterol; 777 mg sodium; .6 gram fiber.

Comfort food at its best
Potatoes

There is probably no comfort food more beloved by Americans than steaming hot, buttery mashed potatoes. Just try them next time your nerves or your soul needs a little soothing.

Potatoes are made up of complex sugars that are very quickly absorbed into the bloodstream—even more quickly than bread, but nobody ever mentions a "potato high."

Spoon into a pottery bowl, sit in an armchair or rocker, and enjoy.

*M*ashed Potatoes from Scratch

Steam your face over the potatoes for a two-minute beauty treatment.
～

6 medium-size baking potatoes, peeled and cut
   into ½-inch pieces (about 2 pounds)
5 cloves of garlic, unpeeled
½ cup butter, melted (1 stick)
¼ cup half-and-half or whipping cream
   Salt and freshly ground white pepper
4 strips of lean bacon, rendered, drained, and diced, optional
¼ cup minced parsley, optional

Cook potatoes and garlic cloves in boiling, salted water until just tender when pierced with a wooden skewer or small, sharp knife, about 15 to 20 minutes. I like to cook nearly everything in a pot with high sides to prevent spillage and make clean-ups easier. Avoid overcooking. Drain; return potatoes to the pan over heat, and shake the pan until excess moisture evaporates. Mash potatoes with potato masher (leaving a few lumps to fully enjoy the homemade quality) or use a ricer and press into a large bowl. Stir in melted butter and cream; beat on medium speed with an electric mixer until smooth. Salt and pepper to taste. Add bacon and parsley, if desired. Makes 6 servings.

Per ⅔-cup serving: 286 calories; 3 grams protein; 32 grams carbohydrate; 16 grams fat; 10 grams saturated fat; 45 mg cholesterol; 170 mg sodium; 1.2 grams fiber.

I love homemade mashed potatoes as much as anyone, but I rarely take the time so have learned to compensate with a good brand of instant mashed potatoes and some extras.

Heavenly Instant Mashed Potatoes

Spike instant mashed potatoes with key condiments such as extra butter, cream, sour cream, cream cheese, whipping cream, and minced garlic. Then, if I'm adventurous, I might give it some chopped herbs like fresh basil, parsley, sage, tarragon, dill, saffron, or curry, maybe grated parmesan, or even goat cheese!

Southern Mashed Potatoes: Add crisp, crumbled bacon.

German or Polish Mashed Potatoes: Add sauerkraut, sausage chunks, and chopped onion.

Light Cheesy Mashed Potatoes: Drop 2 slices of fat-free cheese into the hot water before adding the potato flakes.

Bugs Bunny Potatoes: My mother lured us into eating carrots by cooking and mashing them together with the potatoes. How beautiful they are! Mash cooked carrots with potato masher. Blend in instant mashed potatoes. Garnish with chopped parsley.

Improve instant gravy mix by using a lowfat creamer or evaporated milk, for example, instead of water.

❦

You might turn up your nose at these, and then again you might like the idea of serving mashed potatoes as pancakes.

Old-Time Potato Pancakes

All you do to make them is to start with leftover mashed potatoes, add a bit of fresh parsley if you like, and moisten with milk, if potatoes are stiff. (Feel as you go.) Using your hands, form into ½-inch thick pancakes. Pan-fry in a medium skillet until lightly brown.

Gravy is nourishing from the inside out. Open a can of homemade gravy, or make it from scratch.

Homemade Gravy

1 cup chicken or turkey broth
2 tablespoons flour
¼ cup skim (or richer) milk
Sliced mushrooms, optional
Salt and pepper to taste

Heat broth in saucepan over medium heat. Combine flour and milk in a jar and shake until mixture is well blended and free of lumps. Add to broth. Cook over medium heat, stirring constantly until thick. Stir in mushrooms, if desired. Add salt and pepper, reduce heat, and continue to cook, stirring to desired thickness. Makes 1 cup.

Per ⅓ cup serving: 80 calories; 7 grams protein; 9 grams carbohydrate; 2 grams fat; .7 gram saturated fat; 4 mg cholesterol; 577 mg sodium; .3 gram fiber.

If you have two or more teenagers, you may want to invest in a freezer. Not only will that make it possible for them to prepare their own meals when you're not available, but it will also teach self-sufficiency. Stock frozen dinners, microwavable hamburgers on a bun, pizzas, chicken breasts, shrimp, and all kinds of novelty frozen foods now available.

～

This is my kind of dinner when what I am really wanting is dessert.

Baked Sweet Potatoes

Sweet potatoes
Whipped butter
Brown sugar, optional
Crushed pineapple, optional
Flaked, sweetened coconut, optional

Prepare as for baked potato and serve with butter. For extra garnishing, sprinkle on the brown sugar and crown with a few spoonfuls of crushed pineapple and coconut.

For 1 baked sweet potato: 117 calories; 2 grams protein; 28 grams carbohydrate; 0 gram fat; 0 gram saturated fat; 0 mg cholesterol; 23 mg sodium; 3.4 grams fiber.

The perfect baked potato is a versatile, wholesome comfort food, eaten plain, with salt, salsa, Dijon mustard, plain yogurt, sour cream, or whipped butter. Or stuff it with one of a million fillings, such as chicken chili, tuna salad, or chilies and cheese; see Index under potatoes.

The Perfect Baked Potato

To Microwave: Scrub well and pierce with a fork. Cover with Saran Wrap if you wish to have an extra-moist potato. Arrange potatoes 1 inch apart on a paper towel. Turn over and rearrange after half the time. To open, cut an X just through the skin.

AMOUNT	MICROWAVE TIME	STANDING TIME
1	3 to 5 minutes	5 to 10 minutes
2	5 to 7½ minutes	5 to 10 minutes
3	7 to 10 minutes	5 to 10 minutes
4	10 to 12 minutes	5 to 10 minutes

Look for what you want to see (ignore the rest)!

To bake: Start with a baking potato, say a russet. Wash and dry it and rub with a little oil. Pierce with a fork and bake at 400 degrees about 45 minutes (for 6-ounce potatoes) or up to 70 minutes (for larger ones).

To slow cook in Crock-Pot: Wash and grease small baking potatoes with margarine or butter and place in Crock-Pot. Cook at low 8 to 10 hours, or at high 4 to 6 hours.

~

Devoting time to your family and friends is the best investment you can make.

~

Whatever You Acknowledge Will Bring You More of It

When you look around your home, what do you look for? How beautiful it is? Or what's right about it? Or do you see dust, clutter, or that it isn't nice enough? Normally I look for things to pick up or rearrange, but since I started appreciating how pretty and clean my apartment looks, the landlord said I could get new carpet, I found some great track lighting for a little bit of nothing, and a friend brought over a huge bouquet of flowers. We get what we wholeheartedly put our attention on. Look for what you want to see!

When you're on your deathbed, what are you going to wish you did more of? Clean the house? Work harder on that project? Heck no! You'll probably wish you spent more and better time with your family, friends, your significant other, and kids. Now keep that in mind next time you do housework!

Dull women have immaculate homes.

—A WELL-LOVED LICENSE PLATE FRAME

Create a Healing Environment

The kitchen isn't just a place where food is cooked, it is a place to live. Make it your own private universe—a place where you can please yourself and others. Surround yourself in your kitchen with things you love. Perhaps a television set, stereo speakers, an old fashioned lamp, framed prints of food or your loved ones. The most natural things to decorate with are wire baskets of fruit, crockery jars filled with kitchen tools, and so on, but don't be limited by typical kitchen paraphernalia if that doesn't suit you

Make it more of a gathering place with couches—or more like a den with books—or a living area with flowers if you like that. If you don't have a window at the stove or the sink, place a painting or a photograph that stirs you wherever you spend the bulk of your time.

Paint the kitchen a happy color; don't make it look sterile and institutional unless you like it that way. Create it to fit the way you cook and want to live. If you create an environment that vibrates with who you are, you will want to be there.

Love Your Body;
Love Your Self

Service yourself. A hand massage with lotion takes only a minute. We tune up our car because a car is a necessity we trade in after a time. What about our bodies? Respect your beautiful body by grooming and taking good care of it.

Give your arm, your hand, your shoulder, a kiss! I dare you. (No one else has to know.)

Get in tune and stay in tune with your feelings. You may never have to diet and always have an inside edge.

Only look in the mirror at a part of your body that most pleases you. Give that area most of your attention.

Buy clothes that are attractive and that you like now—don't wait until you lose weight. Resume an activity that you enjoyed when you were thinner.

Nibble throughout the day: Eat five to as many as nine mini-meals and you won't overeat at night. (Women need on the average only 400 calories past 6 P.M.)

Snack on the foods that you love and you won't binge.

Take pride in your body and in your sexuality. Acknowledge the need for physical touch and the need for sexual expression. Promise yourself that you will meet both your physical and sexual needs responsibly.

Have a favorite bowl. Perhaps it is wooden or a heavy ceramic that feels good with your fingers wrapped around it. Eat your mashed potatoes in it, curled up in your most comfortable chair.

~

De-stress Your Chores

If you've got to clean, there are ways to have a good time doing it, or at least to make it interesting! I'll combine unlike chores, and that way I get a heck of a lot done. For example, ironing takes no conscious thought for me, so when I iron, I can listen to a tape, brainstorm a new idea, plan the week, think through a problem, and make decisions. Or I could be watering the lawn, letting my toenails dry, backing up the computer, or whatever—you've got the idea. That way ironing could almost be called interesting!

How To Make Housecleaning Easier (and Maybe Even Fun)

Praise yourself for every accomplishment, no matter how seemingly insignificant.

Change the way you look at it. Stop pushing for perfection. So what if your floors aren't clean enough to eat off of—when is the last time you wanted to? Do the things that really matter, and give yourself a break on the rest.

Play the kind of music that energizes you as you work.

Get a timer and clean by the clock—say, fifteen or thirty minutes a day instead of by the job.

Make housework equivalent to a workout. Strap on the ankle weights as you dust and vacuum; mop and scrub with rhythm and gusto; do sit-ups between chores; put your whole body into a single task and use all your muscles as you stoop to pick up clothes or scrub a countertop.

Get the book *Speed Cleaning* by Jeff Campbell and the Clean Team (Dell Publishing Co., Inc., New York) to find out how to clean a house in forty-two minutes! Then make an apron as directed in the book or buy a carpenter's apron that hangs around the neck and fill it full of cleaning supplies. This will take hours off the job.

Don't sacrifice peace of mind. Buy time for yourself.

And Hire Househelp!

Don't waste dollar time on penny jobs. If your life and mental health are too important to clean up things that will be dirty two days later, hired househelp may save your sanity.

Paying for housecleaning is only a waste of money if you're not making good use of the time you've saved. But if you're spending time thinking or even reading a magazine or newspaper for ideas, the time is well spent! The cost may not be as much as you think. Private cleaners generally charge less than cleaning companies. Homeowners pay individuals wages ranging from thirty to seventy dollars—a small price to pay to remove a major stressor (particularly if you are sharing a house), have a sparkling space to come home to, and have more leisure time. Often a biweekly cleaning is enough.

Consider other services such as a tailors, a laundry service, and part-time cooks who will prepare meals and freeze them for rest of the week.

Want To Get Help with Housework?
Here Are Some Tips:

Don't be afraid to ask. Often people don't pitch in because they are not noticing, don't realize you expect them to help, or don't see it as a priority.

Assign specific tasks.

Get out of their way.

Don't feel sorry for them or get angry at them because they don't look happy while they are doing chores.

Don't criticize their work.

～

Spend at least fifteen minutes per day doing something with each child—quality time with just the two of you.

～

TAKE CONTROL OF YOUR ENVIRONMENT: IT LOWERS STRESS!

Keep lists.

Take notes.

Get it off your mind!

It gets it off your mind and you've got the information. Keep a notebook and a peel-and-stick pad in your purse and scrap paper everywhere. Make a list with what you wish to accomplish that day the night before or that morning, then number according to priority. When I number them, organization cuts through the confusion and I also am more likely to accomplish them—and faster, too.

～

Today's packaged potato mixes are rather magnificent—rich with cheese and plenty of butter, which are a breeze to make and taste like Mom's. You can add a cup or two of sliced or chopped ham to either packaged mixes or homemade to make this a meal.

Creamy Scalloped Potatoes

3 tablespoons butter
2 pounds (6 medium) boiling potatoes, peeled and thinly sliced
1 teaspoon salt
1 cup coarsely grated extra-sharp cheddar cheese
2 cups milk or half-and-half
Bread crumbs, optional

Your real niche in life is not what you do but who you are.
—REV. DOREEN RING

Preheat oven to 350 degrees and butter a 2-quart shallow baking dish. Overlap the potatoes in 3 layers, sprinkling each layer with a little salt and one third of the cheese. Pour the half-and-half over the potatoes, just enough to cover them, and dot the top with the remaining butter.

Note: Scalloped potatoes may be prepared up to this point 2 hours ahead and kept covered.

Bake for 1 hour and 15 minutes, covered. Halfway through, spoon milk over the top layer of potatoes and sprinkle bread crumbs on top. Finish baking, uncovered, until potatoes are tender and top is golden. Serves 4.

Variations: Fold in bits of crispy fried bacon, jalapeño peppers, herbs and sour cream, mushrooms, or other flavoring ingredients you love.

Per serving: 349 calories; 8 grams protein; 51 grams protein; 13 grams fat; 5 grams saturated fat; 28 mg cholesterol; 747 mg sodium; 1.8 grams fiber.

All right, all right—who wants to make a pizza, you ask? Because making pizza can be fun and creative, too. Design it by halves, or in six sections with different toppings: Seafood, pepperoni, anchovies, prosciutto, ham, Swiss cheese, different colors of bell peppers, pesto, mushrooms, and different kinds of cheese. Got the picture? Whether you buy it or make it, tomorrow morning you can wake up to leftovers and be just six seconds away from total bliss!

And if you're having company, pizza may be your number one consideration. Pizza is considered "the top food for bringing people together," according to a national poll, and America's preferred lunch and dinner entrée.

Homemade Pizza

1 refrigerated pizza crust or precooked Italian bread shell
1 (15-ounce) jar pizza sauce
6 ounces part-skim mozzarella cheese, grated
2–3 cups fresh sliced vegetables such as sliced mushrooms;
    chopped green or red pepper; broccoli florets;
    sliced tomato; onion; and spinach
    Optional toppings: shrimp; pepperoni; sliced, chopped ham;
    cooked sausage; prosciutto; sliced olives; anchovies; capers;
    pine nuts; fresh or dried basil; oregano; fennel seed;
    assorted cheeses such as fontina, smoked mozzarella,
    grated Parmesan, Romano, Gruyère, Gorgonzola, blue,
    mild goat cheese; and all kinds of mushrooms, cut into
    thin strips and drizzled with olive oil

Place dough round on oiled pizza pan. Pour pizza sauce over crust and sprinkle with cheese. Prebake pizza at 450 degrees for 3 to 4 minutes. Remove from oven and arrange desired toppings. Return pizza to oven and bake 15 to 20 minutes or until crust is lightly brown and cheese is melted. If desired, remove from oven and sprinkle with more mozzarella cheese, and return to oven just until cheese melts. Makes 8 servings.

Per serving, with cheese and vegetables: 188 calories; 9 grams protein; 24 grams carbohydrate; 6 grams fat; 2 grams saturated fat; 12 mg cholesterol; 450 mg sodium; 1 gram fiber.

STOCK UP!

Good food is an investment in your physical and emotional health. To save time, eat more nutritiously, and feel good knowing you have a potential meal at home, stock up! Keep these items on hand:

Packaged salad and sauce mixes

Seasoning packets and prechopped garlic

Salad fixings for tossing a salad in a flash

Fast-cooking rice, pasta, and grains, such as couscous (cooks in two minutes!)

Instant pasta mixes

Black beans

Canned soups

Chili

Tuna

Tomatoes

Cold cereal

Already grated or shredded cheese

Yogurt

Fruit

Breads and rolls

～

With pesto and a good crust, who needs sauce?

Pizza Nuda

Make or buy the best crust you can find—perhaps a thin Italian bread shell. Spread a thin layer of pesto over the shell, followed by mozzarella or an Italian cheese mix. Top this with your choice of topping: sliced fresh tomatoes and fresh herbs, such as thyme, oregano, sage, parsley, cilantro, and so on. (No sauce, just pesto, cheese, and toppings.)

Jewish comfort food, but you need not be Jewish to love it.

Grandma's Chopped Liver

2 onions, sliced
¼ cup oil
2 pounds chicken livers
4 large mushrooms, sliced
1 apple, peeled, cored, and sliced
2 tablespoons brandy or cognac
2 hard-cooked eggs, peeled
   Salt and pepper

Sauté onions in oil until lightly browned. Add livers, mushrooms and apple and sauté, turning livers until brown on both sides. Do not overcook. Add brandy and simmer 5 minutes. Coarsely grind or chop liver mixture and eggs together. Season to taste with salt and pepper. Line mold with wax or parchment paper and spoon in liver mixture. Cover and refrigerate. Serve with crackers. Makes 10 servings.

Per serving: 229 calories; 24 grams protein; 11 grams fat; 3 grams saturated fat; 6 grams carbohydrate; 614 mg cholesterol; 106 mg sodium; .5 gram fiber.

Layered comfort food: Perfect for a party and everyone loves it. All you need to add is garlic bread and a salad. If there are any leftovers, they freeze well.

Vegetarian Lasagna

    1   (26-ounce) jar spaghetti or marinara sauce
   10   lasagna noodles, cooked and drained
    1   (15-ounce) container light ricotta cheese
    2   cups part skim mozzarella cheese, shredded
   ½   cup Parmesan cheese
    2   eggs
    2   tablespoons dried basil or ½ cup chopped fresh basil
   1¼   teaspoons garlic powder
    3   packages (10 ounces each) frozen chopped spinach,
            cooked in microwave and well drained
    1   (15-ounce) jar roasted red peppers

In bottom of a 12 by 8-inch baking dish, place ½ cup spaghetti sauce, spreading evenly. Top with a layer of 2 noodles.

In a bowl, mix together ricotta cheese, ½ cup mozzarella cheese, parmesan cheese, eggs, basil, and ¾ teaspoon garlic powder until well blended. Remove 1½ cups and set aside. Spread remaining ricotta mixture evenly over noodles. Top with another layer of noodles.

Mix reserved 1½ cups ricotta mixture with spinach and remaining garlic powder until well blended. Spread evenly over noodles. Top with another layer of noodles. Then arrange roasted peppers evenly over top of noodles. Cover with foil.

Place on a baking sheet. Bake in preheated 350-degree oven 30 to 40 minutes or until hot throughout. Makes 10 servings.

Per serving: 402 calories; 20 grams protein; 8 grams fat; 4 grams saturated fat; 24 grams carbohydrate; 67 mg cholesterol; 739 mg sodium; .11 gram fiber.

Never assign two or more children to the same task—they'll end up bickering over who isn't doing his or her share. Instead, give each child a separate chore. You'll get a lot more done—with a lot less arguing.

When the family is going through a challenging time, this meal-in-a-skillet can break the tension: It's fun and has mystique. And you may tuck little presents within the crust to bake and transform the tension to joy!

I love this hearty, colorful one-dish meal. The popover is much like eating a biscuit topping.

Chicken in a Popover

2 teaspoons dried thyme
½ teaspoon garlic powder
1½ teaspoons dried tarragon
1½ teaspoons rosemary, crumbled
1 teaspoon onion salt
Dash black pepper
⅓ cup all-purpose flour
1 frying chicken, cut up (skin removed, if desired)
1-2 tablespoons olive oil
1 (15-ounce) can potatoes, rinsed and drained
1 (15-ounce) can carrots, rinsed and drained
1 (15-ounce) can corn, rinsed and drained, optional

Popover batter

5 eggs, separated
2 cups skim milk
2 tablespoons margarine
2 cups all-purpose flour

Combine spices in a jar; cover and shake to combine. Pour flour and half the spices in a paper bag. Drop chicken pieces into bag and shake to coat thoroughly. Spray skillet with nonstick vegetable spray and olive oil. Brown chicken over medium-low heat.

Meanwhile, beat egg whites in a large, clean glass, aluminum, or copper bowl. Add milk, egg yolks, and margarine. Sift flour into liquid and beat until blended.

Coat a 10-inch cast-iron skillet (or 4 smaller ones) with nonstick vegetable spray. Place in 425-degree oven for 5 minutes or until it smokes. Pour batter into pan. Arrange chicken in batter. Dump vegetables on top of chicken. Sprinkle with remaining herb mixture. Bake at 425 degrees for 30 minutes (and no peeking)! Makes 8 servings.

Per serving: 470 calories; 34 grams protein; 41 grams carbohydrate; 18 grams fat; 5 grams saturated fat; 223 mg cholesterol; 583 mg sodium; 3.1 grams fiber.

~

Easy and elegant, pasta is primarily carbohydrates, which will relax you and encourage sleep. (Thus not recommended for a sensuous evening.)

Pasta with Freshly Ground Cheese

1 pound cooked pasta
2 tablespoons warm olive oil
4 crushed cloves garlic (or use granulated)
¾ cup freshly grated Parmesan, Romano, or Mizithra cheese

Toss pasta with olive oil, garlic, and cheese. Makes 6 servings.

Per serving: 368 calories; 13 grams protein; 60 grams carbohydrate; 8 grams fat; 2 grams saturated fat; 8 mg cholesterol; 226 mg sodium; .15 gram fiber.

Keep parsley fresh by inserting stems in a glass filled with water, like a little bouquet, then covering with a plastic bag. This same technique will keep celery fresh for weeks.

Create a day in the Ozarks with this menu: Spicy oven-fried chicken; cheesy mashed potatoes (add a few cheese slices to hot water when making instant); creamed corn; tossed salad (prebagged); and rolls. Put on some honky tonk or Cajun music such as "Honky Tonk Cajun Songs" by Jole Blon or "Alabama's Greatest Hits" by Alabama, a jug or Mason jar of apple wine, a checkered tablecloth or patchwork quilt—why not make it a picnic in the living room? Now disconnect the phone.

In less than an hour, you can have crispy chicken, sans the fat and the work. This juicy oven-fried chicken is sensuously comforting to eat alone or with loved ones around your table (children love it). Be sure to save some white meat for a sandwich tomorrow.

Spicy Oven-Fried Chicken

The only mark there is to leave is Love; all else is a watermark.

—REV. DOREEN RING

1 envelope chicken coating mix such as Shake 'n Bake, or:

½	cup enriched white or yellow cornmeal
½	cup all-purpose flour, sifted
1	teaspoon onion salt
¼	teaspoon pepper
½	teaspoon oregano, crushed
2	teaspoons chili powder
¼	teaspoon garlic powder
1	(3½-pound) frying chicken, cut up and skinned
¼	cup butter or margarine, melted

Turn oven to 375 degrees. Pour commercial chicken coating or the first 7 ingredients into a paper bag. Place chicken pieces, one at a time, in bag and shake to coat.

Place chicken on a large, shallow baking sheet and drizzle with melted margarine or butter. Bake for 45 minutes or when juices flow clear when pierced with a fork. Makes 8 servings.

Per serving: 525 calories; 55 grams protein; 12 grams carbohydrate; 27 grams fat; 7 grams saturated fat; 212 mg cholesterol; 327 mg sodium; .67 gram fiber.

Make a big pot of something, then you know there's always enough. The "something" Mom would make is goulash. My sister Tina and I still love it and make it for ourselves, but now I substitute bow tie pasta for the elbow macaroni and add the colored peppers for flair.

My Mother's Goulash, Dressed Up

2½ cups (6 ounces) bow tie pasta
1 pound lean ground beef
1 (15-ounce) can tomatoes with juice
1 (8-ounce) can tomato sauce
1 onion, chopped
1 clove garlic, minced
1 green, 1 red, and 1 yellow bell pepper, chopped
1 (4-ounce) can sliced mushrooms
1 (10-ounce) can whole kernel corn, drained,
    optional (Mom's addition)
1 (4-ounce) carton lowfat sour cream, optional
2 teaspoons basil, crushed
2 teaspoons paprika
    Garlic salt
    Your favorite herbal seasoning
    Parmesan cheese

This above all: to thine own self be true.

—WILLIAM SHAKESPEARE

Cook pasta in boiling, salted water until tender; drain. Meanwhile, coat skillet with vegetable spray and brown ground meat, stirring to keep fine until grey in color. Add tomatoes and break up with a wooden spoon while adding tomato sauce, onion, garlic, chopped peppers, and mushrooms (and corn, optional). Simmer for 30 minutes or until peppers are soft. Add pasta to meat mixture in pan and stir to combine. Stir in sour cream if you're using it; cook and stir until warmed through. Season to taste with basil, paprika, garlic salt, and herbal seasoning. Serve with Parmesan cheese. Makes 6 hearty servings.

Per serving: 292 calories; 22 grams protein; 22 grams carbohydrate; 13 grams fat; 5 grams saturated fat; 62 mg cholesterol; 564 mg sodium; 3 grams fiber.

Time-Saving Cooking Hints

Be prepared for the labor of weeknight dinners by having timesaving items stashed away on your shelves.

Make salad for a week. Clean, dry, and tear enough greens and vegetables for salads. Refrigerate greens in a plastic bag or airtight container for up to five days.

Place a combination of chopped celery, onions, and sweet peppers in small freezer bags, then seal, label, and freeze. Add as a quick, no-mess flavoring to soups, stews, and stir-frys.

Cook up a big batch of rice, pasta, or dry beans, then divide it into family-size side-dish portions and freeze for reheating in the microwave oven another day.

Shred some cheese or buy preshredded for topping pasta, potatoes, casseroles, salads, and soups during the week.

When freezing ground meat, place ½ pound in a gallon-size plastic food storage bag and then press until it is very thin. Expel the air, seal, and freeze. Meat freezes and thaws faster or cooks quicker from the frozen state.

Keep a storage container in your freezer to store small amounts of leftover vegetables. When you're in a pinch for dinner, you'll have the makings for vegetable soup right in the freezer.

Get a jump on chilled salads or desserts by keeping cans of frequently used fruits, vegetables, and meats on hand in your refrigerator.

Don't cook!

Your approach to life determines if you win or lose.
—REV. DOREEN RING

～

*Now what were your mother's recipes that you loved most?
Think about several foods that you used to be crazy about
when you were a child. Choose your favorites, write them
down here, and make them in the next few days.*

～

This is lovely, old-timey chicken and biscuits: A dish that gives you more of what you cook for! Allow yourself up to two hours for this dish to bake and enjoy the time therein: Make chocolate chip cookies using only your hands (no spoons) to mix the batter, balance your checkbook with Beethoven, stretch your gorgeous body to Natalie Cole. Whatever you do, do it sensually. Serve with cream-style corn and a green salad.

Buttermilk Chicken and Biscuits

- 1 (3½-pound) frying chicken
- 1 stalk celery
- 2 cups buttermilk
- ⅓ cup all-purpose flour
- ¼ teaspoon salt
- ⅛ teaspoon pepper
- 1 tablespoon parsley
- 2 teaspoons cornstarch

Biscuits

- 2 cups all-purpose flour
- 3 tablespoons freeze-dried chives, optional
- 2 teaspoons baking powder
- ¼ teaspoon baking soda
- ¼ teaspoon salt
- ¼ cup chilled light margarine, cut into small pieces
- ¾ cup buttermilk

Cut chicken into pieces, reserving the back, wings, and giblets. Soak the chicken for half an hour in buttermilk. Meanwhile, to make the gravy, cook the back, wings, giblets, and a stalk of celery in a pot with enough water to cover. Bring to a simmer. Reduce the broth until fully flavored, thicken slightly with cornstarch, and pour into a 9 by 13-inch pan.

Remove the pieces from the buttermilk and drop into a bag containing the flour, salt, pepper, and parsley. Coat a large skillet with butter-flavored vegetable spray and slowly brown chicken pieces until golden. Pour the remaining buttermilk in a 9 by 12-inch baking dish and add the browned chicken. Bake, uncovered, in a 250-degree oven until tender, 1½ to 2 hours or until tender.

Meanwhile, prepare the biscuit dough:

Combine flour, chives (optional), baking powder, soda, and salt in a bowl; cut in chilled butter or margarine with a pastry blender until the mixture resembles coarse meal. Add buttermilk and stir just until dry ingredients are moistened.

Turn dough out onto a floured surface and knead 4 or 5 times. Roll dough to a ¼-inch thickness; cut with a biscuit cutter and place them next to each other right in the 9 by 13-inch pan containing the broth. Bake at 450 degrees for 12 minutes or until golden. Makes 1 dozen biscuits.

The chicken will be deliciously crisp, and a good gravy for the biscuits may be made by adding milk to the drippings, thickening with flour or cornstarch if necessary. Makes 8 servings.

Per serving: 590 calories; 54 grams protein; 27 grams carbohydrate; 28 grams fat; 8 grams saturated fat; 193 mg cholesterol; 449 mg sodium; .90 gram fiber.

With a little planning, you have immediate gratification!
Slow and Easy: The Crock-Pot

If you love to come home to good food but don't love the time or work it takes, you're crazy if you don't start using a Crock-Pot. Dispassionately throw a variety of ingredients into the crock pot before you go to work and the combination will have magically transformed to a whole new identity six to nine hours later when you walk through the door. Think of it as a live-in cook. They bring harmony to a piece of meat, vegetables, and herbs, melding flavors magically together while you play or do something more meaningful. Soups, stews, chili, roasts, beans, steamed breads, puddings, meatloaf, and even hot punch can be made in a Crock-Pot.

∼

GENERAL RULE OF THUMB:

Use the low setting when you leave a slow cooker unattended. If you are at home and eager for dinner, switch it to high. Exact timing is not critical.

Fast Advice on Slow Cooking

Crock-Pots can cut down on actual preparation time by cooking in large batches for you to put up half in the freezer.

Buy a larger Crock-Pot than you think you'll need because a Crock-Pot cooks more efficiently when it is half full.

Don't worry about leaving the Crock-Pot unattended. It cooks slowly so no steam escapes, so food will not burn.

Different settings on the Crock-Pot offer flexibility. At a higher setting, foods may be ready in two to three hours, while on low these dishes may need twice the time—perfect for a regular work day (eight to ten hours).

For better color and flavor, brown meats and other ingredients in a frying pan before you place them with liquid and seasonings into the Crock-Pot.

Sprinkle vinegar—any kind of vinegar—over tougher cuts of beef or pork while they're cooking to tenderize them.

Sauces may be thin because steam hasn't escaped and they have not been allowed to reduce. To heighten flavor and improve appearance, boil sauces down on top of the range just before serving, or thicken them with flour.

In adapting your favorite recipes, add less liquid. All the liquid you place in the pot is likely to be there when you finish. Use three-quarters of the liquid normally required for soups.

When making stews, place vegetables under meat because they tend to cook more slowly in Crock-Pots and the highest heat is at the bottom of the pot.

Foods cooked on low may need more seasoning because they haven't been allowed to reduce. Experiment. You can always adjust seasoning at the end.

～

I've always thought of Sunday as a day to wear lace and drink champagne—and that all men should dance and wear after-shave. Although I can ensure only half of that equation, sometimes I get lucky and find a man who thinks like I do. This easy, easy meal can make Sunday special while giving you a day of rest (and lace). To save more work, buy chicken pieces already cut up or do it yourself with a pair of kitchen scissors (a must-have). Do serve this with a bottle of sparkling champagne.

Roasted Chicken à la Crock-Pot

1 whole chicken, 2½ to 4 pounds*
  Salt and pepper
¼ teaspoon each marjoram and thyme, or
2–3 cloves garlic and
2–4 sprigs rosemary, plus
1 teaspoon chopped rosemary, or
1–2 teaspoons dried rosemary
1 (12-ounce) bag frozen mixed vegetables

Remove giblets and thoroughly wash chicken. Pat dry with paper towel to assure good browning. Sprinkle cavity with salt, pepper, and marjoram and thyme. Or, if using garlic and rosemary, add the garlic and rosemary sprigs to the cavity and under the skin.

Invert a 2 to 4-inch ovenproof dish and place it on the bottom of the Crock-Pot. (The dish will allow fat and juice to drain from the chicken). Set chicken on top of dish. Cover with vegetables. Cover Crock-Pot and cook 6 to 8 hours on low. Serves 6.

*Remove skin from chicken to minimize the grease.

Chicken 'n Noodles. Add 2 cups water to Crock-Pot along with the chicken. Cover and cook on low 8 to 10 hours (high: 4 to 5 hours). Remove chicken from broth. Turn Crock-Pot to high and add noodles. Debone chicken and cut up meat. Stir chicken into noodles. Cover and cook 30 to 45 minutes, stirring occasionally.

Chicken 'n Dumplings. Add ½ cup white wine to Crock-Pot with the chicken. Cover and cook on low 5 to 6 hours. Stir in 1 cup lowfat sour cream, and 1 (10-ounce) can small white onions, drained. Turn control to high. Combine 1 cup of biscuit mix with 2 tablespoons of fresh parsley, if you have it; in a separate bowl, combine ¼ cup milk with 1 beaten egg. Stir into biscuit mixture to form sticky dough. Drop dough by rounded teaspoons into simmering liquid. Cover and turn heat to low and simmer 15 minutes. Remember—no peeking! Lifting it for even a second allows the steam to escape and lowers the cooking temperature. Makes 6 servings.

Using a 3-pound fryer: 307 calories; 35 grams protein; 0 gram carbohydrate; 18 grams fat; 5 grams saturated fat; 137 mg cholesterol; 93 mg sodium; 0 gram fiber.

～

The way to slow down in a hectic world is not to find even more ways of saving time, but to look for ways to spend it.

～

GOAL SETTING THAT WORKS

Goals can limit us by being too rigid. When we don't reach our goals, we can get really discouraged.

A better strategy: Set goals from your core beliefs, and choose the outcome underlying the specific goal. For instance, instead of saying, "I'll go to the gym every night," make your goal to get in good physical shape. This way, if you don't make it to the gym every night you intended, you can find a way to still get in shape and not be limited by the original goal.

Most men love pot roast. They'll feel they're back at home with mama and there's nothing wrong with that—as long as you express the other sides of yourself as well.

Pot roast is so very easy to make so don't hesitate to begin your own Sunday supper ritual. Did you know that it takes exactly the same amount of time to cook a pot roast as it does to go to church, or to take a long bicycle ride? A beef or pork roast are both cost and time effective. After you put them in a pan and season them, they will happily roast, sensually filling the house with an enriching aroma. Then after you've eaten a satisfying meal, you can enjoy the leftovers. How practical can you get?

Instead of using water, combine 1 envelope Lipton onion soup mix with 2¼ cups water—or pour in a cup of red wine and a teaspoon thyme. Or pour in a can of beef broth instead of the water with a pinch of brown sugar.

Whenever worry, fears, or anxiety rear their heads, mentally put them aside. Worry is pointless, like a squirrel running around in a cage. Get rid of worry by talking to a friend, by writing it out, or by giving it to God. The truth of the situation is always made clear at the proper time. Hasn't it always been so in the past?

～

Sunday Pot Roast and Gravy

1   bottom round roast (3½ pounds or larger for leftovers)
    Celery, carrots, and potatoes
    Salt and pepper
1   large onion, sliced
2   cloves garlic, sliced
    Water or red wine

Gravy

2   tablespoons all-purpose flour
2   cups water

Preheat oven to 450 degrees. Place beef, fat side up, on a rack in a roasting pan; surround with chopped celery, carrots, and potatoes. Season with salt and pepper; top with onion and garlic slices. Add enough water or red wine to cover the bottom of the pan. Put beef in oven and immediately turn oven down to 350 degrees and bake for 3 to 4 hours or until tender. For gravy, mix flour with water; stir into pan drippings, cooking over medium heat, until gravy has thickened. Makes 8 servings.

Per serving without gravy: 516 calories; 53 grams protein; 0 gram carbohydrate; 32 grams fat; 12 grams saturated fat; 159 mg cholesterol; 124 mg sodium; 0 gram fiber.

Workday Crock-Pot Pot Roast
The easy way to cook while you're working

Place roast, vegetables, your choice of seasonings (a can of mushroom soup combined with dry onion soup mix is wonderful), and cook 8 to 9 hours on low, then come on home to a home cooked meal. With the leftovers, here are some suggestions:

First day: Pot Roast with Vegetables. Place peeled carrots, potatoes, rutabagas, and/or turnips in with the roast during the last hour of cooking. Bring a roast beef sandwich to work tomorrow.

Second day: Sweet and Sour Beef. Heat chunks of leftover beef in sweet-and-sour sauce and serve over cooked noodles. To make sauce, saute ½ cup chopped celery and ¼ cup chopped onion in 1 tablespoon butter until tender. Stir in 1 tablespoon flour. Add ¼ cup sugar, ¼ cup vinegar, and ¼ cup water. Stir until slightly thickened. Add beef chunks. Canned mushrooms are good too. Toss together with hot pasta and maybe some sliced tomatoes or salsa for a nice lunch tomorrow.

Third day: Stir fry. Combine all leftover chopped beef. Heat 1 tablespoon of sesame oil in a wok or skillet. Add meat and stir-fry 2 minutes. Add all leftover vegetables you have on hand (or a bag of frozen stir fry vegetables). Stir-fry 3 more minutes. Serve over rice sprinkled with toasted sesame seeds and soy sauce. Reserve 1 cup stir fry and stuff a potato with it for tomorrow's lunch.

Fourth day: Beef Stew. Heat gravy and chunks of beef in a pan, along with leftover potatoes and carrots. Bring a bowl to lunch tomorrow.

Fifth day: Pot Pie. Place leftover meat chunks, gravy, peas, and carrots in a pie plate. Top with your favorite pie crust, or make a biscuit dough from Bisquick, or top with instant mashed potatoes. Bake at 350 degrees for 30 to 45 minutes or until crust is golden. Go out for lunch tomorrow.

The secret to perfect roasting is a hot oven. With high heat you get the browning of the surface that makes for rich juices and flavors.

It feels so delicious to recreate a "pot of something" that your mother made. What did your mother make that you loved? My Polish mom prepared much the same foods that her stepmother did: Potfuls of boiled cabbage, sauerkraut, pork, and mushrooms, served with horseradish and rye bread. Should you have Slavic roots or just like simple foods, you may love this too!

Pork Chops and Sauerkraut

1 quart sauerkraut, drained
½ cup brown sugar
2 dashes garlic powder
Dash of salt
2–3 apples, peeled, cored, and diced
1 teaspoon caraway seeds
6 (or more) pork chops

Preheat oven to 350 degrees. Sprinkle the kraut into a 9 by 13-inch pan and then sprinkle the brown sugar, garlic powder, salt, apples, and caraway seeds over this. Put the chops on top and bake for 45 minutes to 1 hour, or until chops are well done. Makes 6 servings.

Per serving: 427 calories; 20 grams protein; 34 grams carbohydrate; 23 grams fat; 8 grams saturated fat; 77 mg cholesterol; 1,553 mg sodium; 2.6 grams fiber.

PLAN FOR JOY AND PASSION!

Make a list of specific fun things to do every month for the rest of the year. This list should not include any other goals such as career, family, spiritual, or social goals—only the things you really enjoy, that exhilarate you, that make you feel happy!

How does one develop passion? Look for things to appreciate—and act as though you do until you find it!

Find Private Time
(Schedule escape!)

Have you noticed that what you give your time to is what you value? It follows, then, that we value ourselves when we take the time to be and to feel good. This is how we exemplify how valuable we are to ourselves!

Whatever activity you choose, portion out some time each day to spend freely without constraints, rules, or regulations. Here are the required guidelines:

1. Do it.

2. Do it alone.

3. Do it 100%, without a shred of guilt.

Rule #1:
Do what you love.
Rule #2:
See rule number one
and do it several times
a day if you can.

A twelve-year study of 1,200 men and women attending a night-school program found that students who didn't take private time had more illness and were less likely to exercise and eat healthfully than whose who relaxed regularly.

Physical Escapes

Get up early to allow yourself time before the rest of the family's needs are urgent. Read the paper, go for a jog, take a bath.

Be a child again. Go to the library for pleasure only. Sit in the children's section and read children's books to regain a fresh, innocent perspective.

Take a break before everyone comes home. Turn on the answering machine. Stretch out on the bed and read. Or take a shower and put on something attractive. Take a walk with the dog.

Lay in a patch of tall green grass and make out cloud images. Eat a cherry Popsicle.

Mental Escapes

Worrying works: Ninety percent of what we worry about never happens. Don't worry, be happy!

If you have to worry about something, give yourself a set time each day to do it, say thirty minutes—then stop! If it is still difficult to clear your mind, visualize it as a television set, then unplug it.

Believe (instead). See the issue resolved in your mind, one way or the other. Or at least visualize that you know the answer and are happy with it.

Don't waste time wondering what will happen in your life, and do not concentrate on what you don't have! Thoughts are energy and we get in our life what we think about. Think about what you want, instead! When you do, your vibratory rate will change and you actually begin to attract it to you. (Remember when you were in love, then suddenly men were attracted to you? Your vibratory rate changed.) You can bring about change by changing your conditions through appreciating, thinking, and feeling what it would be like to be or to do or to have what you want. When you put yourself in those thoughts and feelings, you draw situations that vibrate with what your new vibration is.

If you're not having fun, don't do it!

In the movie *Smokey and the Bandit II,* Sally Field's character lived in a filthy, cluttered house crammed full from floor to ceiling with old furniture laden with dirt and cobwebs, but she was happy—pristinely happy! She spent the day filing her nails, primping herself, looking beautiful, oblivious to the contrast of the messy house around her. How I'd like to be like that!

There is nothing more attractive—or healthy—than feeling good. She did this by not making everything a job. She didn't answer the phone just because it was ringing. (Let the answering machine pick it up or, if you don't have one, you know that if it is important, they will call back.) Don't open the mail or wash the dishes just because they're there.

Be more like the character Sally Field played and live in your own sense of time. Open it when you want to. Don't be a slave to your "to-do" list, your Day Runner, or your home.

GO WITH YOUR GUT

If you're not sure about whether or not to go for a particular thing, follow this simple formula: Feel how you're feeling about it. Does the thought of it fill you full of energy? If not, "it"—the situation or the person—is probably not for you. Validate yourself. You are your most important barometer.

⁓

What do you remember most about growing up? Maybe it was a certain dress. Maybe it was a doll, or finally getting to cook a dessert you loved. I remember making banana pudding. This style of pudding originated in the Deep South, where bananas and desserts are taken very seriously. To save time, simply prepare a package of sugar-free vanilla pudding mix and pour it over the bananas and vanilla wafers you've layered in a bowl. Chill and, if you would like to, serve with whipping cream.

Old-Fashioned Southern Banana Pudding
or 'Nanner Pudding

1 (3¼-ounce) package vanilla pudding and pie-filling mix
2 cups lowfat milk
1 teaspoon vanilla
18 vanilla wafers
4 medium bananas, cut in ¼-inch diagonal slices
2 egg whites
2 tablespoons sugar
  Flaked coconut, optional

Life is not lost by dying; life is lost minute by minute, day by dragging day, in all the thousand small uncaring ways.

—STEPHEN
VINCENT BENET

Combine pudding mix and milk in saucepan. Cook and stir over medium heat until mixture comes to a boil. Remove from heat and blend in vanilla. Line a 1½-quart glass casserole with wafers; add layer of bananas. Pour pudding over bananas.

In a large bowl with an electric mixer, beat egg whites until stiff; gradually beat in sugar until stiff peaks form. Spoon over pudding and sprinkle with coconut. Bake pudding in preheated 350 degrees oven 12 to 15 minutes, or until meringue is light brown. Makes 6 servings.

Per serving: 360 calories; 6 grams protein; 76 grams carbohydrate; 4 grams fat; 1 gram saturated fat; 14 mg cholesterol; 572 mg sodium; 1.39 grams fiber.

Rent "The Big Chill" and serve these again.

Kellogg's® Rice Krispies Treats®

3 tablespoons margarine or butter
1 (10-ounce) package (about 40) regular marshmallows or
   4 cups miniature marshmallows
6 cups **Kellogg's® Rice Krispies®** cereal

Melt margarine in large saucepan over low heat. Add marshmallows and stir until completely melted; remove from heat. Add cereal, stirring until well coated.

Using buttered spatula or waxed paper, press mixture evenly into buttered 13 by 9 by 2-inch pan. Cut into 2-inch squares. Makes 24 squares.

Peanut Krispies: Stir 1 cup raisins or 1 cup peanuts (or a combination) into the mixture along with the cereal. Stir ¼ cup peanut butter into the marshmallow mixture just before adding the cereal.

Chocolate Krispies: Add ¾ cup chocolate chips to the melted margarine and stir until completely melted.

Peanut Butter Krispies: Add ½ cup peanut butter.

Per square, using the original recipe: 77 calories; 10 grams protein; 16 grams carbohydrate; 1 gram fat; 1 gram saturated fat; 4 mg cholesterol; 93 mg sodium; .13 gram fiber.

BE POSITIVE!

Accentuating the positive is more important as we age. As children we run, jump, play, and believe solidly in our dreams. The older we get, we tend to experience more losses, and the physical world seems to hold us down more, thus it is more important to lift ourselves higher by focusing on the positive.

Next time you feel you deserve a pat on the back, whether you're turning forty, returning to school, or getting a new cat, why not go all out and throw yourself a party? Accentuating the positive will enrich relationships and increase appreciation of life and of each other. Go for what is good in life, and that is what you will get!

～

To me, the best pie crust is one someone else's mother has made. Today, if you feel like me and your life is too busy to make pie crust, no one has to know you've bought it when you buy the unfold-and-roll-out variety found in the dairy section of the supermarket. Just unfold it and tuck into your own pie pan.

Here are two versions, because pie crusts are like politics and religion: Someone else always has a better, or different, idea of what is best. And, by the way, you can always make pie crusts ahead and freeze them.

Perfect Pie Crust I

For a 9-inch regular pie pan

1	cup all-purpose flour
¼	teaspoon salt
3	tablespoons cold butter or margarine, in ½-tablespoon chunks
3	tablespoons cold solid shortening, in ½-tablespoon chunks
3–4	tablespoons ice water

In a bowl, stir 1 cup of the flour (use 1¼ cup for larger crusts) and salt with a pastry blender. Cut in butter, then shortening, until particles are pea sized; occasionally scrape fat from pastry blender and use it to scrape bowl and gently stir in flour.

Add the minimum amount of water 1 tablespoon at a time; stir with a fork just until flour is evenly moistened. Gently squeeze a handful of dough; it should hold together and feel like clay. If not, add water ½ tablespoon at a time.

Gather dough into a ball. Flatten into a 4-inch disk, wrap in plastic, and chill at least 1 hour or up to 2 days.

Lightly dust a countertop, the dough, and a rolling pin (if you can't find it, a wine bottle works well) with flour. Using short, gentle strokes, and working from the center of the dough outward, roll dough to the size circle required (2 inches greater than the diameter of a regular pie pan).

The difference between a so-so cake, cookie, or muffin and a moist, sublime experience can be how soon you remove it from the oven! Be mindful to remove them just at the brink of doneness, as all food continues to cook a bit before it cools down.

Make it fun and easy: Use a food processor and substitute brandy for half the water (delicious)!

Perfect Pie Crust II

4 cups all-purpose flour
2 teaspoons salt
1 tablespoon sugar
1¾ cup shortening
½ cup water
1 egg, beaten
1 tablespoon vinegar

Combine all ingredients as in recipe above and roll out as needed. Makes 2 or more crusts, depending on size of pan.

～

Take too many photographs of your loved ones.

～

Woman grounds herself in being as she claims her time, moment by moment to be within it, as if she could touch it and hold it in her hand . . . as she claims her time to be, not forcing into an hour more than that hour can hold, but listening, with a sense of balance and restraint, that each task be quietly fulfilled with pause before and after . . . an interlude for her to reflect, to be present to herself.

—JUDITH DUERK, "CIRCLE OF STONES: WOMAN'S JOURNEY TO HERSELF"

I used to watch Aunt Lucille make her wonderful pies, knowing her best cookies would soon also be hot out of the oven. These were snapped up immediately!

Aunt Lucille's Best Cookies

Leftover pie crust
Jam or jelly

Roll out the leftover pie crust and cut out 2-inch circles with a round cookie cutter. Place a spoonful of jam or jelly on one side. Fold dough over filling and pinch shut. Bake with whatever you are baking in the oven until they are lightly brown. Check for doneness when you smell them, about 8 to 12 minutes. If the pie crust dough is superb, these will be the richest, flakiest cookies ever.

To save time making drop cookies, empty cookie batter into a large zip-top bag. Cut one corner and squeeze the desired amount of cookie dough onto the cookie sheet.

Exercise regularly and you'll need less sleep!
Move How You Want To— But DO Move It!

Three out of four women flip on the tube instead of choosing exercise. Are you one of those? I know you worked all day, but if you can use a little more discipline for yourself in addition to what you gave at your job, you'll be adding to yourself as a person. Women who consider themselves to be very active are more likely to see themselves as physically strong, assertive, sexy, and fashionable.

Think of exercise as moving your body. When you look at it this way, it can be pure pleasure when you choose how to move. Start small. Exercising (dancing, walking, tai chi) daily at fifty percent of your capacity will give you maximum energy. For instance, if you are able to run ten laps, only run five. You'll feel energetic and, over time, your capacity will increase as you increase your workout.

I once dated an auto-body man with a very nice one. He claimed it became that way through his job. It wasn't that his work was particularly body building, he just made it that way. He threw himself into every movement. For instance, when he bent down to pick up a part, he stretched his back, his legs, and his reach a little further. When he sanded, he would flex his stomach muscles a little more. We can all do this with a job as simple as putting paper in the copier to cleaning the house or the car. Often it's the simplest things that are the most overlooked—and effective.

Double Your Pleasure

Whatever form of exercise you choose, double your satisfaction by combining it with other things you love to do, such as: As you walk or ride your bicycle down a country road, listen to a symphony through your earphones and pick a few wildflowers . . . walk or run with a friend . . . walk the treadmill while watching the news on television . . . listen to a tape while riding a stationary bicycle . . . let your favorite song take your mind off sit-ups. . . stretch while watching TV . . . clean the house to Eric Clapton . . . bellydance . . . lift weights to aerobic videos . . . dance to a juke box. I often hike a well-known mountain road and read a small, easy-to-carry book. I'm sure you can think of more.

We lose more weight, feel better, and eat less when our metabolism is elevated throughout the day by exercising in some way for ten minutes here than there rather than one thirty-minute chunk.

～

You Need to Play!

Do you remember how? Play is fun. Play is our inner spirit expressing itself. Play is joy. Play is necessary!

Your inner spirit actually is as sensitive as a child and will come out to play only if she thinks she is safe: If you'll open up a space for her or if there's a playground! Let her know that she can come out and that you will take care of her.

If we work too much and too often, our spirit goes on strike, so half of us isn't with us anyway. We may experience this by feeling spacey, confused, in a mist, or in a daydream. That is when we should have followed our bliss and found a way to take a few hours or the day off.

Don't postpone joy!

This easy-to-make pie is a chocolate lover's dream. Lighten the calories by using lower-fat or nonfat pudding, milk, or whipping cream. Beautiful and primally tempting with a rose tucked into the whipped cream, eat it with someone you love.

Double Chocolate Pie

If you've had a really bad day, complete it in the privacy of your own home. Pick up some really good take-out food, and run your bath water soon after you walk through the door. Put on some really elegant or sexy pajamas that are also comfortable and spend a candlelit evening enjoying your solitude or with your boyfriend.

- 6 ounces (1 cup) semisweet chocolate morsels
- 1 (8-ounce) package light cream cheese, softened
- 1 (3.9-ounce) package chocolate instant pudding and pie filling
- 1½ cups 2% cold milk
- 1 ready-made 9-inch graham cracker or cookie pie crust
  Aerosol whipping cream or frozen whipping cream, thawed, optional
  Grated bittersweet chocolate (or a candy bar) for garnish, optional
  Miniature roses for garnish, optional

Place chocolate morsels in microwavable bowl. Microwave on high 1 to 2 minutes, stirring every 30 seconds, until smooth. With electric mixer, beat together cream cheese and melted chocolate until smooth. Add pudding/pie filling and milk. Beat 2 minutes at low speed, scraping bowl occasionally. Pour mixture into crust and chill several hours or overnight. Before serving, garnish with mounds of whipped cream and miniature roses, or grate chocolate over the top. Makes 8 servings.

Per serving: 334 calories; 7 grams protein; 41 grams carbohydrate; 17 grams fat; 3 grams saturated fat; 22 mg cholesterol; 529 mg sodium; .37 gram fiber.

Form these into "itsy-bitsy" or "giant" size. To make giant cookies, use a ¼-cup measuring cup to scoop dough onto cookie sheet. For an itsy-bitsy size, spoon half a teaspoon per cookie. I also like to throw in a little fruit, such as chopped apples, crushed bananas, blueberries, drained crushed pineapple, or dried cranberries or dates.

Famous Oatmeal Cookies

¾ cup margarine or butter, softened
1 cup brown sugar
½ cup granulated sugar
1 egg, beaten
¼ cup milk
1 teaspoon vanilla
1 cup all-purpose flour
1 teaspoon salt
½ teaspoon baking soda
3 cups oats, uncooked
1 cup raisins
1 cup chopped nuts

Blend together margarine and sugars. Beat in eggs, milk, and vanilla. In another bowl, sift flour, salt, and soda together. Add to first mixture and beat until smooth. Blend in oatmeal, raisins, and nuts. Drop by spoonfuls onto greased cookie sheet. Bake at 350 degrees for 12 to 15 minutes. Makes about 4 dozen.

Per cookie: 100 calories; 2 grams protein; 13 grams carbohydrate; 5 grams fat; 2 grams saturated fat; 12 mg cholesterol; 90 mg sodium; .7 gram fiber.

My Aunt Lucille was brought up during the Depression, where every-thing from toilet paper to ice cream was rationed. When she made us choco-late chip cookies, you would think she was still cutting back because we were lucky to find the chips! Now I go a little crazy and sometimes double the amount of chips and nuts just remembering the "good old days."

These chocolate chip cookies are identical to Pecan Sandies, with choco-late chips added. They freeze beautifully and seem to thaw instantly. They are her kids', her kids' kids', and my all-time favorite chocolate chip cookie.

Rosie's Chocolate Chip Sandies

  1 cup white sugar
  1 cup brown sugar
  1 cup margarine or butter
  1 cup vegetable oil
  1 egg
  1 tablespoon milk
  1 teaspoon vanilla
  1 teaspoon cream of tartar
  1 teaspoon salt
  1 teaspoon baking soda
  ½ cup chopped nuts
  1 (12-ounce) package milk chocolate chips
3½–4 cups flour

Combine all ingredients and drop by teaspoonfuls on ungreased cookie sheet. Bake at 350 degrees for 15 to 20 minutes and drink in the aroma of one of the most heavenly smells on earth. Makes 8 to 9 dozen cookies.

Per cookie: 87 calories; 1 gram protein; 10 grams carbohydrate; 5 grams fat; 2 grams saturated fat; 7 mg cholesterol; 42 mg sodium; .16 gram fiber.

This recipe also makes delicious cupcakes. To vary it, throw in some grated orange rind and substitute orange juice or orange liqueur for part of the pineapple juice.

Pineapple Upside-Down Cake

Topping

5 pineapple rings
6 maraschino cherries
3 tablespoons butter or margarine
6 tablespoons dark brown sugar

Cake batter

¼ cup butter or margarine
¼ cup sugar
1 egg, separated
1 cup sifted flour
1½ teaspoons baking powder
¼ teaspoon salt
½ cup pineapple juice
½ teaspoon vanilla

Spray a cast-iron skillet with vegetable spray and arrange pineapple rings and cherries on the bottom.

For the topping, melt butter in a saucepan and add brown sugar. Cook over low flames until well blended. Pour over pineapple rings.

In another bowl, cream the butter, add the sugar, and beat until fluffy. Beat the egg yolk and add. Sift the flour, baking powder, and salt together; add alternately with the pineapple juice. Add vanilla. Beat the egg white until stiff and fold into the batter. Pour the batter over the topping and bake in a preheated 350-degree oven for 25 minutes. Cool, then turn cake carefully onto a cake plate, pineapple side up. Makes one cake (12 servings), 2 dozen miniature or 1 dozen regular cupcakes.

Cupcakes: Use ½ cup crushed pineapple instead of rings. Pour about a teaspoon of this topping in the bottom of each greased miniature muffin cup, and add a sliver of red cherry.

Per serving: 119 calories; 1 gram protein; 17 grams carbohydrate; 7 grams fat; 4 grams saturated fat; 36 mg cholesterol; 165 mg sodium; .21 gram fiber.

These are like family: I often forget how good they are—and how effortless they are to make! Baked apples have that old-fashioned appeal and are an inspiring breakfast alternative with vanilla yogurt or a healthy dessert smothered with light whipping cream or ice cream.

aked Apples

4 cooking apples, such as Granny Smiths
⅓ cup brown sugar
2 teaspoons lemon juice
½ teaspoon ground cinnamon
2 tablespoons raisins
2 teaspoons butter or margarine
¾ cup water

Heat oven to 350 degrees. Core apples, leaving ¼-inch shell at bottom. Pare 1-inch peel from around top. Mix brown sugar, lemon juice, and cinnamon in a small bowl; fill apple cavities with raisins, then spice mixture, and butter or margarine. Place apples in 8-inch square baking pan and pour the water around apples. Bake, uncovered, for 40 minutes, or until soft. Makes 4 servings.

Variation: Fill apples with chopped walnuts.

Crock-Pot Baked Apples: Prepare apples as above and place in Crock-Pot. Pour water on bottom of Crock-Pot, cover, and cook on low setting for 7 to 9 hours.

Microwave Baked Apples: Prepare apples as for baking, then set in a microwave-safe dish. Add 2 to 3 tablespoons of water to dish. Cover with vented plastic wrap and zap on high 4 to 5 minutes, or until tender.

Per apple: 239 calories; 1 gram protein; 53 grams carbohydrate; 3 grams fat; 3 grams saturated fat; 0 mg cholesterol; 39 mg sodium; 5.8 grams fiber.

In our logical world we are given the distinct impression that there is one correct method to cooking. Recipes, simply having finite ingredients with exacting directions, imply that they must be followed to the letter—yet that should never be the case. Here is a recipe to loosen your left brain and create your own personal masterpiece using leftover bread. It's almost impossible to make a "mistake" (and so what if you do?)—follow the basics of eggs, sugar, milk, and bread, then run with it. For instance, rather than bread, substitute leftover birthday cake, day-old French rolls you brought home from the restaurant, the cake that fell, or leftover toast. Taste your way through it. Add a portion of cream, eggnog, piña colada, or margarita mix for the milk, if you're moved to.

Bread pudding can also be made into a denser cake-like dessert and served in slices. For this version, add half again as much bread and bake in an 8-inch springform pan or cake pan. Ice as you would a cake, or enjoy with whipped cream, ice cream, or whiskey sauce. It also makes a fabulous breakfast!

HERE'S A TIP:

Men's athletic socks are thicker and more durable than women's socks, so I buy bags of the same white quality socks and I never need to match them up!

～

Design Your Own
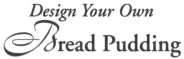read Pudding

4	eggs or 1 cup egg substitute
2½	cups lowfat milk (or half-and-half for a more succulent pudding)
1	teaspoon vanilla
½	cup sugar
½	teaspoon nutmeg or cinnamon
⅛	teaspoon salt
8–10	slices of firmly textured white bread
	Coconut and cinnamon to garnish, optional

Beat eggs or egg substitute. Beat in milk, vanilla, sugar, nutmeg, and salt. Mix in the bread (and any additions that sound good to you). *Note:* Mix bread cubes with the liquid using your hands in a large mixing bowl so that liquid is well distributed. For best results, the bread must absorb all the liquid as evenly as possible before being transferred to the baking dish. Some breads do this more quickly than others. Turn into a deep-dish glass pie pan or a 1-quart casserole. Sprinkle with cinnamon and coconut, if desired, and bake at 325 degrees for 45 minutes or until set. Makes 8 servings.

Per serving: 156 calories; 7 grams protein; 24 grams carbohydrate; 4 grams fat; 2 grams saturated fat; 110 mg cholesterol; 174 mg sodium; 2 grams fiber.

Variations on Bread Pudding

Bread pudding is whatever you want it to be: homespun or haute cuisine. If you're going for the latter, be creative and have fun choosing interesting ingredients—and be sure to name it appropriately. For example, if using chocolate chips and macadamia nuts, name it Chocolate-Macadamia Bread Pudding, or Bourbon Bread Pudding should you stir in a swig of bourbon. Other delicious additions are:

For white bread, substitute any type of bread—buns, croissants, leftover rolls, cinnamon raisin bread, brioche, and so on.

Grated lemon peel, orange peel.

Cherries, crushed pineapple, strawberries, raspberries, or other fruit or fruit purée.

Dark or golden raisins, currants, chopped dates, figs.

Chopped walnuts, pecans, hazelnuts, almonds.

Chocolate or butterscotch chips, chopped chocolate bars.

Shredded coconut.

Chocolate-covered cherries.

Most any liqueur: Bourbon, whiskey, rum, coffee, and so on.

Half-and-half, cream, or whipping cream.

Piña colada cocktail mix.

Margarita cocktail mix.

～

Pamper yourself inside and out
Wear What You Love

Buy one great, horrendously expensive piece of clothing such as one gorgeous suit that makes you feel powerful and attractive. I bought an expensive suit and wore it to every job interview where I sincerely wanted to get hired. To this day, it has worked. (It also helps to strongly believe in your "magic" piece of clothing!)

As often as possible, wear the kind of clothing that makes you feel good. Think about it! How do blue jeans, loosely fitting pants, calf-length dresses, suits, or elegant black velvet gowns make you feel?

What colors do you love? Does something in pink or some other soft and cozy color allow you to relax and let the "real you" emerge? Perhaps white or a slightly dressy pants and top would elevate your mood as it does mine. Each color actually has a vibratory rate that affects us on a feeling level: black tends to conserve energy, while red generates it, for example (note how red shoes or socks make you feel).

Let's always wear clothes that we love, be it at home or at work. Always dress with the idea that every moment counts and your clothes can improve these moments. When we feel good, we attract good things and people.

> Wear a loose-fitting shirt with happy memories attached to it, or something soft (fleece, mohair, velour), or something big, loose, and roomy.

> Or dress beautifully and comfortably, perhaps all in white, or lace, or put on some energizing bright stripes!

> Dressing well need not cost a lot: Shopping outlet stores, consignment shops, good quality second-hand and yard sales in better neighborhoods can yield surprisingly good clothing.

> Buy lots of quality underwear and socks to avoid the need for frequent laundry trips.

～

Self-Help for PMS

A teacher of mine used to say that PMS stood for Pretty Mad Somebody. Whatever causes the symptoms, sixty-two percent of violent crimes by women are committed in the week before menstruation, compared with two percent in the week after, according to a study done several decades ago. Another study has found that more than half of suicide attempts by women occur during this time. Experts suggest the following alternative approaches may be of help:

> Have a romantic evening with your lover. Sexual stimulation boosts endorphins and promotes the release of estrogen and progesterone, smoothing the fluctuation in these hormones that some researchers believe is the underlying cause of PMS. It also tends to relieve cramps and headaches.
>
> Express your feelings.
>
> Have a massage.
>
> Get more sleep.
>
> Get regular aerobic exercise.
>
> Lay on a heating pad or lounge in a hot bath.
>
> Brew a cup of raspberry leaf tea.
>
> Increase your intake of complex carbohydrates, which leads to an increase of serotonin—a brain chemical that eases stress and tension. Avoid salty foods, which aggravate fluid retention.
>
> Increase calcium, a natural relaxant that is helpful for alleviating cramping. A study showed that a daily ingestion of 1,200 milligrams of calcium taken for three months slashes PMS symptoms by an average of fifty percent. Nearly a third of the women achieved seventy-five percent lessening of symptoms.
>
> Increase magnesium—Research also indicates that consuming 600 milligrams daily from food helps reduce mood changes, water retention, and breast tenderness.

Limit alcohol, which as we all know can bring out anger and moodiness.

Limit caffeine. We don't need stimulants when we are irritable.

Drink decaffeinated coffee or tea to encourage calmness, and lots of fresh water.

～

Chapter 3

What we think determines what we feel

❦

Morning Pleasures

Start the day as you want it to go

Waking up can be like a deliciously dreamy Maxfield Parish painting or it can feel like The Rocky Horror Picture Show, but one thing's for certain: I am free to guide how the day will continue. I decide to see the best in life, or to allow people, weather, or my own negative thoughts to influence me feeling sad or insecure. Since what we think determines what we feel, to feel happy I'll put more into my mornings, with a mind-and-emotion-over-matter routine that centers me before I run off in ten different directions. This is what I do:

When I take my morning walk, or sometimes in the shower, I think about the day ahead and focus on each demand, visualizing myself meeting them easily and well. I remind myself that I can meet them with peace, harmony, and calm. I think about those things I have in my life, then those things I want to exist. I'm thankful for my cat, Baby, snuggled next to me, for the good time I had dancing last night, and for coffee. I'm *very* grateful for coffee. Then I go on to envision those things I want to have happen. I walk through the day in my mind, experiencing it both visually and emotionally as I prefer it to be. For example, if I want to close a real estate deal or to complete a chapter in my book, I imagine these easily

Bless what blesses you.
—REV. LINDA SCHNEIDER

❧

completed, feeling good about it, even excited, seeing myself autographing stacks of books, smelling the flowers that I'll buy to celebrate, and so on, simultaneously feeling grateful that this will happen.

It's true that we tend to attract to us what we think about and feel strongly about. I utilize this natural law by feeling good—by feeling grateful in advance for what I want to have occur that day. In other words, I decide what my day will be like by appreciating what I already have, then by directing my thoughts to what I want to have happen. Finally, I go through my day looking for these conditions and, by doing so, they eventually do manifest.

This "exercise" is prayer, meditation, and positive thinking all rolled into one. It's quite practical. It not only gives me focus, direction, and a sense of control, but once I create in my consciousness a mental reality, a natural, inevitable process can gradually make it happen in the physical world as well. Fifteen minutes of imagining can be more productive than eight hours of work.

You transform your life by transforming yourself into the person you want to be. Every morning is a new beginning. We've got what it takes to create a castle or a cubbyhole and we do this with every thought, feeling, word, and deed. Sports professionals, such as golfer Jack Nicklaus, have used visualization for years to improve their game. In his mind, he imagines the ball's perfect flight before every swing. We can also train our mind in this way to improve our own lives.

I call this technique "emotional imaging" and have found it to be one of the most effective exercises I can do to mold my life—and it's all internal. Sometimes we women forget that there is more to power than physically conquering the world (which is our *animus,* or male energy). Traditionally female power is the power to attract, to draw to us what we want, which is our *anima,* or female energy. To be most effective, we should use both.

～

It is just as important to imagine our lives as we wish them to be as it is to physically produce because the mind cannot create what it cannot see.

And we attract to us what we give our attention to.
Consciously look for things you like and your life
will be filled with more of them.

～

Breakfast is a Smart Investment in Your Mood and Productivity

Or, if you don't take care of your body,
where are you gonna live?

Have you noticed the difference when you eat well? Studies show that both school children and adults who have a good breakfast perform better intellectually. This is also true for lunch, of course, but usually it is not as noticeable. To increase your energy and feel more alert, which is simply feeling better, try eating a breakfast high in protein and low in fat. Protein foods wake you up better than coffee, as long as you don't follow it with a glazed doughnut. It might be a Spanish omelet made with egg substitute or a breakfast sandwich of lean sausage and eggs. Grilled ham and cheese—if only a half sandwich—will wake up those neurons, as will light cream cheese and strawberries lavishly spread over an egg bagel.

There really are ways to make a good breakfast happen almost without thinking. Flour tortillas can wrap up a good breakfast that you can walk out the door with. Make a breakfast quesadilla like this: Sprinkle grated lowfat cheese with lean breakfast sausage or leftover sliced meat, chiles, and so on over a flour tortilla; microwave until cheese melts. Or spread the tortilla with peanut butter and roll up a banana, burrito-style!

Two servings of fruit will provide a natural sugar boost so that we don't need that chocolate doughnut. Half a cup of berries, melon chunks, a piece of fruit, a glass of juice, or bowl of Raisin Bran counts as one serving.

Sweets and starches such as a Danish or a doughnut kick up blood sugar levels, which slide back down lower than they were when you were hungry in an hour or two, leaving you edgy and a prime candidate for another quick fix. A nutritious breakfast also keeps you from overeating at lunchtime.

Consider taking a vitamin/mineral supplement every morning, especially if you consume fewer than 2,500 calories per day or are under stress. Even marginal nutritional deficiencies can adversely affect your mood.

❦

Beloved Cereal

Few pleasures make it all the way to adulthood. Today Captain Crunch sticks to my teeth—but hey, Life cereal, Cheerios, and Rice Krispies still hold their charm, as Lucky Charms once did. Which cereal was and still is your favorite? Buy a box of whatever it is. Eat a cereal you haven't eaten in years. I dare you. Use your memories to bring you back to being a kid. Most of us could use it. I'll munch frosted, bite-sized shredded wheat any time of the day, right out of the box, while glued to my computer, or in my cobalt blue jelly jar with milk. Foods that you really love deserve special dishes or at least distinctive containers. See for yourself if a brandy snifter doesn't transform Special K into dessert status.

For cereal to be complete, it needs fruit. We all know what fresh fruit such as bananas, berries, and sliced peaches can do for cereal, but try canned fruit too. In the winter months my Aunt Lucille would keep home-canned peaches and pears on the breakfast table for us to spoon over cold cereal. Sublime!

If schedules are tight for dinner together, try breakfast, brunch, lunch, or even a late-night snack.

Unbeatable Ways with Cereal . . .

Combine several boxes in a large covered glass jar—like an old-fashioned pickle jar. Or just combine them in your bowl. I like the combination of Wheat, Corn, and Rice Chex.

Eat hot or cold cereal from long-stemmed goblets. Add a dollop of whipping cream to cold cereal.

Instead of eating plain cereal, slice a banana and top with sour cream and cinnamon sugar.

Have on hand an assortment of miniature boxes—a snack pack, they call it. These can be transported easily anywhere.

⁓

Wake up to hot oatmeal like Grandma's. This is better than instant, with higher food value than oatmeal made with water. Using a Crock-Pot, you can feed and please the whole family, regardless of different morning schedules.

Oatmeal in a Crock-Pot
à la Grandma

  1 teaspoon margarine or butter
  2 cups nonfat or lowfat milk
  1 cup light creamer or half-and-half
  1 cup rolled oats
 ¼ cup raisins or other dried fruit, optional
1–2 apples, unpeeled, chopped, optional
     Dash of salt

Rub the inside of the Crock-Pot with butter or margarine. Bring the milk and light creamer to a boil on the stove and pour into the Crock-Pot. Stir in the oatmeal, raisins or other dried fruit, and apple, if desired. Add salt. Cover and cook on low setting 6 to 8 hours or overnight. Pour oatmeal into your bowl and lean over it for a free facial with breakfast. Makes 4 servings.

Thermos method: Before you go to sleep, bring the milk or water to a boil and put into a wide-mouthed thermos along with the cereal and salt. Add cut-up dried fruit or raisins, if you'd like. The cereal will be cooked and warm the next morning. Sweeten to taste and, if it is too thick, stir in some milk. Take to work or use this method when camping.

> Per serving using lowfat milk: 297 calories, 11 grams protein; 49 grams carbohydrate; 6 grams fat; .7 gram saturated fat; 2 mg cholesterol; 101 mg sodium; 4.9 mg fiber.

MAKE MORNINGS TO REMEMBER

Have a favorite bowl. Perhaps it will be wooden—or maybe an oriental rice bowl or a heavy ceramic bowl that feels good to your hands. Use it now for your oatmeal.

Self-indulge with a Little Sweet Creativity On Your Oatmeal

Sprinkle with brown sugar.

Swirl in a teaspoon of low-sugar jam or syrup.

Add plain yogurt and light molasses.

Add a dab of butter and sprinkle with cinnamon
and toasted pecans.

Garnish with strawberries, raspberries, and blueberries.

Serve with a scoop of light vanilla ice cream or frozen yogurt.

*Write a friend
at breakfast.
Prestamp postcards
and keep them near
the breakfast table.
These are nice for
keeping in touch with
long-distance friends.*

*Like oatmeal with a nuttier flavor, couscous makes a yummy hot cereal
on cool mornings. It cooks in a heartbeat, is light yet hardy, and is good with
a little butter and light cream.*

Easy, Soothing Hot Couscous

¼ cup boiling water
¼ cup couscous

Simply pour boiling water over couscous. Cover and let it sit there a couple
of minutes. If you eat it immediately, you'll have the texture of Grape Nuts.

Tina and I made this when we were kids and we still love it.

Hole-in-the-Wall Toast

1   slice of bread
1   egg
    Salt and pepper

Spray skillet with nonstick vegetable spray. Tear out a hole in the piece of bread and place in pan. Break egg over the hole, letting the white spill over onto the pan. Break yolk (that's what most of us do) and fry both sides until done, seasoning with salt and pepper or with your favorite seasonings. You might like to melt cheese on top, or eat with salsa or a splash of Worcestershire sauce, for example. Makes 1 serving.

> Per serving: 154 calories; 9 grams protein; 15 grams carbohydrate; 16 grams fat; 1.7 grams saturated fat; 212 mg cholesterol; 313 mg sodium; 0 gram fiber.

Crisp Bacon in the Microwave

The microwave is the only way to cook bacon because there is much less to clean up. Simply lay bacon slices on a double thickness of paper towels and cover with another paper towel. Microwave on full power for about 45 seconds to 1 minute for each slice. Let stand for 2 minutes to crisp.

Note: Crisp, lean bacon isn't really such a high cholesterol food when chosen and prepared well. Choose lean and cook crisp. Yes, there's fat in it, but you need some anyway.

BACON TIP

To stop bacon grease from spattering in the frying pan, toss a few celery leaves into the pan with the bacon.

～

Do give this a try: Soft and sweet, surprisingly satisfying. If you don't want to fuss, simply place the banana—peel and all—in the oven for 20 minutes; unpeel and sprinkle with cinnamon sugar for a preview of how good it can be! Serve one to your lover or friend—with their eyes closed.

Baked bananas make an exotic and very chic dessert too. Try your skill at making them marvelous. Spit the banana open and then begin with ginger, coconut, cocoa, vanilla, honey, liqueur, or whatever.

Baked Bananas

⅓ cup butter, melted
3 tablespoons lemon juice
6 ripe bananas, peeled
⅓ cup sugar
1 teaspoon cinnamon
¾ cup grated coconut

Combine melted butter with lemon juice and pour on the bottom of a shallow baking pan that will hold 6 bananas. Turn bananas in dish until well coated with butter and juice mixture. Sprinkle sugar and cinnamon evenly over bananas. Bake at 375 degrees, turning once halfway through. Sprinkle coconut over bananas about 5 minutes before they finish cooking. Makes 6 servings.

Per banana: 270 calories, 2 grams protein; 2 grams carbohydrate; 5 grams fat; 0 gram saturated fat; 27 mg cholesterol; 139 mg sodium; 6.1 grams fiber; 758 mg potassium.

GOOD MORNING!

If you really love coffee, buy the best and begin the day with it. For best results, never guess, always measure. In general, 1 rounded tablespoon to 6 ounces of water makes a medium-strength cup.

I might read a few pages from a favorite poetry or inspirational book (my favorite is *A Course in Miracles*) then take a short walk in the early morning light.

Begin the day with an attitude of accomplishment even before the day begins. Expect it to come true.

"Feel Good" Breakfasts

"Feel good" food can certainly be nutritious. *Feel* what foods you need and want and you will choose wisely. Here are some less-traditional ways to begin the day.

The moment you wake up, ask yourself what you can do to make yourself happy today!

Have baked apples with plain yogurt, sour cream, or a rich cream.

Eat a piece of pie, any kind of pie.

Have leftover beef stroganoff over toast.

Make grilled steak and eggs when you need a jump-start or if you drank too much last night.

Hot brown sugar Pop Tarts.

Slices of brie, heated to melt in microwave, served with whole wheat toast and strawberry jam (*Note:* slices of brie can be frozen and popped into the microwave!).

Leftover cold pizza.

Leftover pizza, reheated.

Buttered toast, biscuit, or bagel with whipped cream, sprinkled with cinnamon sugar.

Fruit-filled turnovers baked hot from the oven.

Eggs scrambled with smoked salmon.

To find the beautiful, we must carry it with us.

—AUTHOR UNKNOWN

If you're having a time getting motivated, lovingly jump-start that beautiful brain of yours with French toast drizzled with cognac, Grand Marnier, or Frangelica, or one of your favorite liqueurs. (You know you can always use frozen French toast and dress it up.) Then think positively about today over a cup of good strong coffee with whipping cream. Absolutely everything is how you look at it—so step back and strive for a higher perspective!

Fabulous, fast

French Toast

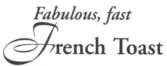

2 eggs, beaten, or ½ cup egg substitute
½ cup lowfat milk
1 teaspoon vanilla
4 slices day-old white, whole wheat, or your favorite bread
   Nonstick vegetable spray, butter, or margarine
   Optional toppings: Confectioners' sugar, brown sugar, syrup, honey, jam, jelly, freshly cut-up fruit, or flavored liqueur such as Amaretto, Kahlua, cream whiskey, Grand Marnier, or Frangelica

Have breakfast for dinner tonight! Capitalize on the cozy feeling of breakfast food and order bacon and eggs or a vegetarian omelet for dinner when you especially need a softer touch.

In a shallow bowl, combine eggs, milk, and vanilla. Dip bread into egg mixture, coating both sides.

Coat skillet with nonstick spray and cook bread over medium heat for 2 to 3 minutes on each side or until golden brown. Spray more vegetable spray or add more margarine or butter as needed.

Serve with your favorite topping on a pretty plate. Garnish with a flower, berries, or what have you. Eat with your fingers or linger over it with a knife and fork.

Microwave method: Follow recipe above, then place bread on a paper plate and microwave, turning bread with a spatula after 45 seconds or so, then let it cook until egg firms up, or about 1 more minute.

Per slice using whole wheat bread: 121 calories; 7 grams protein; 14 grams carbohydrate; 4 grams fat; 1 gram saturated fat; 225 mg sodium; 107 mg cholesterol; 3 grams fiber.

Using a carbonated beverage makes these pancakes extra light with a touch of sweetness. Pancakes look and taste even better served with fresh fruit such as sliced bananas (why don't you throw some ham into the batter?). I love to see pancake batter in my refrigerator at all times. You might also prepare a big batch (use up all the batter) and freeze them in a covered container, each pancake separated with a piece of waxed paper. Then pop pancakes into the microwave for a wonderfully quick, no-mess breakfast during the week.

7UP Pancakes

1 egg (or ¼ cup egg substitute)
1 tablespoon margarine, melted
1 cup 7UP, regular or diet
1 cup buttermilk pancake mix

Beat egg or egg substitute well. Add margarine and half of 7UP. Blend; stir in pancake mix, then add remaining 7UP and mix until almost smooth. Pour onto hot, lightly greased griddle. Bake until lightly browned, turning only once. Makes about eight 4-inch pancakes.

Variations: Add slices of medium-ripe banana, chopped pecans, fresh or frozen blueberries, or well-drained crushed pineapple to the batter.

Per 2-pancake serving: 71 calories; 2 grams protein; 10 grams carbohydrate; 2.3 grams fat; 0 grams unsaturated fat; 8 mg cholesterol; 210 mg sodium; 0 gram fiber.

Buy a box of greeting cards and write them all out at the beginning of each month.

Ma made us breakfast every morning and she often would include her warm, sweet oatmeal muffins. Today I've found my own piece of morning heaven: Scones. They're the trendy crunchy-looking cakes you often find in the case at fancier coffee shops, and they are delicious to eat throughout the day, not just for breakfast. Scones are similar to biscuits, but made with real butter and the addition of eggs and sugar. Then comes the fun part—add your favorite dried fruit, chocolate, spices, and sugary glazes and they're more like cake. Divide the dough into two batches and make one of them a nice little surprise gift for the person who fixes your computer, your car, or touches your heart.

MAKE CHILDHOOD MEMORIES

At least once a week, invite younger children to help create a meal. They can set the time, add the vegetables to soup, or shape the hamburger patties. Ask them to help set the table or assist in other responsibilities— and there will be less likelihood that you will be waiting on them when they're grown!

～

Scones
with raisins and nuts

2 cups all-purpose flour
4 teaspoons baking powder
¼ cup sugar
⅓ cup butter, cut up
½ cup buttermilk
1 large egg, lightly beaten
½ cup chopped nuts
¼ cup raisins

Glaze

1 tablespoon milk
1 tablespoon sugar

Combine first four ingredients; cut in butter with a pastry blender until crumbly. Add buttermilk and egg, stirring just until moistened. Fold in nuts and raisins. Turn dough out onto a lightly floured surface, and knead 5 or 6 times. Divide dough in half and pat each portion into a 6-inch circle. Cut each circle into 8 wedges and place 1 inch apart on baking sheet lightly sprayed with vegetable spray. Brush with milk, and sprinkle evenly with 1 tablespoon sugar. Bake at 425 degrees for 12 to 15 minutes or until scones are golden brown. Makes 16 servings.

Lemon-Poppy Seed Scones: Add 2 teaspoons grated lemon rind and 1 teaspoon poppy seeds to flour mixture. Substitute lemon yogurt for the buttermilk. Omit milk and sugar topping. Combine 1½ tablespoons fresh lemon juice and 1 cup sifted powdered sugar; drizzle evenly over warm scones.

Mocha Hazelnut Scones: Add 1 teaspoon instant coffee powder to buttermilk, stirring to dissolve, and ½ cup chopped hazelnuts and ½ cup mini-chocolate chips (optional) to dry ingredients.

Note: Reheat scones in a 400-degree oven for 5 to 7 minutes to keep their crispness.

Per scone using original recipe: 137 calories; 3 grams protein; 19 grams carbohydrates; 19 grams fat; 2.6 grams saturated fat; 24 mg cholesterol; .21 gram fiber.

Toast: Perfect As Is

I think of a slice of toast as a blank canvas. I use my creative license and choose a topping that fits my mood, state of hunger, or whatever looks pretty: maybe cream cheese and blueberries, or sliced bananas over a layer of peanut butter. Or I'll fill a bowl with marmalade and settle in for the simplest, most satisfying of breakfasts. Toast tastes much better cut into small squares or "fingers" or interesting shapes made with a high-edged cookie cutter. After all, life is short. It's the little things that count.

~

Learn to say "no" in many languages: German (nein), Spanish (no), French (non), Polish (nie). Say these with an accent and an attitude: Russian (nyet), Pig Latin (oh-nay). And for those of you who need it in English: No.

Auntie Eve taught me how to make these pancakes when I stayed with her during the summer. Potato pancakes are wonderful for dinner too! I like them flavored with dill weed and served with sautéed mushrooms and lean sausage.

Auntie's Potato Pancakes

4 cups shredded peeled potatoes (about 4 large)
1 egg, lightly beaten
3 tablespoons flour
1 teaspoon salt
¼ teaspoon pepper
¼ teaspoon dried dill, optional
1 tablespoon grated onion
   Butter-flavored cooking oil or vegetable cooking spray
   Applesauce, maple syrup, light sour cream, optional

It's love that keeps the wolf from the door.

Drain potatoes well, blotting excess moisture with a paper towel. Gently toss together potatoes and egg. Combine dry ingredients and onion. Stir in potato mixture. Drop by tablespoons onto preheated greased skillet. Brown lightly on both sides. Serve warm with applesauce or syrup. Makes sixteen 4-inch pancakes.

Per pancake, using vegetable spray: 75 calories; 2 grams protein; 16 grams carbohydrate; 0 gram fat; 0 gram saturated fat; 13 mg cholesterol; 142 mg sodium; 1.5 grams fiber.

Here is an unsophisticated sandwich to bring you back to simpler times. Fit for a busy woman or a lazy Saturday, it can be put together in the time it takes to put on your makeup. Use the best coarse-grained bread you can find (it's more like homemade) and a fresh egg, if possible. This sandwich is wonderfully messy to eat. Don't forget to wipe the plate with your crust.

Country Egg and Green Onion Sandwich

1 tablespoon whipped butter
1 large fresh egg
2 slices whole wheat bread
1 green onion with tops, chopped
1 teaspoon chili sauce
Salt and pepper

For the perfect fried egg, put a little butter (diet or whipped is fine) into a nonstick skillet. If you want it sunny-side up, put a cover on and the steam will cook the egg. If you want it over-easy, flip the egg over and count to five slowly. Remove egg and wipe out pan.

Spray skillet with vegetable spray. Fry 2 slices of bread by first lightly buttering one side only with remaining butter and sautéing until golden. Slip the egg on one slice and cover generously with finely chopped green onions. Dot fresh chili sauce over the onions. Salt and pepper to taste. Cover with second slice of bread.

Per sandwich: 286 calories; 12 grams protein; 28 grams carbohydrate; 15 grams fat; 6 grams saturated fat; 230 mg cholesterol; 626 mg sodium; 6 grams fiber.

I used to wonder why my mother bothered to bake her coffeecake at all because the batter always tasted better than the cake. Not true with this one.

Butter Streusel Coffee Cake

¾ cup butter, softened
¾ cup sugar
¾ cup light brown sugar
3 cups flour
1 teaspoon cinnamon
1 teaspoon nutmeg

Blend butter with sugars and add in flour and spices. Reserve 1 cup of mixture. Add to the remainder and beat until smooth:

2 eggs, beaten
1 cup buttermilk, soured milk or sour cream
1 teaspoon baking soda
1 teaspoon vanilla

Fold in one or more of the following:

½ cup chopped nuts
½ cup raisins
1 ripe banana, mashed
2 cups blueberries, cleaned and drained

Pour into pan and top with cup of remaining mixture, which will be the streusel. Bake at 325 degrees for 45 to 50 minutes. Serve warm or at room temperature. Makes 15 servings.

With all additions, per serving: 236 calories; 5 grams protein; 48 grams carbohydrate; 3 grams fat; 0 gram saturated fat; 28 grams cholesterol; 113 mg sodium; 1.3 grams fiber.

LIVE FIRST!

My friend Elmer would tell me, "Don't get out of bed until you can find something to be passionate about." If the only reason you get up is fear of losing your job, you're doing it backwards: Work to live.

Live first! Do what you love and your passion will get you up.

Luxury Weekend Breakfasts You Need Once In Awhile

Seize the day with more or less virtuous breakfasts during the week and throw caution to the wind on the weekends. Planning your crazy times and structure (you need both) is comforting. And if you keep the following ingredients on hand, you're more likely to attract the conditions to use them!

Sunday morning brunch can be the happiest meal of the week. Take the time to enjoy it. Forget calories. Take a bike ride, invite over a friend, put on Mozart, Billie Holiday, or Waylon Jennings; celebrate Sunday morning a bit like a modified Saturday night. Splash a bit of Irish cream in your coffee, make a quick omelet with bits of last night's steak thrown in, toast a bagel, or plan ahead with some enticing Danish. Get out the espresso machine or microwave some milk and add it in equal parts to strong coffee. Top it with whipped cream and shaved chocolate.

Keep These Stocked in Your Refrigerator

A bottle of good champagne.

A bottle of cheap champagne (to make mimosas).

Frozen orange juice (combine with champagne to make mimosas).

Whipping cream.

Nice breads such as bagels, scones, or flavored biscuits (in the freezer) and good crackers.

Caviar.

Smoked salmon.

Cream cheese.

In summer: Fresh berries, peaches, and nectarines.

Sound decadent? That's the point.

GREAT TOAST TOPPINGS

Peanut butter and sliced banana

Lemon curd

Any kind of berries with whipped cream

Nutella (a hazelnut and cocoa spread) and cream cheese

Whipped honey butter

Whipped cream cheese flavored with strawberries or pineapple

Jams and jellies

Ricotta cheese

Fresh fruit

Cheesecake for breakfast? Heavens yes! When you use fat-free cream cheese, you've got a lean, mean nutritious breakfast wrapped up in a seductive package. One slice is equal to the protein of a bacon and egg breakfast, but with less fat! You can choose to use a combination of fat-free and reduced-fat, or keep it rich by using regular cream cheese. However, the lower the fat, the more protein is available—and that can help to keep emotions balanced and energy steady, which on a work day is preferable to a fat indulgence.

Breakfast Cheese Pie

2 packages (8 ounces each) cream cheese, Neufchâtel cheese, or fat-free cream cheese, or any combination thereof

½ cup sugar

¼ cup light cream or half-and-half

1 teaspoon vanilla extract

2 tablespoons lemon juice

2 eggs or ½ cup egg substitute

½ cup graham cracker crumbs or 1 prepared graham cracker crust, 6 ounces or 9 inches

¼ cup red raspberry preserves

For Impressive Muffins:

Prepare the batter from a box of yellow cake mix and bake with a streusel topping, or add fruit or nuts and then bake in huge muffin tins. Freeze any extra. Sliced while frozen, they taste like cheesecake!

Beat cream cheese, sugar, light cream, and vanilla with electric mixer until well blended (the secret to creamy fat-free cheesecake is to beat until blended, then beat another 5 minutes). Beat lemon juice into eggs or egg substitute; mix just until blended. Do not overbeat after adding eggs. Spray a 9-inch pie plate with nonstick cooking spray and sprinkle bottom with crumbs (or use prepared crust).

Pour cream cheese mixture into prepared pie plate. Spoon preserves into a glass or plastic bowl and microwave for 5 to 10 seconds or just until preserves are liquefied. Dot top of cheesecake batter with preserves. Cut through batter with a knife several times for a marble effect. Bake at 325 degrees for 45 minutes or until center is almost set. Cool. Refrigerate 3 hours or overnight. Garnish with fresh raspberries, strawberries, lemon or orange slices, and mint, if desired. Makes 8 servings.

Lemon Cheesecake: Add ¾ teaspoon lemon extract, ½ teaspoon grated lemon rind, 2 to 3 drops of yellow food coloring, and increase the sugar to 1 cup.

Fruity Cheesecake topping: 1 (27-ounce) can cherry, raspberry, or blueberry pie filling. Spoon contents of can of pie filling over slices of cheesecake. Refrigerate until serving.

Note: Or top with any fresh fruit.

Per serving using fat-free cream cheese and prepared crust: 217 calories; 9 grams protein; 29 grams carbohydrate; 6 grams fat; 1 gram saturated fat; 24 grams cholesterol; 292 grams sodium; 0 gram fiber.

∼

Breakfast in Bed

Call in sick for a day to remember. Snuggle under the covers and lose yourself in a good book or catch up on all the magazines you've been looking forward to reading. And don't feel guilty! It's a good time for breakfast in bed!

Breakfast in bed is necessary from time to time. Do you remember when you last honored yourself with a tray of Danish and coffee? Or maybe cereal with fresh, sliced strawberries? Or brought yourself some hot, buttered blueberry muffins? Do take a moment to give special attention to details: Serve a good-flavored coffee, tuck a flower or note to your loved one into the napkin. Serve a mimosa or fruit cup in champagne. Be original. Be fresh. Be inventive. Deliver the morning paper or a book of poetry. Then tell him to move over. Share your talent and love in all ways, and you will have also fed your spirit and your soul.

∼

FREEZE MUFFINS AHEAD

Muffins freeze well for several months if wrapped airtight. To reheat, thaw while still wrapped. Unwrap, place in cold oven, turn oven to 400 degrees, and heat until warm, about 8 minutes or until muffins test done. Or, heat thawed muffins in microwave on medium power until just warm.

∼

This spread is a "smart food." It's light, yet rich—and empowering. Bring some to use as a spread on bagels during break for a real lift, rather than the sugar high from eating doughnuts or sugary muffins.

Chocolate Cream Cheese

8 ounces fat-free or light cream cheese
3 tablespoons unsweetened cocoa powder
3 tablespoons sugar
1 teaspoon vanilla
½ teaspoon almond extract

Using an electric beater, whip cream cheese, then add remaining ingredients and whip until completely blended.

Variations: Stir in fresh, cut-up strawberries, coconut, chopped pecans, or slivered almonds. Makes eight 2-tablespoon servings.

Using fat-free cream cheese, per serving: 47 calories; 7 grams protein; 6 grams carbohydrate; 0 gram fat; 0 gram saturated fat; 5 mg cholesterol, 170 mg sodium; 0 gram fiber.

～

Keep a bag of blueberries in the freezer for muffins, pancakes, fruit cups, and as a snack.

～

To a Midwesterner like me, a week doesn't go by that I don't scramble together a farmer's breakfast. If you're from some other part of the U.S., use your creative license to adapt to your region; for example, a West Coaster might prefer to use all fresh vegetables and herbs, mozzarella, or parmesan cheese, cooked exotic mushrooms, and asparagus spears. The South: seafood, Cajun seasoning, and so on. This is especially nice on a frosty autumn weekend morning or for dinner, for that matter. You might serve it with chilled apple cider and toasted homemade bread.

Farmer's Breakfast
Grand Haven Style

½ cup chopped lean ham, 3 strips bacon (fried crisp—use the microwave for no mess and speed), or sausage (bulk or link—Polish sausage is traditional)

½ medium bell pepper, chopped

¼ medium onion, chopped

1 cup mushrooms, chopped

1 medium leftover baked potato, chopped

2 tablespoons chopped parsley, optional

1 cup egg substitute or 4 eggs

2 slices American cheese

If using bacon or sausage, coat medium frying pan with nonstick spray. Over a medium-high heat, cook bacon until crisp, and sausage until cooked through; wipe out pan and set meat aside. Respray pan and sauté bell pepper, onion, and mushrooms over medium heat until onions are translucent. Add potato and sauté until crispy. Toss in meat; pour egg over all, sprinkle parsley over, and cook over low heat, scrambling with a wooden fork or spoon. Divide among serving plates. Top with halved cheese slices. Serves 2 extremely hungry people.

Using ham, per serving: 286 calories; 25 grams protein; 32 grams carbohydrate; 70 grams fat; 3 grams saturated fat; 22 mg cholesterol; 906 mg sodium; 3.7 grams fiber.

Just for today, make pleasure a part of daily life. Enjoy the feel of the towels as you fold them, the color of the sky as you drive to work. Slow down and smell the roses: Shorten your "to-do" lists and really experience—not rush through—the tasks that remain on it. Pause and look for the pleasure in each activity.

Create-a-muffins: Add a different ingredient to this basic recipe and presto—you've created a muffin! Call them "Muffins Randee" (put your own name in here).

Use the recipe for Favorite Blueberry Muffins, eliminating or reducing the amount of blueberries if you wish. Then add your favorite ingredient(s): Raspberries, strawberries, chopped apple, sliced banana, raisins, chocolate chips, chopped nuts, peanut butter chips, and so on, to measure two cups. My favorite combination is blueberries, raspberries, and chopped walnuts. Pop them in the oven and serve warm, bring them to work, or deliver some to the neighbors.

JAM-FILLED MUFFINS

Make Favorite Blueberry Muffins, eliminating the blueberries. Spoon half of the batter into 8 paper-lined muffin cups. Make a well in the center of each; spoon 2 teaspoons of your favorite jam into it. Spoon remaining batter over jam. Bake as directed in recipe.

Favorite Blueberry Muffins

1¾ cup all-purpose flour

1 tablespoon baking powder

¼ teaspoon salt

2 eggs (or 4 egg whites)

½ cup (fat-free to whole) milk

⅓ cup softened butter or margarine

½ cup plus 1 tablespoon sugar

2 cups fresh or frozen blueberries, or other fruit or favorite ingredient(s) (see above)

1 teaspoon cinnamon

Line 8 muffin cups with paper liners and spray with vegetable spray. Mix together flour, baking powder, salt, eggs, milk, butter and ½ cup sugar. Fold in berries. Divide batter equally among muffin cups. Stir remaining tablespoon of sugar and cinnamon together, then sprinkle scant ½ teaspoon of mixture over each muffin. Place in 425-degree oven and immediately reduce temperature to 400 degrees. Bake until toothpick inserted in center comes out clean, about 35 minutes. Makes 8 muffins. Serve warm!

Per muffin: 285 calories; 5 grams protein; 41 grams carbohydrate; 10 grams fat; 5 grams saturated fat; 74 mg cholesterol; 312 mg sodium; .79 gram fiber.

Invest in Family and Friends
Invest in love

Clark was a boss of mine for a very short time but he struck me as the kindest, most sincere person I've ever met who really loved people. What made him different was the value he placed in other people. A year before I worked for the company, his home and possessions were completely destroyed in the Painted Cave Fire in Santa Barbara, along with many other homes. It is apparent that he found what is of real value.

Invest in the people in your life who really matter. They are your empowerment: that center of peace and balance from which you draw energy, like fresh water from a well. It's all too easy to sacrifice important friendships when you get caught up in networking to help your career, but unless these relationships grow, they are just temporary trails that rarely lead you to what you really need: Love, support, and comfort. Some people use money to bring them security, respect, and freedom, but the real source of these things are your family and friends. Will money hold you or listen to your problems late at night? Building friendships takes time away from other things—but the richness and warmth friends bring are worth it.

Building friend-ships takes time away from other things— but the richness and warmth friends bring are worth it.

Friendship Begins in the Heart

When you feel an honest, warm interest in others, this feeling is somehow communicated to them, usually without words—and usually they will react accordingly. Make at least three new friends every year. We get back what we put in by learning new attitudes and new approaches to the world. New people and experiences give us energy. When we trust our friends, we give them energy. And when they trust us, we are accordingly fed a bit more.

Keep Your friendships in Good Repair

Give them attention to keep them. Keep in touch with friends at a distance by leaving messages on their answering machine and by remembering their birthdays and holidays with a card. Mail them a paperback novel you've enjoyed—or a copy of your favorite tape.

A friend who lives over a hundred miles away can be much closer than an acquaintance close by in this era of e-mail, fax, and competitive phone rates.

Keep stamped picture postcards in a convenient place so that you can whisk off a few thoughts to a good friend at a distance. Tear out articles on your friend's favorite topic, cartoons, or photos without comment, and send it off. My friend Paula bought two beautiful barrettes and let me pick one to keep as a remembrance. Now I think of her whenever I see it. Let them know you're thinking of them.

Give invitations to dinner. It's worth the effort and if you're insecure about how dinner will turn out, do it anyway. With practice, entertaining becomes easier.

Visit or call your oldest living relative; ask them to reminisce about their life, family, and ancestors.

Do you have enough emotional support? If you hesitated even an instant to answer that question, get out your address book. Make it a goal to have four people in your local calling area that you can call, day or night, who make you feel safe.

Choose your friends as though they were your investments—because they help to form you.

～

A Southern tradition, also popular at truck stops. I say this respectfully because I love truck stops!

Best Sausage and Biscuits with Milk Gravy

1   pound lean bulk sausage*
5   tablespoons flour
4   cups lowfat milk
2   teaspoons sage
¼   teaspoon basil leaves
½   teaspoon salt
⅛–½ teaspoon ground black pepper
2   large cans refrigerator or homemade biscuits, prepared
        according to package directions

Crumble and fry sausage until golden brown. Remove sausage from pan and set aside. Add flour to hot pan drippings and allow to bubble 1 to 2 minutes. Remove from heat and slowly add milk. Blend until smooth; cook over low heat until thickened. Add sausage and seasonings. Serve over hot biscuits. Serves 8.

*Or make your own by combining your favorite spices into lean ground chicken, turkey, beef, or pork.

Per serving: 458 calories; 16 grams protein; 36 grams carbohydrate; 36 grams fat; 9.5 grams saturated fat; 56 mg cholesterol; 1,170 mg sodium; .79 gram fiber.

Nothing's as good as a homemade biscuit straight from the oven: the warm, flaky, melt-in-the-mouth texture warms the soul. It takes just a minute to whip up biscuit dough using Bisquick. My neighbor Charlie makes these in the morning and grazes on them all day long.

Charlie's All-Day Biscuits

1¾ cups baking mix such as Bisquick
½ cup fresh ground whole wheat flour (or a close facsimile such as regular whole wheat flour, wheat bran, or 100% bran cereal)
⅔ cup lowfat milk (or half-and-half for richer biscuits)
¼ cup sugar
½ teaspoon cinnamon

If you don't have a biscuit cutter, make one by using a can opener to cut off the top of an evaporated milk can. This "biscuit cutter" is standard equipment in a working hillbilly kitchen.

Combine all ingredients and mix with a wooden spoon until soft dough forms. Roll out ½-inch thick onto floured surface. Knead a few times, then cut out with a biscuit cutter or drop by spoonfuls onto ungreased cookie sheet. Combine cinnamon and sugar and sprinkle lightly over tops of biscuits. Bake 8 to 10 minutes or until golden brown. Makes 8 biscuits.

Per biscuit: 190 calories; 5 grams protein; 34 grams carbohydrate; 5 grams fat; 1.5 grams saturated fat; 3.8 mg cholesterol; 98 mg sodium; .94 gram fiber.

What To Do with Leftover Biscuits

Make shortcake: Split open biscuit, layer the two pieces with lightly crushed strawberries (or other berries) sweetened with honey, and top with a dollop of vanilla yogurt or whipped cream.

Breakfast sandwich: Split open and layer with slices of ham, cheese and a fried egg. Spread with salsa or chutney, if desired.

Crumble in: Crumble biscuits in a glass of cold, sweetened milk. Spread with homemade apple butter: Combine 2 cups applesauce with ½ teaspoon cinnamon and a splash of brandy in a medium saucepan; cook over low heat until reduced to 1 cup.

Tips for Making
Great Biscuits

When baking from scratch, for best results start biscuits with chilled butter, shortening, and liquid ingredients to produce the most delicate texture. Keep the dough cool while working to slow the development of gluten, which will make the biscuits tough.

Shape biscuit dough to please your sense of aesthetics: Use a biscuit cutter for a traditional round form (or use a glass or cut out the bottom of an evaporated milk can). Or cut the dough into squares with a floured knife or drop it by heaping spoonfuls. (For drop biscuits, add 2 tablespoons or more milk to the biscuit recipe.)

Biscuit dough doubles in size during baking. For biscuits with crisp edges, place an inch or two apart on the baking sheet. For soft, pull-apart biscuits, cluster the biscuits together with the sides almost touching, then bake.

For flaky, tender biscuits, used well-chilled butter or margarine. To make it as cold as possible, measure the butter, cut it into cubes as directed in the recipe, then refrigerate for an hour before using. Use a wire pastry blender to knives, working quickly so that the butter stays cold.

All breads, including biscuits, can be frozen or used in a myriad of ways, so don't worry about making too many.

∼

If y'all were raised in the South, your ma may have made gravy with cream and served it with fried red or green tomatoes, sausage, ham, bacon, and grits with biscuits.

Truck Stop Gravy

4 tablespoons flour
4 tablespoons bacon fat or meat drippings
1 cup evaporated milk or cream
1 cup chicken stock

In a medium skillet or saucepan, stir flour into melted drippings. Let flour and fat bubble for 5 minutes, then add milk and stock. Stir constantly until well thickened. Simmer a few more minutes. Makes 2 cups.

Per ¼ cup serving: 240 calories; 6 grams protein; 13 grams carbohydrate; 18 grams fat; 6.7 grams saturated fat; 25 mg cholesterol; 325 mg sodium; .11 gram fiber.

A Southern-Style Breakfast

After I finished my nutrition schooling, I promised myself a train trip across the U.S. One of my stops was Dyersburg, Tennessee, to visit a friend. When the train arrived, he was nowhere in sight, so I accepted a ride from a friendly policeman. A likeable, small-town lawman with a thick Southern drawl, Officer Corbier reminded me of Barney Fife. While driving to my destination, he obliged me with the secret of his good looks, virility, and gumption, which was his mama's breakfast. This is a typical breakfast made by his mama. (Important note: It's a matter of course that Southern cooks set a full and pretty table, so buy or pick a big bouquet of flowers.)

Black ham and fried eggs.

Grits with butter.

Sweet potato biscuits with homemade strawberry jam.

Buttermilk.

Serve this with fried eggs.

Black Ham

2 tablespoons low-sugar apricot preserves or
    orange marmalade
¼ teaspoon dry mustard
1 slice lean ham

Combine preserves or marmalade with dry mustard. Spoon over ham slice and broil until surface is black, 3 to 5 minutes.

> Per serving: 200 calories; 8 grams protein; 32 grams carbohydrate; 7 grams fat; 0 gram saturated fat; 7 mg cholesterol; 302 mg sodium; 4 grams fiber.

As southern as moonlight and magnolias are grits, corn bread, and a well-seasoned cast-iron skillet. Grits are a grain that look much like Cream of Wheat cereal in appearance, texture, and nutritional composition, One cup—without additional butter—checks in at just 131 calories and, being a grain, grits also have a fair amount of B vitamins.

Hominy Grits

3 cups chicken broth
¾ teaspoon salt
¾ cup quick grits
1-2 tablespoons butter

Heat broth and salt to boiling in 2-quart covered saucepan; slowly stir in grits. Cover pan; reduce heat to low. Cook for 5 to 6 minutes, stirring occasionally. Top each serving with a pat of butter. Serves 4.

Breakfast Grits: This is the way I like it. Make as above, but substitute water for the chicken stock. Serve with butter or milk and sugar. Also try it with raisins, cinnamon, or brown sugar.

> Per one serving hominy grits, without butter: 131 calories; 4 grams protein; 23 grams carbohydrate; 2 grams fat; 8 grams saturated fat; 0 mg cholesterol; 429 mg sodium; 3.4 grams fiber.

There ain't nothin' like biscuits with butter, gravy, or, in some parts, such as West Virginia, pinto beans and eggs as a substantial breakfast. If you feel like making biscuits, it's just as easy to make them special, like these.

Golden Sweet Potato Biscuits

1 large sweet potato (½ cup baked or microwaved and mashed)
2 cups all-purpose flour
1 tablespoon baking powder
½ teaspoon salt
1 tablespoon sugar
  A few dashes of nutmeg
3 tablespoons vegetable oil
½ cup milk

Mash the sweet potato. Sift the dry ingredients together into a large mixing bowl. Mix in the oil and sweet potato with an electric mixer until they are evenly distributed. Gradually add the milk, continuing to mix just until ingredients are evenly dampened; do not beat.

Knead on floured board a few moments, just until slightly moistened. Roll out gently to a thickness of ¾ inch and cut out biscuits with a biscuit cutter. Place 1½ inches apart on an ungreased baking sheet. Bake in a preheated 425-degree oven for 12 to 15 minutes or until lightly browned. Makes 8 biscuits.

Per biscuit: 202 calories; 5 grams protein; 30 grams carbohydrate; 7 grams fat; .9 gram saturated fat; 7 mg cholesterol; 302 mg sodium; .12 gram fiber.

The southern United States grows June apples, sweet as honey, grainy, yellow, and great for cooking, which I discovered walking out my friends back door. I created these lightly sweet, delectable pancakes for the two of us and we dined under his apple tree on sweet apple pancakes and sausage.

Sweet Apple Pancakes with Fresh Berry Sauce

½ cup pancake flour
¾ cup quick oatmeal
⅓ cup nonfat dry milk solids
1 large June apple, grated, or substitute
   the sweetest apple you can find
¾ teaspoon vanilla
½ cup diet cream soda
2 egg whites, stiffly beaten

Combine pancake flour, oatmeal and nonfat dry milk. Stir in apple. Add vanilla and cream soda and mix just until combined. Fold in egg whites. Cook over medium heat in a nonstick skillet or keep the house and yourself cool and use the microwave. Pour batter into a shallow 8-inch microwave-safe bowl. Cook on high 4 to 5 minutes. Cake will be spongy. Serve in wedges with fresh berry sauce (next page) on flowered china. Accompany with classical or soft rock music. Makes about eight 4-inch pancakes.

Per pancake: 64 calories; 3 grams protein; 124 grams carbohydrate; .5 gram fat; 0 gram saturated fat; 0 mg cholesterol; 118 mg sodium; .77 gram fiber.

Love always comes back to you, sometimes double.

Berries and cream are what old-fashioned summers are made of.

Fresh Berry Sauce

1½ cups fresh berries such as blackberries, blueberries,
    raspberries, or strawberries
1 tablespoon sugar, or to taste
¼ cup light cream

Wash berries. Sprinkle sugar over berries and add cream. Squash berries slightly with a fork, making a juice that combines with the milk. Spoon berries over pancakes.

Per ¼ cup serving: 39 calories; 0 gram protein; 8 grams carbohydrate; 1 gram fat; 0 gram saturated fat; 0 mg cholesterol; 5 mg sodium; 1.46 grams fiber.

~

Chapter 4

Love is the best comfort food

Food for Love

Comforts to ease frustrations over relationships

Although I don't believe in fairy tales, there had better be some magic in my relationship, or what's the point? Yes, I know that in time love tends to turn into the everyday kind of love that is sometimes referred to as "oatmeal." And it's a secure feeling to know there is some oatmeal in the house—a comforting hug and someone to snuggle with. We often haven't the time to do a whole lot more than show each other that we're paying attention. Yet from time to time I need something a big more nutritious . . . don't you?

To me, romance is an ethereal quality layered with mystery, solitude, imagination, suspense, and, might I add, chemistry. It takes effort to cultivate such formless illusory substance into our fast-paced lives, yet the payoff is worth it. I applaud the line in the movie *The Preacher's Wife* where Dudley was asked what the secret was to keeping the flame going in a relationship. His answer? "You don't let it go out." Add a few raspberries to your oatmeal.

How much more we would enjoy the loves in our life if we could look ahead and see how short our time with them would be.

—Tom Schmidt

All Relationships Begin (and End) with You

As you well know, it's a fact of life that you can be in a room filled with hundreds of people and end up standing next to the man who will ultimately drive you nuts. It is said that we tend to attract and fall in love with people who can best work out our childhood dynamics—our weakness, if you will. Does the man in your life have any similarity to good old dad? Isn't it fun?

Given that we can't fool Mother Nature and attract others who symbolize our self-relationship, it makes good sense to have a solid and dynamic relationship with ourselves first. In that way we always have someone to depend on (ourselves)—because all the support in the world isn't going to be enough if we can't stand up by and for ourselves.

Observe a good relationship and you'll see that both people are whole individuals themselves. In order to have a quality one-on-one relationship, it is a natural law that we must be good for and to ourselves; we must love ourselves first—before the men in our lives, before our jobs—or we'll lose ourselves in the process. So if you're motivated by relationships like I am, approach it backwards: Become more important to yourself to become more important to others. (It actually works that way! Look around you!) You be the gourmet coffee—and let him be the cream. Be a quality person and maintain reasonable quality controls in order to attract the men and women into your life who are responsible and who will support you in being who you are.

Commitment is when the fun starts.
—KEN MICETIC

～

Love is the best comfort food, however, the body requires nutrients that are more basic and thus more important than you might think. Eat well and you'll be and perform well—and romantic love takes a lot of energy! Here is how the foods chosen for this chapter can affect your love life:

Carbohydrates are the primary ingredient in the foods for stress because they calm and stabilize moods through the manufacture of the neurotransmitter serotonin. Just one-and-a-half ounces or thirty grams of pure carbohydrates (which is equal to two cups of Cheerios, half a bran muffin, twenty-eight gummy bears, or a three-quarter cup of pasta) is enough to induce a quick surge of insulin from the pancreas, which in turn begins the soothing process by which serotonin will relax, calm, and focus frazzled nerves within thirty minutes. However, a meal in carbohydrates—a meal high in serotonin—"takes away your sex drive and delays your orgasms," according to Theresa Crenshaw, M.D., in *The Alchemy of Love and Lust* (Pocket Books, 1996).

Protein, as in steak and seafood, builds the body, giving energy and stamina as well as a sharp mind with which to enjoy that person. Alcohol is included in this chapter because we are often full of inhibitions and alcohol tends to temporarily allow us to do what we want to anyway. (**Note:** Moderation is extremely important, even complete abstinence if there is any tendency toward alcoholism.)

Then There's Chocolate . . .

My sister Eve used to tell me that I had to suffer to be beautiful while she was poking spiked curlers into my scalp. She would also tell me, "The harder you work, the more money you'll make," as well as, "Chocolate will make you break out." She was wrong on all counts. As we all now know, chocolate has soothing properties—something of a female health food with more than 400 compounds, twice as many as any other food, which makes it capable of elevating the female mood and spirit. Since ancient times, nuns were forbidden to enjoy it because of its sexual reputation. Priests, however, could consume it without restraint. Chocolate is the number one food craved by women (men most often crave red meat). Chocolate produces endorphins and appears to "power" the female body and mind for several reasons:

> Due to mood swings set off by hormones during and after the menstrual cycle, women tend to biologically crave foods that will stabilize them. Chocolate is half sugar and half fat, therefore half serotonin-producing and half endorphin-producing, for the perfect high: It's a mood-altering food, which both calms and elevates the mood.

> Chocolate contains tyramine and phenylethylamine, which in turn are made into the "stay alert" neurotransmitters, leading to greater alertness and slightly elevated blood pressure. Phenylethylamine is the chemical that being in love releases into the brain and thus induces this wonderful feeling—and it's not addictive!

> Chocolate contains caffeine and theobromine, both of which are stimulants, which increase our alertness and concentration.

> Chocolate contains magnesium, a mineral involved in the manufacturing of serotonin, which stabilizes mood.

Taking care is giving and receiving warm fuzzies strokes affection consideration nourishment sharing appreciation support system trust intimacy compassion understanding communication loyalty thoughtfulness And nice, warm sex The mundane will take care of itself P.S. The definition of Love lies above.

—REV. DOREEN RING

We can eat chocolate every day and not gain an ounce when we make a few trade-offs like skipping the butter on our bread. It's also possible to make nonfattening chocolate products by getting rid of the chocolate fat. Instead of chocolate, which is loaded with cocoa butter, use cocoa, which is what you get when you remove the fat from chocolate. An ounce of unsweetened cocoa is only thirty-six calories! And indulging in a food that really satisfies can boost your diet resolve because you won't feel deprived.

~

Instant gratification—prepare in less than fifteen minutes. Use it for a love (or other) hangover. These were my favorite cookies to make since I could reach the stove. They are chocolaty and delicious—more like candy.

KISSING FACT

Passionate kissing burns 6.4 calories a minute; a Hershey's Kiss contains 25 calories.

~

No-Bake Chocolate Fudge Cookies

1½ cups sugar
⅓ cup unsweetened cocoa
½ cup lowfat milk
¼ cup (½ stick) butter
⅓ cup peanut butter
3 cups quick-cooking oatmeal
1 teaspoon vanilla
½ cup flaked coconut

Combine first four ingredients in a medium saucepan. Bring to a boil, stirring constantly, for 1 full minute. (Remove from heat too soon and cookies will remain soft.) Mix in peanut butter. Add oats, vanilla, and coconut, and blend thoroughly. Drop by teaspoonfuls onto waxed paper. Let cool completely. Store cookies in airtight container. Makes about 36 cookies.

Per cookie: 96 calories; 2 grams protein; 15 grams carbohydrate; 3 grams fat; 2 grams saturated fat; 4 mg cholesterol; 30 mg sodium; .82 gram fiber.

Make cookies together. What could be a chore turns into a playful, messy, sexy way to spend time with him. Let him mix the batter while you feed him chocolate kisses. Move around each other, reaching, tasting, stirring—as your bodies touch, the oven isn't the only thing that's heating up!

Substitute almond-filled kisses!

Chocolate Kiss Cookies

- 1   cup butter or margarine, softened
- ⅔   cup sugar
- 1   teaspoon vanilla extract
- 1⅔ cup all-purpose flour
- ¼   cup unsweetened cocoa powder
- 1   cup finely chopped pecans
- 1   (9-ounce) bag Hershey's Kisses, unwrapped
     Confectioners' sugar

In large mixer bowl, beat butter, sugar, and vanilla until creamy. In separate bowl, stir together flour and cocoa; blend into butter mixture. Add pecans; beat on low speed until well blended. Refrigerate dough about 1 hour or until firm enough to handle. Heat oven to 375 degrees. Mold scant tablespoon of dough around each chocolate piece, covering chocolate completely. Shape into balls; place on ungreased cookie sheet. Bake 10 to 12 minutes or until set. Cool slightly; remove from cookie sheet to wire rack. Cool completely. Roll in confectioners' sugar. Roll in sugar again before serving, if desired. Makes about 4½ dozen cookies.

Per cookie: 94 calories; 1 gram protein; 9 grams carbohydrate; 7 grams fat; 10 mg cholesterol; 2 grams saturated fat; 35 mg sodium; .3 gram fiber.

Make your intention for peace and harmony with yourself, then with others, greater than anything . . . and that is exactly what you'll get.

Cooking can be a canvas for your emotions. Find a recipe that emotionally feeds your hungers, then infuse them into the food as you prepare it, as did the young Spanish girl, Tita, in the movie "Like Water for Chocolate." Tita cooked her passion for the man she was forbidden to love into her rose petal sauce, and everyone who tasted it also sampled her flaming desires— and was likewise transformed through it. Garnish this soup with rose petals or nasturtiums.

Strawberry Soup

1 pint (2 cups) fresh strawberries
1 cup light sour cream
1 cup light creamer or half-and-half
¼ cup sugar
2 tablespoons rum or brandy
½ teaspoon vanilla
  Sour cream, sliced strawberries, mint leaves, rose petals, or nasturtiums to garnish

Place glass goblets in the freezer. Now wash and hull strawberries. Reserve two for garnish. Place berries in blender with sour cream, half-and-half, sugar, rum or brandy, and vanilla; process 30 to 45 seconds until smooth. Serve in chilled glass goblets and garnish with a dollop of sour cream, slices of strawberries, mint leaves, rose petals, or nasturtiums. Instant relief for an incurable romantic. Serves 4.

Per serving: 341 calories; 4 grams protein; 60 grams carbohydrate; 7 grams fat; 4 grams saturated fat; 20 mg cholesterol; 61 mg sodium; 4.97 grams fiber.

Just for you . . .

A Rose Sandwich

Spread miniature bagels with soft strawberry cream cheese, cover with red rose petals, and sprinkle with cinnamon.

Set your standards
Giving to Yourself First

We are always setting our own standard and teaching others how to treat us. When a woman doesn't require her man, children, or girlfriends to cherish her feelings, she will in effect, become the masculine energy in the relationship. So if you're a supermom—doing all the cleaning and chauffeuring with a full-time job, and allowing the children to do what they will instead of having them participate in the household—think of when you won't have the energy. Do you think they'll help you out then? Will they offer to pick up the house or do the dishes? Suppose you were incapacitated. Is it then the loved ones you've been overdoing for will come around? Of course not. You're setting the standard for how you'll be treated *now*.

So many women don't understand how important it is to nurture their inner lives, that feel-good place within themselves. We give our light away as if we were limitless—but guess what, we're not!

～

When you're not tough with love, love can be tough with you.

Single or married . . .
Take Yourself On a Date

Cupid has his own time schedule and there are times it's good to be just with ourselves out on the town, whether married or single, so don't wait for the perfect man or the perfect opportunity. Take yourself out into the world. You're a whole person. Put effort into this—and follow through! Be your own lover: Go anywhere you want to go—a movie, a play, a coffeehouse with entertainment, dancing, a fancy restaurant, or Las Vegas. (Your inner child needs to know it can play—and get what it wants!) Treat yourself as you would want someone else to treat you. Do your nails, put on makeup, buy yourself flowers. Approach your evening playfully and joyfully! Warning: Enjoying yourself by yourself can be good for your emotional health.

Give Love

Every moment we have on this earth is vital! We are here to learn, to share, to love. It feels good to give and giving is precisely how we receive. Remember your priorities and give one hundred percent every day to those you love. Being creative in expressing love shows you took the time and really do care. Here are a few ideas:

Tuck notes, poems, puzzles, and comics into their lunches, backpacks, briefcases, and day-timers that say what you feel.

Just call to say "I love you."

Tell your beloved something so flattering it makes him blush.

Buy presents when you're away—it makes you feel closer to those you love.

Send flowers to your mother on *your* birthday.

Make signs that express how you feel. Five signs spotted consecutively along the road in Topanga Canyon, California, read: (1) Welcome Baby Pearl (2) You (3) Are (4) Very (5) Loved!

∽

The character trait you loved most about him in the beginning is most likely to drive you crazy after you really know him.

∽

No matter how pure the heart or innocent the intent, the notion of pleasure without consequence, intimacy without commitment, sensation without deliberation, is an illusion.

—SAM KEEN,
"THE PASSIONATE
LIFE: STAGES
OF LOVING"

Gifts of food make the heart grow fonder, my mother used to say. If cherries are not in season, use dried cherries. Substituting amaretto for the vanilla might be fun to try, too. Cut the slices thin and spread with whipped cream cheese.

Chocolate Cherry Bread

⅔ cup margarine

½ cup sugar

2 eggs or egg substitute

1 teaspoon vanilla

1½ cups sifted all-purpose flour

¼ cup unsweetened cocoa powder

1 teaspoon baking soda

½ teaspoon salt

¾ cup buttermilk

½ cup chopped walnuts

1¼ cup cherries, pitted and chopped

⅔ cup white raisins, optional

To know what a person wants in a relationship, look at what they give.

With an electric mixer, cream together margarine and sugar. Add eggs or egg substitute and beat well. Stir in vanilla; sift flour with cocoa, soda, and salt. Add to creamed ingredients alternately with buttermilk. Stir in nuts, cherries, and raisins.

Grease five soup cans (one end open, the other sealed) well. Turn batter into cans and place on a baking sheet.

Bake in preheated 350-degree oven for 30 minutes or until bread tests done. Cool cans 15 to 20 minutes on a wire rack, then turn out breads. Makes 5 small loaves to give to the neighbors or freeze. Yield: 20 servings.

Per serving: 143 calories; 3 grams protein; 14 grams carbohydrate; 8 grams fat; 21 mg cholesterol; 156 mg sodium; .11 gram fiber.

The Many Faces of Love

There are many kinds of love and all of them are important to develop and experience (doing so we're not as likely to put all our eggs in one basket): Romantic love, the kind that can make you crazy and takes a lot of energy, and platonic love, which says, "I don't want a relationship with you but I admire you." Then there is friendship love, that wonderful unconditional relationship with a comrade whom we can confide in from our soul. Kindred love is the love of nature and connection with the animal kingdom. Finally, there is the highest love: Spiritual love. Part of learning to love is through the growth of our spirit. We do this when we recognize, build, and implement love, caring, sharing, and taking care of each other.

If it's not yet time to meet that special one, express spiritual love. It and you will make a difference!

SELF/OTHER

One must determine
Self needs
To determine
How much to be
The Receiver
And how much to be
The Giver

—REV. DOREEN RING

Volunteer at a soup kitchen.

Lend a hand.

Give a smile or a touch.

Keep eye contact.

Circulate.

Listen.

Give in.

Express gratitude.

Teach what you know.

Keep the faith.

Be with a child (let them show you how).

Seek out older people and give them the gift of yourself.

～

If food and sex can cure depression, they must mean cheesecake. New York style cheesecake, the popular heavier style, was foreign to me until I was old enough to vote. Way back then my mother made a very light version using cottage cheese that would now be referred to as a "California cheese-cake." This one can be either, depending on whether you use whole fat, low-fat, or fat-free cream cheese and whipped topping.

Five-Minute California Cheesecake

1½ (8-ounce) packages fat-free, lowfat, or
       full-fat cream cheese, softened

⅓ cup sugar

1 (8-ounce) tub frozen whipped topping, thawed

1 (6-ounce) purchased graham cracker pie crust or
       chocolate pie crust

Beat cream cheese with sugar using an electric mixer until well blended. Gently stir in whipped topping. Spoon into crust.

Refrigerate 3 hours or overnight. This is complete as is, but it's good with fresh berries and fruit, too. Makes 8 servings.

Using fat-free cream cheese, per serving: 242 calories; 7 grams protein; 32 grams carbohydrate; 9 grams fat; 6 grams saturated fat; 1 gram cholesterol; 361 mg sodium; 0 gram fiber.

How To Win an Argument

Make your first response to an opposing opinion "yes" and, instead of combating his reasons, agree with him, then offer a solution.

For instance, if he doesn't want to fly to Hawaii, say, "Yes, honey, travel is expensive, but I have an old girlfriend living in Honolulu and we could stay with her."

∼

Here is a beautiful way to romance him. It's food for the eyes and the heart—so pretty poured under or over cheesecake, pound cake, angel food cake, or a slice of chocolate cake. Strawberries may be substituted for the raspberries.

Great-with-Everything Raspberry Sauce

2 cups fresh raspberries (two half-pints) or
1 (12-ounce) package frozen raspberries, thawed
⅓ cup confectioners' sugar
1 tablespoon lemon juice

Treat him as if he were a brand new Mercedes. If we were to treat him as if he were the ever-changing spirit that he is—and as you are—can you imagine how delightful his presence will become?

Place ingredients in a blender and purée until smooth. Place a fine-textured sieve over a bowl or place a piece of cheesecloth over a strainer and pour in a little of the purée. Using a rubber spatula, push the sauce through to remove seeds. Repeat with remaining purée. Taste sauce and, if desired, add a little more confectioners' sugar. Makes 1 cup sauce. Refrigerate (it will keep for about one week).

Per ¼ cup: 57 calories; 0 gram protein; 14 grams carbohydrate; 0 gram fat; 0 gram saturated fat; 1 gram sodium; 1.96 grams fiber.

~

Give to yourself whatever you need to keep your own spirit alive, which is the best way to keep all your relationships alive!

~

If Hillary Clinton can find time to bake cookies, imagine what you have the time to do! Here is her recipe for chocolate chip cookies. "We always look forward to Mrs. Clinton's cookies," says Neel Lattimore, her deputy press secretary.

Hillary's Cookie Recipe

1½ cups unsifted all-purpose flour
1   teaspoon salt
1   teaspoon baking soda
1   cup solid vegetable shortening
½   cup sugar
1   cup firmly packed light brown sugar
1   teaspoon vanilla extract
2   eggs
2   cups rolled oats
1   (12-ounce) package semisweet chocolate chips

Heat oven to 350 degrees. Combine flour, salt, and baking soda. Beat together shortening, sugars, and vanilla until creamy. Add eggs, beating until fluffy. Gradually beat in flour mixture and rolled oats. Stir in chips. Drop teaspoonfuls of batter onto cookie sheets. Bake 8 to 10 minutes. Cool cookies on sheets for two minutes before placing them on wire rack for further cooling. Makes 7½ dozen cookies.

Variation: Substitute 1 (12-ounce) bag M&Ms for the chocolate chips.

Per cookie: 68 calories; 1 gram protein; 9 grams carbohydrate; 3 grams fat; 1 gram saturated fat; 2.3 mg cholesterol; 43.7 mg sodium; .08 gram fiber.

You'll never regret spending too much time with your kids.

Love invents us. Turn around and invent this horrendously decadent, unforgettably impressive hunk of cookie-cake for your love. Head Chef Richard Goetz at the Orange Coast Medical Center often made this cake for us, the kitchen staff, on our birthdays. It's a birthday cake they'll never forget.

Chocolate Chip Cookie Cake

Follow Hillary's recipe above, or buy a bag of Nestle's chocolate chips and follow recipe on the bag for Tollhouse Chocolate Chip Cookies.

Coat two 9 by 9-inch cake pans with vegetable spray. Divide batter between both pans and bake 20 to 25 minutes, or until layers test done (insert a toothpick in the center of the pan and if it comes out clean, it's done).

Fill and frost with 1 (16-ounce) can of prepared chocolate fudge icing.

~

If you plan to ask for help from your husband or family, take it as it comes. Be happy with them doing tasks the way they do it, not the way you would necessarily want them to. If you complain they may never help you again!

~

*T*ransform heartache into laughter by spending more time around funny friends and watching Chevy Chase, Steve Martin, or your favorite comedians on home videos. Laughter reduces stress, relieves tension, soothes anger and yes, even heartache, if you can let yourself go. Or watch a good tearjerker. It's the second-best tension release in town (unless, of course, you've already done enough of that).

Here is a list of my favorite videos for times like this (we don't need any romantic movies just now). So why don't you make a cup of tea, curl up with a friend, and get lost in someone elses' drama?

 EROTICA AND THE
MARRIED LIFE

In a 1993 *Ladies' Home Journal* survey that drew responses from over 40,000 readers, forty-seven percent of the married women surveyed said they use erotic material at least occasionally. Eighty-four percent of the ladies used erotic videos and movies. Thirty-nine percent of wives who use erotic aids say they and their husbands use sex toys, and thirty-four percent choose sexy magazines.

—LADIES' HOME
JOURNAL (FEBRUARY
1993), "THE LOVE
LIFE OF THE
AMERICAN WIFE"

Cheatin' Heart

Leaving Normal

My Cousin Vinny

Housesitter

Steel Magnolias

National Lampoon's Christmas Vacation

Any movie with Steve Martin

Any movie with Chevy Chase

First Wives Club

Housesitter

Black and white classics

Fried Green Tomatoes

Honeymoon in Vegas

～

*Did you know that it takes five positive comments
to neutralize one negative comment?*

～

*Ask your partner:
How am I doing as
a spouse/partner?
Act on the
information you get.*

What to Fix for a Night of Reconciliation

Most aphrodisial foods—oysters, chocolate, anchovies, brains, chiles, ginger (to name a few)—are either stimulants or protein foods, so a steak dinner and coffee is just as stimulating. The secret is to vocalize that what he is eating is known to be a sexually stimulating!

～

*What usually bothers us most about others is the same trait
in ourselves that we do not like. We can give to others
only what we give to ourselves. We can forgive in others
only what we forgive in ourselves.*

～

This stir-fried dish spiced with ginger will fortify both of you for an evening of making up. Or if you don't care to cook, and you both like it hot, take-out food from any Thai or Indian restaurant will do. Serve with Thai beer or an off-dry, low-tannin wine, perhaps a reisling, or a sparkling wine and coffee.

Spicy Beef and Tomatoes

1　pound round steak, cut about ½-inch thick
2　tablespoons soy sauce
2　tablespoons salad oil
1　tablespoon cooking sherry
4　teaspoons cornstarch
½　teaspoon sugar
¼　teaspoon powdered ginger (or grated fresh)
2　medium green, red, and yellow peppers, cut into
　　　lengthwise strips
2　small onions, quartered
2　small tomatoes, cut into wedges
3　cups hot cooked rice

Starting each day new, seeing him fresh—not carrying yesterday's problems, not focusing on your problems, but only what you want— will give you the opportunity to create your relationship as you want it to be.

About 45 minutes before serving, cut steak lengthwise in half; slice halves diagonally into thin slices. In large bowl, combine steak, soy sauce, 1 tablespoon salad oil, sherry, cornstarch, sugar, and ginger; set aside.

Put a sexy ballad on the CD player—say, Ravel's "Bolero." Now pour 1 tablespoon oil into the wok. Over medium high heat, pour meat mixture into pan and stir-fry 2 to 3 minutes, until barely medium rare. Add peppers and onions and stir-fry for 3 more minutes, adding tomatoes halfway through. Serve over rice with optional chop sticks and extra soy sauce. Makes 4 servings.

Per serving: 419 calories; 39 grams protein; 50 grams carbohydrate; 4 grams fat; 73 grams cholesterol; 2 grams saturated fat; 324 mg sodium; 2.2 grams fiber.

Romance Is the Sweet Little Unexpected Things

Be the can opener to a man's soul
by planning a bit of romance
every single day

It helps to know that men fall in love with their eyes (and women with their ears). Slip on a pair of black lace underpants when you get home. One of the best aphrodisiacs is self-confidence!

Sexy thoughts are arousing. Let him know during the day that you have an erotic surprise planned for him that night.

When making love, little additions such as feathers, sheepskin puffs, chocolate body paint (add a bit of whipped cream, maybe a few chocolate chips), and edible oils can be quite nice.

Chilled champagne or flavored vodka and icy oysters set a mood. Feed your lover, your friends, children—or anyone you want to be intimate with—with your fingers.

Have "love snacks." Barbara De Angelis teaches people in her seminars to have little five-minute periods of kissing, holding, caressing, and sustaining eye contact—whatever it is that makes you feel more loved.

To rebond when you've drifted apart, or to simply get closer, try this! Plan two hours of uninterrupted time together without saying a word. Do a bubble bath with candles, incense, even flowers around the tub. Wash each others' hair. Massage and powder each other. Then write a letter to each other and exchange them.

~

SEDUCE HIM ON HIS CELL PHONE . . .

When you know your sweetie is en route to your place, give him a ring on his mobile and whisper sweet nothings into his ear. You can finish what you started once he arrives.

Helps for . . .
Soothing the Pain of a Breakup

Remove attention from him and put it on you. Healing takes place when you finally really let go. Before picking up the phone to call him, have a list of five people to call or ten things you need to do first.

My heart will go on! Although it feels like it, you know it's not the end of the world. Calm yourself with a nice hot bath and be with yourself. Take it one minute, one hour, then one day, at a time. Concentrate on taking care of you. You may not look any different, so people expect you to act the same, but your hurt is no different than having a broken leg or a debilitating illness. The solution is to pamper yourself.

Things to Remember
When Breaking Up

You never find yourself until you face the truth.

—PEARL BAILEY

It's your responsibility to break emotionally with the other person, not the other person's responsibility to free you. Let go of the anger. If you brood and hang onto it, it will not be over. Even if there is a lot of love between you, love is not enough to maintain a relationship. Mutual love is only one element of maintaining a relationship.

Comfort your mind by hiding, avoiding, or throwing away as many triggers to thinking about your relationship as you can. These may include photographs of the two of you, gifts from him, tapes or CDs you enjoyed together, special scents he liked on you, restaurants, and so on. Don't listen to romantic songs, and avoid the places you would go with him for awhile. Remove the food and drink that was "his" in your refrigerator and gradually replace these with new things that say "you."

One of the best ways to be yourself is to reach out. Call your friends, ex-lovers, or family! Move yourself into the flow of people: Touch, speak, laugh. Call, get out, talk. Do it now.

Don't Stop Loving;
Some of These Suggestions May Help:

Spend the night with a good friend.

Get a kitten.

Create comfort for yourself. Now you can justify buying yourself
a lovely quilt, comforter, or set of sheets . . . flowers . . . something
you've been secretly lusting over. Rediscover bubble baths.
Find out what time the local bakery takes its bread out of the
oven so you can buy it while it's still warm. Put a Band-Aid
over your heart.

Rent "woman movies" you've been wanting to see.

Invite your girlfriend over or spend an evening drinking hot
chocolate at a cozy coffee house. Think, write, and talk about him.
In time the whole affair will get old. Go ahead, bore yourself!

Plan on taking off early from work. Rent a good video and take
a hot bath or get a massage.

Buy light whipping cream and top everything with it.

Keep going forward.

*In time the whole
affair will get old.
Go ahead,
bore yourself!*

~

*Find reasons to feel good because what we think, especially
with emotion, we attract to us—whether we want it or not.
When we feel lonely, we tend to attract more loneliness;
when we feel rich, we attract more money, and so on.
Nothing is more important than making yourself feel good.
Make it your number one priority!*

~

Hurt feelings have less power over us when we express them.
Get them out to him or to a confidante. If you won't see him
again, put it in a letter.

Eat. A balanced meal will stabilize emotions and help you feel better able to cope. Carbohydrates (bread, cereal, juice, fruit, and so on) will calm and center. Protein will fortify, make you feel stronger, and have a sharper mind. If you don't feel like eating, start with a beer or glass of wine. Besides the short-term high, it may also tease your appetite.

If you can't eat, drink: Milk, fast food shakes, hot cocoa, tea, diet sodas, water, broth, or soup. Pick up some fat-free ice cream (it contains appreciable protein and comes in chocolate) or your favorite cereal and milk (spoil yourself and add strawberries or blueberries).

People *do* die from broken hearts. Loss and other emotional stress can trigger coronary artery disease. The best prescription is to cry, laugh, or yell. Scream, tell him how you feel and don't hold back, move furniture, run, or lift weights. If you don't, it may well turn inward (depression), or manifest on the skin as a rash or acne.

You can let go, if only you believe you can. If useful, utilize photographs to help you by putting them away, far out of reach, or by ceremoniously burning them. In photographs of the two of you, it may feel right to cut out your own photo and burn the rest. (It feels good and you're worth saving!) But don't make any "thing" more important than you or your healing process.

Divert your thoughts to other things. Accept invitations to be around other people. Start reading a great book. Begin a project. See lots of movies. Dress well. Get your hair trimmed or try a new hair color.

Buy yourself a visual token of your love and support, such as a beautiful bracelet, ring, or necklace.

Anticipate a positive future. Plan on it, expect it—it will come! Be with the sadness, but go about your business. Pain that is resisted persists. The pain will pass.

Plan for those times you know you'll be more vulnerable to sadness—a Saturday or holiday alone. Schedule something for that day that you really enjoy—a movie, a talk with a friend, an afternoon drive. Unrequited love is universal and, unfortunately, natural. Life is neither good nor bad, life includes both good *and* bad—and so did the relationship. Write down all the good things you've gained from this period of time, what did you learn? Perhaps you've learned when to invest your love, when to invest your energy, and when to run like hell.

～

As time goes on, be kind, patient, and gentle with yourself. The grieving process takes time. Spells of sadness will come and go. Remember, life is your adventure and that was just an episode.

～

Celebrate! Believe in happy endings. Just because this relationship didn't work out doesn't mean there isn't still a happily-ever-after ending for you in the future. Conjure up a variety of endings for yourself.

Think of your relationship not as letting go of a person, but instead as letting go of an experience—it was, and experiences are easier to let go of. Think, "It was so nice to have had what we had." You are not mourning for what you had, but for what could have been, thus you're not mourning for reality, but for a dream.

My needs are soooo simple I want a man Who has integrity with a capacity to Love And a capacity for intimacy Only equal to my own.

—REV. DOREEN RING

～

It matters not whether you have left a relationship or someone has left you. There are stages of feelings: Loss and denial, anger, grief, self-awareness, and a sense of freedom, that we all need to move through to begin anew. It is personally mandatory that you act in your best interests and deeply care for yourself through this time. The more say you have about your own life, the more secure you will feel about what's happening to you, the most self-satisfaction you will experience, and the smoother you will move through this experience.

～

Do you have to make everything a challenge?" my friend Guy asked me after I broke up with my boyfriend the twenty-third time. "So you crashed again without a runway." Yes, I did. But nothing that lots of sleep, a few glasses of wine, and a sandwich won't cure. This is the sandwich I'm talking about.

Two chocolate sandwiches. It's certainly no worse than a burger and fries.

Chocolate Cream Cheese Sandwich

1 French roll
  Cream cheese (all you want)
1 chocolate bar with almonds

Preheat oven to 400 degrees. Set roll in oven for 5 minutes, or just until the outside is warmed and crispy. Remove roll from oven and split. Spread cream cheese over the bottom. Break candy bar to fit roll and insert over cream cheese. Press down and let it melt a bit. Makes 1 serving.

435 calories; 10 grams protein; 40 grams carbohydrate; 26 grams fat; 42 grams saturated fat; 7 grams cholesterol; 368 mg sodium; 0 gram fiber.

A recent medical dispatch has indicated that people who eat chocolate live longer that those who abstain. This chocolate sandwich has about the same amount of protein as a McDonald's hamburger, yet is lower in fat! There is always a healthy way to enjoy what we truly love . . .

"Skinny" Chocolate Cream Cheese Sandwich

1 French roll
2 tablespoons fat-free cream cheese
1 chocolate bar
  Fresh sliced strawberries or light strawberry preserves, optional

Communication is the house that love built. When we communicate with anyone we are actually loving them by validating them. Have you noticed that you can fall in love with someone who really listens to you? On the other hand, withdrawing communication deteriorates a relationship.

Preheat oven to 400 degrees. Set roll in oven for 5 minutes, or just until outside is warmed and crispy. Remove roll from oven and split. Spread cream cheese over the bottom. Break candy bar to fit roll and insert over cream cheese. Press down and let it melt a bit. Tuck in a few strawberries or spread some good jam over the chocolate if you like. Makes 1 serving.

350 calories; 11 grams protein; 43 grams carbohydrate; 15 grams fat; 7 grams saturated fat; 15 grams cholesterol; 432 mg sodium; 2 grams fiber.

Note: 1 McDonald's hamburger has 320 calories; 13 grams protein; 34 grams carbohydrate; 21 grams fat; 8 grams saturated fat; 70 grams cholesterol; 820 mg sodium; 2 grams fiber.

Make a Flaming Impression with Coffee

Brew a mocha or other favorite flavored coffee. Fill a spoon with cognac, place a sugar cube on the spoon, ignite, and drop in hot coffee. Then learn about love through some great reading and listening!

Recommended reading

Love is Letting Go Of Fear by Gerald G. Jampolsky, M.D.

Recommended listening

How to Love a Woman by Clarissa Pinkola Estes, Ph.D. Estes explores the idea that all relationships fade and expire only to be reborn in a fresh and strengthened form. Also available in book form.

Dr. Pat Allen, Ph.D. Lecture series on *Training for Effective Relationships* includes cassette tapes and the book *Getting To I Do.* Call 1-800-496-3983 or write Pat Allen & Associates, 3355 Via Lido, Suite 205, Newport Beach, CA 92663 for a brochure.

I think possibly the crowing achievement of femininity is to be able to bring joy, ecstasy, pleasure into life. A man values a woman so highly because she has just this capacity or power. Men cannot find this ecstasy alone, without the aid of the feminine element, so they find it either in outer woman or in their own inner woman. Joy is a gift from the heart of woman.

—ROBERT JOHNSON, "SHE"

Romantica (ro-man-tik-a) is Spanish for "Romantic Experience." Make a romantica out of these chocolate biscuits and feed them to him. Now invite him to feed them to you. Make these with love and enjoy with light whipping cream (or light ricotta cheese) for a breakfast that won't leave you with only a sugar high (unlike some forms of love). This sensual indulgence is food for the body and the soul.

Chocolate Biscuits

1¼ cup all-purpose flour
½ cup wheat bran
1 teaspoon baking powder
3 tablespoons cocoa powder
⅓ cup light brown sugar, packed
   A couple dashes of salt
¼ cup light butter or margarine
1 teaspoon vanilla
¾ cup light sour cream
¼ cup chocolate chips, optional

Combine flour, bran, baking powder, cocoa, brown sugar, and salt. With a fork or pastry blender, break butter down into small pieces. Add vanilla and sour cream. Stir, then knead ingredients into a ball. Knead in chocolate chips. Pat out either in a bowl or on a board 1-inch thick with the palm of your hands. Sprinkle with flour if it is sticky, then cut out biscuits with a small cookie cutter (a fluted champagne glass is perfect, should you have no cutter). Bake at 375 degrees for 20 to 30 minutes or until lightly firm. Makes fourteen 1½-inch biscuits. Be sure and enjoy them with whipping cream!

Per biscuit: 90 calories; 3 grams protein; 16 grams carbohydrate; 2 grams fat; 1 gram saturated fat; 5 mg cholesterol; 39 mg sodium; 1.4 grams fiber.

TREAT YOURSELF

Whether you wake up feeling wonderful or miserable tomorrow morning, it's reason enough to drizzle your French toast with a bit of Grand Marnier, Frangelica, or your favorite liqueur.

Read some inspiring story or literature, pray, think positively, and follow with some good strong coffee adorned with whipped cream.

Soon you will see from a better perspective. Promise.

Pamper your loved one. A make-ahead breakfast in bed is guaranteed to make good memories. Prepare the night before, then bake it in the morning. Serve with champagne and a kiss. By no means follow ingredients exactly. Substitute red wine or champagne, should the mood strike you.

Stay-in-Bed Fruit and Wine Omelet

    1 pound lean turkey sausage
    1 cup mushrooms, cleaned and sliced
    6 eggs or 1½ cups egg substitute
    1 cup good white wine, fruity or dry
    1 cup nonfat milk
    ½ teaspoon salt, optional
    1 teaspoon dry mustard
    3 slices French bread, cubed
    1 cup sliced apples, peaches, and cherries
    1 cup grated lowfat cheese

Brown sausage with mushrooms. Drain off any oil. Beat eggs and add remaining ingredients, including sausage. Pour into a deep casserole or pretty quiche pan and refrigerate overnight.

Bake 45 to 60 minutes, depending on the depth of your baking dish. Omelet is ready to serve when a knife inserted in the middle comes out clean. Good served cold, too.

Note: Leave a good amount of liquid in pan because the bread will soak it up during the night. Also, if using white wine, consider adding shrimp and white bread only. As you know, traditionally red wine goes well with red meat. Makes 6 servings.

> Per serving: 291 calories; 26 grams protein; 9 grams carbohydrate; 14 grams fat; 224 grams cholesterol; 5 grams saturated fat; 529 mg sodium; .21 gram fiber.

LOVE RINGS

Give him a "love ring," a single telephone ring to remind him that you love him and are thinking of him.

Diet by chocolate and knock him dead at the same time with this luscious lowfat chocolate cake laced with liqueur. It's best eaten warm or the same day. Do serve it with whipping cream laced with the same liqueur or ice cream and fresh coffee.

Hot Fudge Sundae Cake

½ cup lowfat milk
4 teaspoons instant coffee powder
2 tablespoons melted butter
2 teaspoons vanilla extract
¾ cup all-purpose flour
¼ teaspoon salt, optional
2 teaspoons baking powder
½ cup sugar
½ cup quick-cooking oats
¼ cup unsweetened cocoa powder
1¾ cups boiling water
2 tablespoons coffee, Frangelica (hazelnut flavored), or other favorite liqueur
Light whipping cream or ice cream, optional
Berries for garnish, optional

*When a man says
he loves you
He promises safety
and protection
When a woman says
she loves you
She promises
to entrust herself*
—REV. DOREEN RING

Heat ¼ cup of the milk. Stir in coffee powder to dissolve. Add remaining milk, melted butter, and 1 teaspoon vanilla extract.

Resift flour with salt, baking powder and ¼ cup sugar in mixing bowl. Add milk mixture to dry ingredients, stirring with fork until blended. Mix in oats. Do not overmix.

Combine remaining ¼ cup sugar, 1 teaspoon vanilla extract, and cocoa powder with boiling water. Mix well to dissolve cocoa. Stir in the liqueur. Pour into bottom of an 8-inch square baking dish. It will look like chocolate soup, but don't worry—it will firm up when it bakes! Spoon on batter by large spoonfuls. Bake at 350 degrees 40 to 45 minutes. Let stand about 10 minutes.

Spoon into dessert dishes and scoop chocolate sauce from pan over each serving. If desired, serve with dollop of light whipped cream or ice cream and garnish with berries. Makes 9 servings.

> Per serving: 99 calories; 3 grams protein; 16 grams carbohydrate; 2 grams fat; 0 gram saturated fat; 1 mg cholesterol; 172 mg sodium; 1 mg cholesterol; 0 gram fiber.

Stir a few chocolate chips, sliced bananas, or chopped nuts into the batter, if you like. Carbohydrates calm the nerves and chocolate has phenylethylamine, the chemical that feels like love. Bake immediately or store in a tightly covered container in the refrigerator for up to two weeks.

Big Batch of Bran Muffins

2	cups water
¾	cup vegetable oil
1	teaspoon salt
2¾	cups sugar
2	eggs
6	cups (a whole box) bran cereal
5	cups all-purpose flour (substitute half whole-wheat flour, if desired)
4	teaspoons soda
1	quart buttermilk

The best way to develop a good relationship is to maintain the relationship you have already developed with yourself.

Combine all ingredients and refrigerate at least 2 hours. Bake at 400 degrees for 20 to 25 minutes. Makes about 5½ dozen muffins.

> Per muffin: 114 calories; 2 grams protein; 22 grams carbohydrate; 3 grams fat; .3 gram saturated fat; 7 mg cholesterol; 59 mg sodium; 2.9 grams fiber.

Perhaps he has his own type of PMS and needs a dietary lift too! If your male companion is about as much company as a hamster on a bad diet, feed both of you a steak. In the movie "Moonstruck," Cher threw a steak in the pan, seared it, and fed it to overemotional Nicholas Cage. There's something inherently sexy about a steak dinner for two. Perhaps the most effective aphrodisiac is a clear, strong mind and body.

Mae West was quoted as saying, "It isn't the men in my life, it's the life in my men." If your man needs a little life, fix him a steak. Red meat increases testosterone.

One of the best ways to become a broken woman . . . is to mother a man. Be sure you are a woman who loves herself before all others. A woman who loves a man more than herself becomes, in a sense, his mother, giving to him without hesitation, as his mother would. Women who mother men often fill themselves with food, booze, or drugs to fill the hole within herself.
—PAT ALLEN, PH.D.

~

Pan-Fried Steak

2   filet mignon, New York, sirloin, T-bone, or Spencer steaks
    Your favorite seasoning
    Salt and pepper

Spray a medium skillet with nonstick spray and turn the heat up. Rub your favorite seasoning (I like a touch of smoke seasoning) lightly over both sides. Get the pan nice and hot and lay the steak in the pan. Fry until one side is seared—about 1½ to 2 minutes—and flip. Fry other side. Slide off onto plate. Serve with whatever you or he likes—steak sauce, Worcestershire sauce, salsa, or nothing at all!

Per 8-ounce sirloin steak: 493 calories, 65 grams protein; 0 gram carbohydrates, 24 grams fat; 10 grams saturated fat; 148 grams cholesterol; 137 mg sodium; 0 gram fiber.

It's soft, nourishing, and sexy. Spoon it over angel food cake or biscuits and top with whipping cream. Swirled with cottage cheese, it's a light meal.

This is a simple, nutritious, old-fashioned comfort for breakfast or late at night.

Open a Can of Fruit

1 cup fruit cocktail (or your favorite fruit) in juice
1 cup lowfat vanilla ice cream
½ teaspoon ground cinnamon
2 teaspoons toasted wheat germ, optional

Layer these ingredients in a parfait glass—or swirl them together in a dish. If desired, sprinkle a little toasted wheat germ on top.

Per serving: 314 calories; 130 mg sodium; 20 mg cholesterol; 4 grams fat; 65 grams carbohydrate; 7 grams protein; 1.51 grams fiber.

～

Every time, I think, it is one's own attitude, not the relationship, on which one needs to work.

It is a fact that in any partnership, if one of the partners becomes quite clear in himself what it is that the situation requires, the changes are it will not even be necessary to voice it; the other will somehow pick up the point and comply, with no words said.

—IRENE CLAREMONT
DE CASTILLEJO,
"KNOWING WOMAN:
A FEMININE
PSYCHOLOGY"

$\mathcal{E}$ndorphins work similarly to serotonin. When endorphin levels are low in the brain, we may feel stressed and fatigued. When the subsequent craving is satisfied with a high-sugar, high-fat snack such as chocolate, endorphin levels rise and spirits lift.

	CALORIES	FAT	PERCENT FROM FAT
Peter Paul Almond Joy, 1.76-ounce bar	250	13.9	59
Hershey's chocolate kiss 1 kiss	25	1.38	50
semisweet chocolate chips, ¼ cup	203	12.6	56
Chocolate-covered cherries, 2 pieces	175	4.5	23
Nestle Crunch, 1.4-ounce bar	198	10.4	47
M&Ms, plain, 1 piece	3.3	.15	41
1.69-ounce package (69 pieces)	229	10.6	42
M&Ms, peanut, 1 piece	10	.52	47
1.74-ounce package (25 pieces)	242	13.2	53
York Peppermint Patty, 1 small patty (.39 ounce)	38	1.0	24

$\mathcal{L}$ove is the greatest refreshment in life.

—PABLO PICASSO

～

Truly a sweet offering for someone you love (even you)!

Strawberry-Rose Cheesecake

⅓ cup vanilla wafer crumbs (7 wafers)
2 teaspoons sugar
1 (8-ounce) package Neufchâtel cheese, softened
¼ cup sugar
2 egg whites, lightly beaten
½ teaspoon vanilla
1 cup plain lowfat yogurt
1 tablespoon sugar
½ teaspoon almond extract
2 cups sliced fresh strawberries
6–8 miniature roses, prepared for cooking*
1 kiwi, peeled and sliced

Spray an 8-inch glass pan with nonstick cooking spray. In small bowl, combine vanilla wafer crumbs and sugar; mix well. Sprinkle crust mixture into bottom and sides of pan. In a medium bowl, beat together Neufchâtel cheese, sugar, egg whites, and vanilla until smooth. Pour into crust. Microwave (medium) 4 to 6 minutes or until a knife inserted in the center comes out clean. In a small bowl, combine yogurt, 1 tablespoon sugar, and almond extract. Spoon over cheesecake. Carefully spread to edges. Microwave (medium) 2 to 3 minutes. Cool on a wire rack, then refrigerate until cold. Before serving, arrange strawberries, roses, and kiwi in concentric circles. Makes 8 servings.

*To make roses tastier to our palate (which means sweeter), they may be candied in the following way:

Whip 1 egg white until frothy but not stiff. With a good paintbrush, brush on egg white, petal by petal. Put about ½ cup of sugar in the blender and let it blend nice and fine to become superfine sugar. Using a teaspoon, sprinkle sugar over flower. Use as you like.

Sometimes I wonder if it is wise to work directly on relationship. What matters is to be centered oneself, willing and ready, always ready for the moments or hours of meeting when they come. Then the relationship can be trusted to take care of itself.

—IRENE CLAREMONT DE CASTILLEJO, "KNOWING WOMAN: A FEMININE PSYCHOLOGY"

Keep Packets of Instant Cocoa Mix At Work
Serve your inner beast some hot cocoa
with whipped cream

Rip open a packet of instant hot cocoa or Ovaltine; pour into your favorite mug along with 1 cup boiling water.

Add half a packet to coffee for a double caffeine lift.

Add marshmallows, whipping cream, and grated chocolate over the top.

When An Emotionally Charged Situation Comes Up . . .

Never let a problem to be solved become more important than the person to be loved.

Neutralize your anger by thinking of your emotion as a raging waterfall flowing away from you. Ask yourself: "What do I want out of this?" and "How do I want to feel?" to guide yourself to the appropriate response—rather than reacting.

Keep them guessing. Do something totally unexpected, such as arranging a surprise promotion party, a picnic (made easy with food from a gourmet deli) to celebrate the first day of summer, or a night away at a hotel with an enchanting ambience.

～

Chapter 5

Spring and Summer Comforts

Creative ways to hurry up spring and ooze into summer

Spring evolves slowly in the Midwest and, to a kid growing up, it felt like years. Walls of snow gradually melted into the sloppy ground, leaving puddles of mud that stained my PF Flyers. Then one day the sun was strong as tiny leaves popped out on the trees, crocuses pushed their way under a crusty blanket of snow, and new life stirred all around: yes, finally spring was here! I was stunned, it almost seemed impossible. It was like my first kiss, or first accepted book proposal.

Everything is better in summer.

❧

This is it! Your life! Not a vague dream, not a story in someone else's book—so don't sleep a moment more! Crawl out from under winter's heaviness and regain your spirit. Feed the excitement that is stirring within your body and soul. Reawaken your heart through your senses: buy a pink shawl, maybe a six-pack of petunias, or crimson tulips for your desk, then find some matching nail polish and lipstick. Here are more ways to hurry up spring:

> Warm up your imagination. Most likely, it's been cooped up too! Start by watching clouds change their formation and decide what their shapes remind you of. Read *Creative Companion* by Sark (Celestial Arts, 1991), an adult's guide to developing creativity.

HOW TO BE REALLY ALIVE!

Live juicy. Stamp out conformity. Stay in bed all day. Dream of gypsy wagons. Find snails making love. Develop an astounding appetite for books. Drink sunsets. Draw out your feelings. Amaze yourself. Be ridiculous. Stop worrying—now. If not now, then when? Make YES your favorite word. Marry yourself. Dry your clothes in the sun. Eat mangos naked. Keep toys in the bathtub. Spin yourself dizzy. Hang upside down.

Daydream creatively: Dream that you've won a million dollars and now have to spend it. That you've been asked to appear on the Phil Donahue show. Or that you're meeting Kevin Costner for lunch.

Buy a jump rope, some bubbles, maybe a paddle ball and jacks. Make use of them. Wear a ribbon in your hair.

Collect all the winter clothes you didn't wear this year (and probably never will), and give them to the Salvation Army or other good cause.

Change the station on your clock radio so that you wake up to something different in the morning—perhaps classical, country western, or the blues.

If it's still too chilly to eat your lunch in the park, have your coffee there instead.

Paint a wall, a closet, or maybe the kitchen stool the color that made you happy as a kid.

Change the perfume you've been wearing.

Eat a mango or a papaya for breakfast. You could even go to the tropical paradise it came from if you really, really wanted to. (Until then, dream!)

Buy an inexpensive music box with a pretty tune.

Give flowers to someone you work with.

Give love; develop a crush. Send a man you like a crazy little gift in the mail—and don't sign your name.

Plan all twenty-two warm-weather weekends between now and Labor Day.

~

Easter is traditionally celebrated with a ham. I think of it as a good investment in leftovers for many meals to come. Chop it for Denver omelets, scalloped potatoes, stuffed baked potatoes, casseroles, pea soup, and, of course, sandwiches. It lasts and lasts, but you could also freeze it.

A very elegant way to serve canned ham is to wrap it in a dress made of refrigerated dinner rolls. Similar in concept to Beef Wellington, this method is easier but equally impressive. Cherry pie filling oozes out from beneath it for a pretty bonus.

Ham in Full Dress

1 (5-pound) fully cooked ham
1 (8-ounce) can light cherry pie filling, or
        fruit sauce below, optional
1 (8-ounce) can refrigerated crescent dinner rolls
        Melted butter, optional

Bake a fully-cooked ham at 325 degrees until completely warmed through (about 20 minutes per pound). Remove it from the oven and cool for 20 minutes. Spoon cherry pie filling over top and sides of ham.

Separate the crescent roll dough into two large rectangles; press the perforations together to seal the dough. Overlap long sides of the rectangles and roll the dough out to form one 13 by 9-inch rectangle. Place the dough over the ham, covering the top and sides. Trim excess dough from the corners and cut the excess into small oval shapes, like flower petals, and position them in groups of three on the crust. Increase oven temperature to 375 degrees. Bake for 10 to 12 minutes, until the crust is lightly browned. Remove the ham and brush with melted butter, if desired. Makes 12 servings.

Per serving: 288 calories; 23 grams protein; 26 grams carbohydrate; 7 grams fat; 3 grams saturated fat; 60 mg cholesterol; 2,255 mg sodium; .58 gram fiber.

Follow a child. Celebrate an old person. Send a love letter to yourself. Be advanced. Try endearing. Invent new ways to love. Transform negatives. Delight someone. Wear pajamas to a drive in movie. Allow yourself to feel rich without money. Be who you truly are and the money will follow. Believe in everything. You are always on your way to a miracle.

THE MIRACLE IS YOU

—SARK, "CREATIVE COMPANION"

Since ham is already cooked, it needs only reheating. Choose a glaze you like, spread it on thick, then microwave or bake it until it's cooked through.

Glazed Ham Slice

1 (8-ounce) fully cooked ham slice
Glaze of your choice (see below)

Honey Mustard Glaze: Combine 2 tablespoons honey, 2 tablespoons lemon juice, ¼ cup brown sugar, and 2 tablespoons mustard.

New Mexico Style Glaze: Combine ½ teaspoon ground chile pepper with ¼ cup honey.

Midwestern Style Glaze: Combine ¼ cup peach jam, 2 teaspoons cider vinegar, and ⅛ teaspoon cinnamon.

New England Style Glaze: Combine ¼ cup sugar-free apple butter, 2 tablespoons honey, and 1 or more teaspoons of brandy.

～

Coloring Easter Eggs

If you loved coloring eggs, like I did, you probably already take the time to do a dozen or two with your favorite kids and have more colored eggs than you know what to do with. Here is a good recipe for egg salad sandwiches—or take them to work and eat them with a salt shaker.

The Best Way to Hard-Boil Eggs

Put eggs in a single layer in saucepan. Add enough water to cover eggs by at least 1 inch. (Add a teaspoon vinegar and ¼ teaspoon baking soda for extra clean eggs, which accept dye better.) Cover pan and quickly bring eggs just to boiling. Lower heat and let simmer for 10 to 15 minutes. Immediately run cold water over eggs or put them in ice water until completely cooled.

LET THEM EAT A CHOCOLATE BUNNY

Children who eat sugar have healthier diets (just like us) and are usually thinner than children who are denied it. Nutritionists found that those who ate sugary foods tended to have a more varied diet and consumed less fat than children who did not.

Egg salad sandwiches make an easily totable, delicate picnic lunch—as well as a great spread over toast for breakfast!

Create Your Own Egg Salad

¼–⅓ cup dressing (see below)
1 tablespoon flavor enhancer (see below)
¼ teaspoon salt
⅛ teaspoon black pepper
6 hard-boiled eggs, chopped
1–1½ cups diced or shredded stir-in options (see below)

Blend together dressing and flavor enhancer. Stir in salt, pepper, eggs, and stir-in options until evenly coated with dressing. Chill to blend flavors. Makes 3 servings.

Dressing Options: Bottled salad dressing, sour cream, mayonnaise, plain or lemon-flavored yogurt.

Flavor Enhancer Options: Chili sauce, chutney, vinegar, pickle relish, prepared horseradish, prepared mustard, seafood sauce, salsa, Worcestershire sauce.

Stir-in Options: Alfalfa sprouts, avocados, capers, carrot, chile or jalapeño peppers, coconut, cooked and chilled green beans, cucumbers, drained canned garbanzo beans, green or red sweet pepper, mushrooms, olives, pickled artichoke hearts, pickles, pimento, radishes, sunflower seeds, tomatoes.

Per serving, using lowfat mayonnaise and pickle relish: 231 calories; 13 grams protein; 4 grams carbohydrate; 16 grams fat; 4 grams saturated fat; 427 mg cholesterol; 349 mg sodium; .43 gram fiber.

It is primarily women who need to keep in contact with the springs of life, with the inseparable connection of all growing things and their eternal continuity through the seasons. Rose, my ex-mother-in-law, picked her own greens for this salad from her front yard in West Virginia. Lucky us—we can buy prewashed greens ready to eat from the market. Wonderfully down-home with country ham and crusty bread.

Wild Woman Wilted Salad

4 cups torn leaf lettuce, packed
4 green onions plus tops
4 radishes, sliced thin, optional
6 strips bacon, cooked crisp and crumbled, drippings reserved
2 tablespoons cider vinegar
¼ teaspoon salt, optional
⅛ teaspoon pepper
1 teaspoon sugar

THE TIME FOR PLEASURE IS NOW

When the evening turns cool, stay outdoors on a roomy lawn chair and cover yourself with a blanket. Read Dickens and sip a glass of chablis with the evening breeze.

Every moment we are choosing how we live.

～

Toss greens, onions, and radishes in bowl. Add vinegar, sugar, salt, and pepper to bacon drippings in the pan where the bacon was cooked. Mix to combine and bring to a boil. Pour over the greens. Place a plate or lid over the bowl a few minutes, then toss. Add crisp, crumbled bacon and enjoy. Makes 3 servings.

Per serving: 88 calories; 5 grams protein; 4 grams carbohydrate; 6 grams fat; 2 grams saturated fat; 11 mg cholesterol; 383 mg sodium; .66 gram fiber.

Hot, steamy soup, chili, or Sloppy Joes in a thermos jug are good insur-
ance against winds that may turn chilly. Bring along some sliced meats and
generous chunks of two or more kinds of cheese for sandwiches as well as a
jug of wine, coffee, blankets and good company for the warmth you need
inside.

Sloppy Joes

1 can Sloppy Joe mix such as Manwich, 1 envelope Sloppy Joe
   seasoning prepared according to directions, or

Homemade version

2 cloves garlic, minced
2 onions, chopped
1 large green bell pepper, chopped
1½ pounds ground beef or turkey
1 cup ketchup
2 teaspoons mustard
1 teaspoon Worcestershire sauce
2 teaspoons cider vinegar

8 hamburger buns, toasted

Coat large skillet with vegetable spray and heat over medium-high heat.
Add garlic, onions, and bell pepper. Sauté until aroma of raw garlic has
disappeared. Add ground meat and brown over high heat. Add ketchup,
mustard, Worcestershire, and vinegar and heat through. Spoon mixture
onto bottom bun and leave open-faced with top bun balancing on side.
Makes 7 servings, ¼ cup each.

> For homemade version, per serving: 189 calories; 8 grams protein; 32
> grams carbohydrate; 4 grams fat; .8 gram saturated fat; 12 mg cholesterol;
> 583 mg sodium; .28 gram fiber.

SPRING PICNICS

Why should you stay
inside when suddenly
the air is soft with
the first warm gush
of spring?

It's time to pack
a picnic and take
to the outdoors.
Find a hillside dotted
with wildflowers and,
if it's breezy, buy a kite
and spend a few hours.
Happiness is the best
possible therapy.

Summer Comforts

I think of summer as a kind of benefit package full of light and laughter, a time to relax, to linger, and to take hold of all the pleasures that surround me.

By nature's design, summer is ripeness, when we naturally enjoy simply being ourselves, and this requires time. Of course, the older I get, the less time I have. So I changed my life around to have more time and more of the basics. Yes, I have less money, but more life—because I now have time to feel, to see, to touch and, of course, to eat: Sweet, ripe strawberries with whipping cream; peaches (a bagful if I want to, they're so low in calories); corn on the cob dripping with butter (we need fat, too!); grilled steak; tall salt-frosted glasses of margaritas. . . .

I rediscovered my summer loves and take temporary escapes: Lacy summer tops; an afternoon off work at the beach with an ice chest full of wine coolers; one great bathing suit; red toenails; afternoon naps; and hopefully an occasional romantic picnic. It is near impossible to not feel good slipping on a sundress and walking barefoot in the grass or lying on a blanket, surrendering to the heat of the sun—it's almost like making love with nature, without the strings attached.

Yippee!

⁐

⁐

*W*hat was your perfect summer's day when you were a kid? What did it smell like, feel like, taste like? What did you long for? Now fold these summer memories into this year's vacation—peanut butter and banana sandwich and all. I do this whenever we grill hot dogs . . .

My sister Tina and I grew up in the country, thirteen miles from Grand Haven, Michigan. When I was six years old, the county officially constructed a park of the land across the street. I immediately decided it was "my" park. Almost every day, we would go to the park and picnic. Tina and I filled Dad's red Coca-Cola bag with a jug of Kool-Aid, hot dogs, ketchup, and mustard. Loaded down with supplies, we hiked to our favorite picnic table with a grill, usually still hot with leftover white coals. Since the grill was hot with someone else's leftover white charcoal, we didn't need our own. We arranged the wieners on the grill and cooked them until they were plump and slightly black. Buns were for people who lived in town. We happily wrapped our hot dogs in a slice of bread.

The best part, our reward, was eating our creations under the shade of the crabapple tree and watching the motorboats go by, safe in knowing that tomorrow would be the same.

Grilled Steaks and Burgers

Next time you have an outdoor barbecue, plan ahead to make up extra grilled hamburgers so that you can enjoy them later in the week. Just stuff them into grilled buns, wrap, and freeze individually in waxed paper. Then whenever you're ready for that same smoky flavor, just zap it in the microwave.

Stuff Your Burgers

Make plain ol' hamburgers gourmet by simply stuffing them. Fillings can be cubes of cheese, green or black olives, tomato slices, chopped green chiles, sautéed mushrooms, blue cheese mixed with cream cheese, or just about anything.

Stuff them like this: Divide 1 pound of ground meat into 8 equal parts and form thin patties, about 4 inches in diameter. Place filling on four of the patties, spreading almost to the edge. Top with remaining patties. Pinch to seal.

～

A summer moment: The first bite of buttery corn on the cob. The best corn is just harvested, so buy it from a farm stand or from someone with a full load in the back of their pickup. Look for ears that have bright green, fresh-looking husks. If you pierce a kernel with your fingernail, milky juice should spurt out. It takes just minutes to prepare on the stove or in the microwave. Considering the fiber and enjoyment factor, they're quality diet food—melted butter and all.

Corn on the Cob

Rinse husked corn. Wrap each ear of corn in microwave wrap or in waxed paper (it can also be microwaved in the husks, then peeled and eaten). Microwave corn on high until tender, rearranging corn after half the cooking time. Let stand 5 minutes. Unwrap corn; serve with melted butter or dill butter.

Dill Butter: Mix ½ cup softened butter or margarine with 1 tablespoon dried dill.

Amount	Microwave Time (in minutes)	Standing Time (in minutes)
Fresh cob, 1 ear	3 to 5	5
2 ears	7 to 10	5
3 ears	6 to 12	5
4 ears	12 to 16	5
Frozen cob, ½ ear	2½ to 3	3
1 ear	5½ to 7½	3
2 ears	5 to 8	3
4 ears	10 to 12½	3

How to roast corn over a barbecue grill

1. Peel husks to base without detaching and remove silks.

2. Raise husks, tying together at top with kitchen string.

3. Submerge in cold water for ten minutes so husks won't burn on the grill.

4. Roast over hot coals 30 minutes, turning frequently.

When I'm new in town in the southern or the western states, I usually ask a local where the best barbecue in town is, then make it a point to go and experience it. Barbecue is pure comfort food. Pork is the pick east of the Mississippi River, while beef is preferred in the cattle country of the west. As for sauce, Southerners choose vinegar-based concoctions, while Midwesterners favor tangy tomato-based recipes and Southwestern sauces use regional spices, such as red and black peppers.

Oven-Barbecued Chicken or Ribs

1½ cans of beer (your favorite brand, I like Miller Draft Light)
  1 bottle barbecue sauce (again, your favorite), minus ½ cup
    Chicken or ribs (your favorite parts)

Combine beer with barbecue sauce in a large bowl. Swirl to mix and marinate overnight. If you forget or haven't the time to marinate overnight, it can also be done last minute while coals are getting ready. Brush chicken on one side with reserved barbecue sauce. Place chicken or ribs, sauce side down, on hot grill and sear on one side until partially cooked, about 7 to 8 minutes.

Brush meat generously with more sauce, turn, and continue grilling until cooked through, another 7 to 9 minutes for chicken, 12 to 15 for ribs.

Oven directions: Place chicken or ribs on a rack in a shallow roasting pan. Roast in a 350-degree oven for 1 hour. Drain off fat. Spoon some of the sauce over meat. Roast, loosely covered with foil, for 30 to 60 minutes more or until well done, occasionally spooning marinade over meat.

Flavor variation: Substitute Italian salad dressing (8-ounce bottle) with ⅓ cup Dijon mustard for the barbecue sauce.

> Per each 6-ounce chicken breast covered with ¼ cup barbecue sauce: 374 calories; 54 grams protein; 20 grams carbohydrate; 8 grams fat; 2 grams saturated fat; 146 mg cholesterol; 570 mg sodium; 0 gram fiber.

> Per each 3-ounce lean beef rib covered with ¼ cup barbecue sauce: 416 calories; 19 grams protein; 20 grams carbohydrate; 29 grams fat; 11 grams saturated fat; 73 mg cholesterol; 974 mg sodium; 0 gram fiber.

Slip into your second childhood. It isn't summer without . . .

The Perfect Summer Pasta Salad

2 (6½-ounce) cans solid white or chunk light tuna in water
1 small yellow or green pepper
1 (7-ounce) package elbow macaroni or your favorite pasta
(2 cups raw), cooked and drained
1 tomato, seeded and chopped
½ cup whole pitted ripe olives
8–10 radishes, sliced, optional
⅓ cup sliced onions
¼ cup fresh parsley, chopped
¾ cup bottled creamy Italian dressing
1 teaspoon seasoned salt
2 teaspoons Dijon mustard

Drain and chunk tuna. Cut pepper into strips. Combine macaroni, tuna, tomato, pepper, olives, radishes, onions, and parsley. In small bowl, blend remaining ingredients. Add to salad; toss gently. Cover, chill thoroughly. Toss again and put in lettuce-lined bowl. Makes about 6 servings.

Per serving: 195 calories; 21 grams protein; 22 grams carbohydrate; 3 grams fat; .3 gram saturated fat; 20 mg cholesterol; 898 mg sodium; 4 grams fiber.

AN EMBROIDERED REMINDER THAT OUR LIFE IS PERFECT!

When my girlfriend Sharon was a little girl, a friend of her mothers gave her a 4 by 4-inch tapestry that she had embroidered and told Sharon to keep it as a reminder that, like a beautiful piece of embroidery, God sees our lives as perfect.

We tend to see our lives like the underside tangle of threads: Chaotic.

How much more would you appreciate each day if you knew all along how few you really have? How might your daily life be different?

This is so pretty and classy. Use a flavored spaghetti if you like, such as lemon, pesto, or sun-dried tomato.

Pasta is one of those feel-good foods I've always felt I could overeat on. You know, something that tastes too good or feels too good that you can't stop? True enough, pasta is just 100 calories per half cup. But who in the world eats a half cup? It's more like two to three cups, plus sauce, which often includes lots of oil! Back in my dieting days, I would pour the hot spicy sauce over cool, crisp, shredded lettuce. Though it sounds terrible, it was pretty darn good! After all, it was the flavor of the sauce that I wanted, and that was what I got. Today I realize that I can eat spaghetti or any kind of pasta, allowing myself to enjoy it and trust that I will know how much of it I can have.

Mediterranean Pasta

- 1 large red onion, thinly sliced
- 1 each red, yellow, and green bell peppers, thinly sliced
- 2 tablespoons olive oil
- ¾ pound spaghetti
- ½ cup halved, pitted Greek olives
- 6 ounces crumbled goat cheese
- ½ cup chopped parsley

Sauté onions and peppers in olive oil (or use vegetable spray to eliminate fat calories). Cook spaghetti; drain. Toss with remaining ingredients. Serves 6.

Per serving: 370 calories; 19 grams protein; 38 grams carbohydrate; 17 grams fat; 8 grams saturated fat; 30 mg cholesterol; 144 mg sodium; 8.8 grams fiber.

LISTEN

Go for a walk alone on a full moon night, keeping your flashlight off as much as possible.

Listen to the night sounds. Listen to your heart. Listen to your fears. Listen to God.

My college roommate mixed chocolate chips into all her quick breads. If that sounds like a good idea to you, there are some new strains of chips such as mint, raspberry, and butterscotch that would certainly add your own personal touch.

Or turn this into a Chocolate Fruity Zucchini bread by melting two ounces unsweetened chocolate, allowing it to cool, then stirring it into the zucchini mixture. Either way, you might make several batches and freeze a few for housewarming or hostess gifts during the year.

Fruity Zucchini Bread

**FUN WAYS
TO BURN
300 CALORIES**

Jog to a tape of your favorite songs for twenty-seven minutes (one side of a tape).

Swim for about thirty-six minutes.

Walk with someone you would like to know better for forty-five minutes.

~

3 eggs
1 cup vegetable oil
1½ cup sugar
2 cups packed unpeeled, shredded zucchini
¾ cup canned fruit such as crushed pineapple, finely chopped peaches, pears, apricots, or fruit cocktail in juice, drained thoroughly
1 tablespoon vanilla
3 cups all-purpose flour
½ teaspoon salt
1 tablespoon baking powder
1 teaspoon cinnamon
½ teaspoon cloves
1 cup finely chopped nuts or mixture of chopped nuts and currants

Beat eggs until light in color and creamy. Add oil, sugar, zucchini, fruit, and vanilla. Mix lightly but well. Combine flour, salt, baking powder, and spices together. Add to egg mixture and blend well. Fold in nuts or nut-currant mixture. Spray two 9 by 5-inch loaf pans with nonstick spray and sprinkle with flour. Bake at 350 degrees for 50 minutes to 1 hour or until done. Cool in pans 15 minutes, then turn out and cool completely. Makes 2 loaves, approximately 10 slices each.

Per slice: 256 calories; 4 grams protein; 32 grams carbohydrate; 13 grams fat; 2 grams saturated fat; 11 mg cholesterol; 200 mg sodium; .9 gram fiber.

Summer Musts

All year we await the gift of these long days. Take advantage of the extra sunshine and plan at least one outing for the family or with a companion that's fun each week—a picnic, a day at the beach, a bike ride. Take a walk and beautify the landscape, go to the county fair, or fill up a child's swimming pool with water and sit in it. Watch clouds. Dream a dream. Pop a citrusy cologne spray in your purse for a refreshing head-to-toe spritz. Make love with abandon. Make a glorious idiot out of yourself. Memorize one poem that says something you feel or would like to. Read *Illusions* by Richard Bach. Eat corn dogs.

Corn Dogs

Hot dogs deep-fried in a cornmeal batter then slathered with ketchup and mustard are, to many of us, reminiscent of summer. Or do you prefer the Southern-style hot dog on a bun doused with coleslaw and chili? I grew up in Grand Haven, a town on the west coast of Lake Michigan, where one could mark the seasons by the "Pronto Pup" corn dog stand that operated from June through Labor Day. My sister and I didn't always get one. Maybe that's why I would like to have one now.

Jump in your car and drive down to the market. Corn dogs are in the frozen food section. Heat them per directions (we can microwave, bake, or deep-fry them) and serve with ketchup and a spicy mustard, or be more sophisticated and serve with chutney.

～

Also known as elephant ears or funnel cakes, they're wildly popular at state fairs all around the country. God or the Great Spirit knows who created these, originally using flour and yeast, but frozen bread dough or rolls will work just fine. Comfort the entire family with this hefty dessert (or entrée). It will feed a houseful of family and friends and they will love you for it! Serve them plain with cinnamon sugar, honey, or confectioners' sugar, or create some high drama and turn them into Navajo Tacos by piling on the refried beans, salsa, cheese, and lettuce.

HAVE A PICNIC

A picnic is a ritual, a ceremony in sharing food with friends. Dining outdoors makes the experience distinctive and exhilarating.

Have you noticed that your senses are heightened (you most likely eat more) and that everyone is in the best of spirits?

Find occasions to do it often (and it doesn't have to be a lot of work).

～

Indian Fried Bread

1 (1-pound) package frozen dinner rolls, thawed
   Oil for frying

On a lightly floured surface, roll out each ball of thawed dough to form a thin 4 to 5-inch circle. Heat oil to good and hot, about 365 degrees. Slip in dough circles, 1 or 2 at a time, and fry for about 1 minute or until the bottom is golden brown. Turn with tongs and fry other side for another minute. Keep warm in 300-degree oven while frying remainder.

Sift with confectioners' sugar over the fried bread, or top with honey or cinnamon sugar. Another option is meat sauce. Makes 12 fried breads.

Cinnamon sugar

½ cup sugar
2 teaspoons ground cinnamon

Meat sauce

1½ pounds lean ground beef
1 (16-ounce) can refried beans
1 cup tomato juice
1 tablespoon taco seasoning
1 tablespoon chopped onion
1 teaspoon chili powder
1 cup water

Brown ground beef and drain off the fat. Stir in remaining ingredients and cook until warmed through. Cover fried bread with meat sauce. Garnish with sour cream, shredded cheese, and chopped tomatoes.

Per serving with cinnamon sugar: 296 calories; 6 grams protein; 48 grams carbohydrate; 9 grams fat; 2 grams saturated fat; 0 mg cholesterol; 625 mg sodium; .43 gram fiber.

Per serving with meat sauce: 484 calories; 250 grams protein; 55 grams carbohydrate; 18 grams fat; 5.2 grams saturated fat; 61 mg cholesterol; 926 mg sodium; .91 gram fiber.

～

Some Ideas For the Lazy Romantic

Doesn't food taste better if someone else makes it? Even more reason to pick up food from the deli: Antipasto salad, fried chicken, potato salad, coleslaw, baked beans, ribs, pizza, tossed salads.

Hollow out a loaf of bread, halve horizontally, and fill with a variety of tempting ingredients such as turkey, tomatoes, shredded lettuce, cheese, and salsa. Or cream cheese, curried cheddar, roast chicken, chutney, green onions, and parsley. Refrigerate topped with a plate and a five-pound weight for several hours if there is time, and then cut into thin wedges.

Make a box supper. Fill a cake box full of sandwiches, salads, fruit cups, and brownies and tie it with a fancy ribbon.

Pick up steamed crab, clams, or lobster from the wharf. Sensuality is important, so bring some melted butter and a can of Sterno to keep it warm.

Place dressing and sauces in containers with leak-proof lids. For added protection, place containers in securely tied plastic bags.

Bring salads in plastic bags, add dressing and toss in the bag before serving.

Add condiments to sandwiches at the picnic site to prevent soggy sandwiches.

COOKING TIPS

Sometimes the secret to the feeling of home-cooked food is cooking it for a long time: It's simply the process.

Cooking, of course, can be done while balancing the check-book, exercising, or making whoopee, like my mama used to say.

So don't always let time be your excuse—plan ahead. Food will take on a whole new, richer dimension. Watch and see.

These picnic pleasers add crunch to any meal.

Stuffed Celery

Cleaned, trimmed celery stalks
Choice of fillings:
  Peanut butter
  Cream cheese mixed with sliced green olives
  Any soft cheese in the deli case

Fill celery with one of these fillings. Great for picnics or for the lunchpail.

～

Are any two words more evocative than "summer afternoon?" Celebrate your senses this weekend and let yourself feel.

Picnics Are a State of Mind

Have you noticed how much better food tastes outdoors? Tonight make dinner a nighttime picnic. Arrange to eat dinner in the backyard, under the stars. Carry the dining room table out-of-doors or throw down a blanket. Spend time making it look glorious and even leftovers will seem heavenly. Light candles in colored votive glasses, get out the sparklers, play classical music, and drink champagne or a glass of your favorite vino or grape juice.

This weekend, plan a daytime picnic. Pack a quilt, pillows, your favorite music, a bottle of wine, ice, cookies, fruit, Brie, baguettes, a container for wild flowers, perhaps a washcloth sprayed with your favorite perfume to refresh yourself with, then tossed into the ice chest, and set up your picnic near a field of flowers. Make it a family affair: Bring kites to fly or butterfly nets. Start a photo scrapbook of leaves and flowers. Or buy a plain white paper tablecloth for kids to draw on while the food is being prepared.

～

A sensuous Mediterranean meal for two: Hearty, yet light and sexy.

Salad Niçoise

2 small potatoes, boiled, skinned, and sliced
1 head iceberg, red leaf, or butter lettuce
½ pound green beans, cooked
1 small onion, or ½ red onion, sliced
1 tomato, sliced
¼ cup black olives
2 tablespoons parsley, chopped
   Pinch of salt
   Freshly ground black pepper
2–4 tablespoons low-calorie Italian dressing
1 (6¾-ounce) can water packed tuna, drained
2 anchovy fillets, optional
2 hard-boiled egg whites, chopped

Cook potatoes in boiling salted water until tender. When cooked enough to handle, quarter the potatoes and transfer to salad bowl lined with lettuce torn into bite-sized pieces.

In another bowl, combine green beans, onion, tomato, olives, parsley, a pinch of salt and the pepper. Pour dressing over salad and toss gently but well. Transfer mixture to salad bowl. Flake the tuna over the salad and arrange anchovy fillets, if you use them, in a lattice pattern over the tuna. Garnish with chopped egg whites.

Now put the salad plates in the freezer while you put on your best dress and paint your fingernails red. Makes 2 servings.

Per serving: 385 calories; 38 grams protein; 37 grams carbohydrate; 10 grams fat; 2.3 grams saturated fat; 240 mg cholesterol; 684 mg sodium; 4.4 grams fiber.

Dub this summer your second childhood summer, or your sensual summer, or your expanded self summer, where you're going to get out and be more. Look for ways to live your theme. Here is another sexy dish for a sensual summer. Serve it hot or cold and it makes for great leftovers. Add a carafe of wine and a baguette of French bread. For a heartier meal, throw in a few links of spicy Italian sausage—and if at all possible, eat outside on a midsummer's day with yourself and someone else you love (or would like to).

Ratatouille

2 small onions, peeled and chopped
2 cloves fresh garlic, chopped
1 tablespoon olive oil
1 medium eggplant, peeled and cut into 1-inch cubes
4 small zucchini, cut into ½-inch slices
3 medium tomatoes, peeled and diced
1 large green pepper, cored and cut into ¼-inch strips
3 tablespoons fresh parsley, chopped
Salt and pepper to taste

The zoo is a great place for a date and to be a child again.

Coat skillet with nonstick spray (olive-oil flavored is good) and sauté onions and garlic in olive oil over low heat until golden (sometimes I use both oil and spray for maximum taste and minimum calories). Add remaining ingredients, cover, and simmer 15 minutes. Uncover and simmer ½ hour longer, stirring occasionally, or until vegetables are tender and sauce has thickened. This may also be baked in a roasting pan. Serves 4.

Per serving: 166 calories; 5 grams protein; 21 grams carbohydrate; 4 grams fat; .5 gram saturated fat; 0 mg cholesterol; 28 mg sodium; 2.9 grams fiber.

There's no substitute for real fried chicken, for many of us who remember it. It really doesn't take that long to fry—less than an hour—and if you use a high-sided pot or deep fryer, it won't spatter all over the place. Most cooks have a secret ingredient—ma's was thyme and my aunt's is Old Bay seasoning, though any poultry seasoning will do. What's yours? Invite a few appreciative souls to share the nostalgia and the fat.

Real Fried Chicken

  1   (2½ to 3-pound) frying chicken, cut into serving pieces
1½   teaspoons salt
 ¼   teaspoon pepper
1½   cups unsifted all-purpose flour (or use half cornmeal)
1½   teaspoons thyme, poultry seasoning, or Old Bay seasoning
1½   teaspoons paprika
       Vegetable oil for frying

Wash chicken pieces in warm water, leaving some moisture. Sprinkle with salt and pepper. Combine flour and spices in a paper bag. Drop a few pieces of chicken at a time in bag and shake until evenly coated.

In a Dutch oven or large skillet (with high sides to keep the spattering fat in the pan), pour vegetable oil to depth of 2 or 3 inches. If oil sizzles when a drop of water hits it, drop in the coated pieces. Fry until golden brown, then drain on paper towels. The oil can be strained and used again.

Per 6-ounce breast without skin: 322 calories; 58 grams protein; 1 gram carbohydrate; 8 grams fat; 2.2 grams saturated fat; 156 mg cholesterol; 136 mg sodium; 0 gram fiber.

Per 4-ounce chicken leg with skin: 285 calories; 30 grams protein; 3 grams carbohydrate; 16 grams fat; 4.4 grams saturated fat; 105 mg cholesterol; 99 mg sodium; 0 gram fiber.

Don't forget to save the wishbone to make a wish!

Make Some Memories

My friend Patrice and I often spent summer afternoons in the White Mountains of northeastern Arizona. We drove through the rural towns of Strawberry and Pine, stopping at the country store for a long-necked bottle of soda or an iced tea, and maybe some Cracker Jack or a Moon Pie. Then we found this great old barn (that we now call Patrice's Barn). I photographed while she sketched or wrote poetry to her latest love. We picked wild flowers, browsed through antique stores, stopped for gingerbread and ice cream, then took more pictures. These pastel memories are now comforts that last.

~

By trying some of the more exotic fruits, you can travel the world without leaving town. And have you priced a ticket to the Caribbean lately?

Be aware of, then follow, your true feelings to eat "right"!

~

When work is over, make it a point to turn off the thoughts and live the rest of the day from your feelings. Ask yourself, "What do I really want to do? Am I hungry or do I just need a break? If I'm hungry, what do I really want to eat?" We always know what is best for us when we are centered.

~

Who can resist a whipped-cream enveloped fruit salad? Bring it to the potluck, and you may as well bring the recipe with you. They're going to ask you for it.

Fluffy Fruit Salad

2 cans (20 ounces each) crushed pineapple
⅔ cup sugar
2 tablespoons all-purpose flour
2 eggs, lightly beaten
¼ cup orange juice
3 tablespoons lemon juice
1 tablespoon vegetable oil
2 cans (17 ounces each) fruit cocktail, drained
2 cans (11 ounces each) mandarin oranges, drained
2 bananas, sliced
1 cup heavy cream, whipped

Drain pineapple, reserving 1 cup juice in a small saucepan. Set pineapple aside. To saucepan, add sugar, flour, eggs, orange juice, lemon juice, and oil. Bring to a boil, stirring constantly. Boil for 1 minute; remove from heat and let cool. In a salad bowl, combine pineapple, fruit cocktail, oranges, and bananas. Fold in whipped cream and the cooled sauce. Chill for several hours. Makes 10 generous servings.

Per serving: 264 calories; 3 grams protein; 40 grams carbohydrate; 11 grams fat; 6 grams saturated fat; 75 mg cholesterol; 47 mg sodium; 1.1 grams fiber.

GETTING BACK TO YOURSELF

Take a moment out of each hour during the day and ask yourself, "What do I want now?" "What decisions am I making now?" "What am I doing now?"

This practice focuses an inner awareness. It is a tuning in to your very essence that will give you the freedom of choice at 360 degrees.

—FROM "EMMANUEL'S BOOK," COMPILED BY RODEGAST AND STANTON

Most everyone has their version of potato salad and, of course, it is the best. If you haven't the time to cook, buy potato salad from a deli and spruce it up with flavorings and condiments of your own, such as sweet or dill pickles, whole or cut up; minced onion; fresh or dried dill; celery seed; Dijon-style mustard; sliced radishes; chopped peppers; seasoning salt; and pepper. This one is slimmed down so you can be, too.

My Best Potato Salad

    6 medium potatoes
    ½ cup Italian dressing
    2 medium stalks celery, sliced (about 1 cup)
    1 cup finely chopped red bell pepper
    1 cup finely chopped green bell pepper
    1 cup coarsely chopped parsley
    1 cup finely chopped green onions
    6 radishes, thinly sliced (about ½ cup), or
           1 cup ripe olives, sliced
    4 hard-boiled eggs, chopped, optional
    1 cup lowfat mayonnaise

To Make Your Potato Salad to Die For . . .

Blend real cream together with the mayonnaise before mixing it into the salad.

～

Bring a large pot of water to a boil and add potatoes. Reduce heat to medium-high and cook, with lid ajar, 25 minutes or until potatoes are tender. Drain and cool slightly. Peel potatoes, if desired, and cut into cubes. Toss warm potatoes with Italian dressing in a 4-quart bowl. Cover and refrigerate at least 4 hours.

Add celery, red and green pepper, parsley, onions, radishes or olives, and chopped eggs to potatoes. Pour mayonnaise over top; toss. Refrigerate until chilled. Immediately refrigerate any remaining salad. Makes 10 servings.

Per serving: 209 calories; 3 grams protein; 31 grams carbohydrate; 7 grams fat; 1 gram saturated fat; 9 mg cholesterol; 241 mg sodium; 1.44 grams fiber.

Grow Something!

Monet was quoted as saying, "More than anything, I must have flowers, always, always." Beauty and earthiness are something we can all use to get back to ourselves. If you haven't the time to plant from seed, do as you would in the kitchen—buy a cake mix, or in this case, buy potted plants. I like six-packs and flowers that will bloom all summer long as well as flowers and herbs that we can eat. Pansies, roses, carnations, and nasturtiums may be used to garnish plates or throw in salads for color. (Dipping them in salt water will deter bugs.) Be sure and plant whatever you love in an appropriately sunny area where you can see them when you get home. Or buy some plants for the office. The only requirement is that you love them—because they'll know it and respond for the benefit of both of you.

Gardening is great exercise and good for the soul. Raking and weeding burn about the same amount of calories per hour as a brisk walk. Being in touch with nature à la having a garden can be grounding and improve our psychological well-being.

Plant pretty and practical borage. Their blue petals may be used to float on cold soups or toss in salads—and so can rose, pansy, violet, and nasturtium petals.

Plant often-used herbs such as parsley, mint, chives, basil, and oregano in hanging baskets, tucked beside the flowers.

Grow flowers or herbs in pots on the balcony, on the front porch, or in a window box. Even in a single window box we will use all five senses and bring out our deepest experiences of nurturing, creativity, and catharsis.

Buy six-packs of flowers: pansies, daisies, dianthus, and so on, and set in baskets for immediate bloom (and they're cheaper than cut flowers). Look for compact plants with good leaf color. Leaves should be perky, not limp or wilted. Pass by any plants that are rootbound or straggly. If they are perennials, plant outside after they've lost their bloom.

RECOMMENDED READING:

*Growing Myself:
A Spiritual Journey
Through Gardening*
by Judith Handelsman.

∼

Create a living work of art. Purchase a flat of long blooming perennials and plant them together in one area—they will be more likely to flourish and spread.

Plant a flowering tree.

Get your hands dirty. (Drag your fingernails over a bar of soap first to keep the dirt out.)

Plant the same kind of flowers your mother used to plant. Plant a multitude of them—it will do your heart good.

Next time before you plant a garden, work for an hour in your head, visualizing it first. See how much more beautiful it can be.

Keep on nurturing and loving your plant or your garden: Water, fertilize, and weed it. See it through its entire life cycle for your greatest satisfaction—and it will love your attention.

～

Gardening burns 5.6 calories a minute if you're weeding and 8.6 calories a minute if you're digging—more if it's hot outside, according to the Berkeley Wellness Center.

～

If your garden does not give you exquisite pleasure, you have not planted enough flowers.

Honor the Why-The-Hell-Not Spirit of Summer!

Look for opportunities to celebrate life! There is great joy in the smallest of things, but there are days when we need to throw a glitzy dress over the everyday and raise our own spirits. Taking time to find it is as important as eating a balanced diet or having a balanced checkbook. The no-fail diet for happiness: Feed on joy rather than on worry.

～

This dish evokes for me images of a relaxed, tranquil country lifestyle where Mason jars stuffed with wild flowers adorn a rustic kitchen table and the back porch is a front row seat to rolling emerald hills and a deep azure sky. Serve with cornbread.

Green Beans and Ham in Potliquor

¼ pound lean boiled ham, cut up, or bacon
1 pound fresh green beans
1 cup water
½ teaspoon salt
⅛ teaspoon pepper
2 medium-sized potatoes, diced

If using bacon, dice and brown lightly in a small skillet; drain off any grease and set between paper towels.

Clean green beans—or teach the kids how—then place them in a large saucepan with the bacon or ham, water, salt, and pepper. Cook for a few minutes, then add potatoes. Cook, covered, for 30 minutes or until all is tender. Ladle the vegetables and their juices (called "potliquor") into sauce dishes and eat with a spoon. Makes 4 servings.

Per serving: 177 calories; 10 grams protein; 32 grams carbohydrate; 2 grams fat; 1 gram saturated fat; 9 mg cholesterol; 629 mg sodium; 2.92 grams fiber.

To keep flowers longer, trim stems every day and add lemon-lime soft drink or lemonade to the water.

I used to love to sift through Aunt Eve's cookie jar. Although I couldn't see them, my hands felt the layers of store-bought cookies. There were Fig Newtons, vanilla sandwich cookies with the yummy creme centers, Lorna Dunes, and if you dug deep enough you could usually find some of these buttery sugar cookies, our homemade favorite. I'll bet you could make some little girl happy by baking a batch of these cookies. It's very summer.

Auntie's Sugar Cookies

1 cup butter, room temperature
2 cups sugar
2 eggs
1 teaspoon lemon extract
1 teaspoon vanilla extract
2½ cups all-purpose flour
2 teaspoons baking powder
¼ teaspoon salt

Often we unwittingly place limits on our pleasures. Why don't we consider disturbing the universe? Picnic on Monday mornings or give flowers to the postman. Why not try a bow tie or plaid socks?

Cream together butter, sugar, eggs, and extracts. In another bowl, combine flour, baking powder, and salt; pour flour mixture into batter and stir to combine.

Roll dough into ¾-inch balls and place about 3 inches apart on ungreased baking sheets. Flatten them with a fork or the bottom of glass dipped in additional sugar. Or roll out and use cookie cutters in your favorite shapes. For cut-out sugar cookies, pat dough into a ball, cover, and refrigerate at least 1 hour. Heat oven to 400 degrees. Roll ⅛-inch thick on floured board. Cut with cookie cutter. Another idea is to make hugs and kisses by rolling dough in your hand into Xs and Os. Place on ungreased baking sheet. Bake at 375 degrees for 6 to 8 minutes or until lightly browned. Makes about 4 dozen cookies.

Per cookie: 90 calories; 1 gram protein; 13 grams carbohydrate; 4 grams fat; 3 grams saturated fat; 19 mg cholesterol; 68 mg sodium; .78 gram fiber.

More delicate, melt in your mouth, easy to swipe cookies.

Cinnamon Cookies

2 cups all-purpose flour
1 teaspoon cinnamon
3 teaspoons baking powder
½ cup butter
1 cup sugar
½ cup lowfat milk

Sift flour, cinnamon, and baking powder into medium mixing bowl. Cream butter and sugar in large mixing bowl. Add flour mixture, combining alternately with milk.

Chill dough until firm. Roll dough very thin. Cut into fancy shapes. Bake on greased baking sheet at 375 degrees about 7 minutes. Makes about 5 dozen cookies.

Per cookie: 43 calories; 1 gram protein; 7 grams carbohydrate; 2 grams fat; 1 gram saturated fat; 4 mg cholesterol; 35 mg sodium; .12 gram fiber.

SWING INTO PERSPECTIVE

Remember porch swings, tire swings, and tall rope swings tied to a tree that would reach to the sky?

Swing after work, or on a moonlit night. Public parks and schools have swings—and they're probably right in your neighborhood. Pump yourself as high as you can.

For the ultimate freedom experience, if you dare, swing on a swing nude at a nudist resort. (Rocking in a rocking chair or in the arms of a loved one is a gentle alternative!)

For some reason the men in my life tend to prefer blondes and lemon meringue pie. Apparently they are the most impressive looking and so very easy (I'm talking about the pie) especially when you use premade pastry and packaged filling. Meringue is a breeze if you follow egg white basics: use a clean metal or glass bowl and don't leave a drop of egg yolks in the whites. Do this by first breaking each egg into a small (also clean and oil-free) dish so that you can inspect it for yolks before combining it with the other egg whites.

Quick Lemon Meringue Pie

1 (4.3-ounce) package cooked lemon pudding,
    prepared using 2% milk
Lemon zest from 1 large lemon
1 prepared 9-inch pie shell, baked and cooled
1 meringue recipe, below

Preheat oven to 400 degrees. Prepare pudding per package directions. Finely grate the lemon rind (important ingredient!), and stir into filling. Allow to cool about 10 minutes before pouring into cooled shell (if shell isn't cool, filling may separate and water will form under the crust). Top with meringue and bake for 15 to 20 minutes, until golden brown.

Meringue

4 egg large eggs, separated
¼ teaspoon cream of tartar
½ cup confectioners' sugar

Separate the yolks from the whites (I feed the yolks to my cat). Drop egg whites into a clean glass or metal bowl. Add the cream of tartar and beat until barely stiff, using an electric mixer on high speed continually. Add the confectioners' sugar and beat until it forms soft peaks.

Spread meringue over pie, taking care to cover entire surface, including the exposed crust, to keep the meringue from shrinking as it stands or bakes. Swirl the top to make it pretty (or spoon meringue into a large pastry bag fitted with a star tip and decoratively pipe whites over filling).

Place in center of oven and bake 12 to 15 minutes, until meringue is golden brown. Remove from oven and cool on a wire rack. Makes 1 pie, about 6 to 8 servings.

> Per 1/8 of a pie: 250 calories; 7 grams protein; 34 grams carbohydrate; 10 grams fat; 3 grams saturated fat; 8 mg cholesterol; 283 mg sodium; .59 gram fiber.

Poison Ivy/Oak Remedy

There are countless remedies for poison oak and poison ivy but nothing seems to work very well. Just last year I was looking for something I had tossed in a field behind my house and for the third time that year I contracted poison oak. Poison oak spreads like wildfire on my skin so I immediately went to the emergency room. The doctor was an Army doctor who gave me a cream that he said had "cured an entire branch of the Army." Hey, this stuff does work! If you know someone who really suffers with this rash, you might want to suggest this cream (below) to your doctor. It's available only through prescription and they don't all know about it.

Leave your shoes at the front door and vacuum your floors half as often.

❦

Wash area with a strong laundry detergent such as Tide.

Ask your doctor to prescribe Triamcinolone Acetonide Cream UPS, 0.5%. It is a cream that will dry up the rash in as quickly as twenty-four hours.

The third best is a cortisone shot, if taken early enough.

You're needing lots of love. If you're contagious to people (if the rash has broken), hug your dog or cat. Visualize pink light all around you.

～

It's easy to forget how refreshing a tall glass of real lemonade can be.

Homemade Lemonade

1   cup fresh lemon juice, chilled (about 6 lemons)
3   cups water
½–¾   cup sugar, depending on your taste
Lemon wedges

Roll the lemons back and forth on a hard surface to break down the fibers, then squeeze the juice and pulp out of the fruit. Combine water, sugar, and lemon juice and pulp in a pitcher. Put some of the lemon rinds in the pitcher to bring out more flavor. Serve over ice, and garnish with some of the wedges. Makes 1 quart.

Easy variation: Use canned lemonade or a lemonade mix and add sliced lemons, limes, and oranges.

Orangeade: Add ½ to ¾ cup orange juice plus 2 more cups of water.

Strawberry Lemonade: Add ½ cup defrosted strawberries, puréed, or 6 large, fresh, very ripe strawberries, puréed.

Using ½ cup sugar, per cup: 108 calories; 29 grams carbohydrate; .18 gram fiber.

How to Make Pretty Ice Cubes

They're practical too (well, sort of). At least they'll notice them. Fill an ice cube tray one-third full of water. Place any of the following in each segment before slipping back into the freezer:

Herb leaves such as mint, lemon basil, or fennel.

The zest or peel of an orange, lemon, or lime.

Edible flowers such as miniature roses, violas, pansies, or nasturtiums.

Berries: Raspberries, strawberries, blueberries, or blackberries.

～

Remember sangria? It's so refreshing on a hot day, and a great way to use that day-old wine.

Sangria of the Gods

1   small orange, unpeeled, thinly sliced
1   red apple, cut in half, cored, and thinly sliced
1   cup sliced strawberries
1   (750-ml) bottle dry white wine or medium red, such as
     Lambrusco, chilled
2   cups lemon-lime soda, chilled

Combine all ingredients and pour into a pitcher and serve in glasses half filled with cubed ice. Makes 6 servings.

> Per serving: 126 calories; 1 gram protein; 11 grams carbohydrate; 0 gram fat; 0 gram saturated fat; 11 mg cholesterol; 6 mg sodium; 2.9 grams fiber.

Save your morning coffee for this afternoon delight.

Spiked Iced Coffee

8   cups strong coffee (regular or flavored)
⅛   teaspoon almond or vanilla extract for each cup of coffee
½   cup evaporated milk for each cup of coffee
1   shot cognac or Irish cream liqueur for each cup of coffee

Blend 1 or 2 cups of coffee at a time with the other ingredients in a blender. Pour into a thermos with a few ice cubes.

> Per cup: 84 calories; 1 gram protein; 1 gram carbohydrate; 1 gram fat; 0 gram saturated fat; 2 mg cholesterol; 0 mg sodium; .17 gram fiber.

Berries

There is a time for everything . . . yet they're here today, gone tomorrow. Like people, you can't take them for granted. What I'm talking about are berries. High summer is a languid time when living is simplified and there for the taking, along with summer fruits.

Make it a day trip if you must, but do find some pails and go blackberrying or blueberrying with your family or your favorite child—and take your camera. (The best possible setting to photograph children—and adults—is outdoors in summer, when we feel most free. And of course it makes for wonderful memories.) My sisters and I would take one day and pick a few pails, then make jam or cobbler together, or simply pour half-and-half over them and call it dinner.

If you can't go out and pick them today, make blackberry cobbler using frozen berries or buy a frozen cobbler in the grocery store and bake it, don a house dress, and sit on the steps of the back porch in the late afternoon sun and eat a bowlful with a big scoop of vanilla ice cream.

~

Do you think Sophia Loren worries about how she looks in a bathing suit? Why should you? Wear whatever and bare whatever! There's nothing sexier than self-confidence. If you find that you're still not happy with how your body looks, don't sit around and think about it. Instead, get up and use it. Feel your muscles as you play with your kids, feel the water against your skin while you swim, or feel the fresh air in your lungs as you walk. Get a massage. Book a manicure. Buy new makeup. Focus on who you are on the inside (let your inner light shine!) and know your own distinct beauty.

~

Everyone will love this rich, fruity, old-fashioned dessert that you only have to clean one bowl for. Simpler than a cobbler, this recipe comes from my neighbor, Donna Anderson.

One-Bowl Clafouti

¾ stick butter
1 cup flour
1 cup sugar
¼ teaspoon salt
2 teaspoons baking powder
¾ cup lowfat milk
3 cups canned, frozen, or fresh fruit, drained
Whipped cream, optional

Heat oven to 350 degrees. Put butter in a 1-quart ceramic bowl (like your mother or grandmother had) in the oven until just melted, 3 to 5 minutes. Remove from oven and set aside. In separate bowl, whisk flour, sugar, salt, and baking powder until combined. Add milk and whisk briskly until well blended. (Batter will be rather thin.) Pour batter over melted butter in bowl. Cut through two to three times with rubber spatula so butter is somewhat distributed but not mixed in entirely. Place fruit over batter and bake about 50 minutes, until top is crisp. Serve warm or cold with whipped cream. Makes 6 servings.

Suggested fruit: Peaches, nectarines, apricots, plums, or any kind of berries, or a combination of all of them.

Per serving without whipped cream: 307 calories; 2 grams protein; 49 grams carbohydrate; 13 grams fat; 8 grams saturated fat; 35 mg cholesterol; 268 mg sodium; 1 gram fiber.

Little pleasures can turn life right-side up because one thing is guaranteed: Feelings change. Comfort yourself until they do with what present L.A. Times Editor Russ Parsons claims to be the "perfect shortcake"—and, at least once this summer, don't short yourself with anything less than real whipping cream.

Ultimate Strawberry Shortcake

4 pints strawberries, rinsed and hulled
¼ cup sugar
10 individual shortcakes
2 cups whipping cream, whipped

Cut strawberries in half and toss with sugar. Set aside for 30 minutes.

Split each shortcake while still warm. Spoon plenty of strawberries over bottom of each shortcake, top with generous spoonful of whipped cream, and set top half of shortcake on top. Makes 10 servings.

Shortcake

2 cups flour
1 tablespoon baking powder
3 tablespoons sugar
Dash salt
½ cup chilled butter, cut into 8 pieces
1 cup whipping cream

Preheat oven to 400 degrees. Sift together flour, baking powder, sugar, and salt into medium mixing bowl. Cut in butter. Stir half of cream into dry ingredients with fork. Add remainder of cream, bit by bit, until a mass forms that pulls cleanly away from the bottom and sides of bowl. You may not use all of the cream.

On lightly floured work space, quickly and lightly knead dough until smooth and cohesive. Gently roll out ½-inch thick. Cut out biscuits with 3-inch biscuit cutter or lightly floured juice glass. Gather leftover dough together, knead briefly, and roll out again. Cut remaining biscuits.

THINK LIKE A KID

When I was a kid, Aunt Stella stopped whatever she was doing, got a round gallon of vanilla ice cream from the deep freeze, and planted a couple of scoops into a sugar cone. Well, back then it was really a treat!

Needless to say, we loved to visit Aunt Stella. Kids, like adults, have agendas, needs, likes, and loves. To get to know one, or to simply have them think of you fondly, think like a kid again and always keep a box of ice cream cones in the cupboard. They can also be filled with layers of ice cream punctuated with nuts, berries, a bit of homemade jam, or whipping cream!

～

Place biscuits on ungreased baking sheet and bake until light brown and slightly crusty, about 10 to 15 minutes. Remove from oven and cool slightly before splitting and serving. Makes 10 biscuits.

> Per serving: 486 calories; 5 grams protein; 43 grams carbohydrate; 34 grams fat; 21 grams saturated fat; 114 mg cholesterol; 227 mg sodium; 3.8 grams fiber.

> Or if you must have a sponge cake-style strawberry shortcake with ½ cup fat-free whipped cream: Per serving: 116 calories; 2 grams protein; 24 grams carbohydrate; 1 gram fat; 0 gram saturated fat; 39 mg cholesterol; 93 mg sodium; 0 gram fiber.

A quick and fluffy lemon variation on whipping cream for strawberries.

Lemony Whipped Cream

½ cup heavy whipping cream
⅓ cup sifted powdered sugar
½ cup lemon lowfat yogurt

In a chilled mixing bowl, beat whipping cream and sugar until soft peaks form. Fold in the yogurt. Serve immediately or refrigerate, covered, for up to 4 hours. Makes 1⅓ cups.

> Per ⅓ cup serving: 147 calories; 2 grams protein; 11 grams carbohydrate; 11 grams fat; 1 gram saturated fat; 41 mg cholesterol; 29 mg sodium; .12 gram fiber.

Read a childhood favorite under a tree such as Charlotte's Web, The Boxcar Children, *or* Little Women.

～

Learn to say "no" to things you really don't want to do.
(It's difficult at first, but the more you do it,
you'd be surprised how easy it gets!)

～

Ice Cream
(or a guilt-free facsimile)

You only live once (that we distinctly remember), so do not shortchange yourself on people, places, or foods that you really do want. When I desire ice cream, but ignore the craving and choose frozen yogurt or a lighter version of ice cream instead, I keep eating anyway because it's not what I want—perhaps not what I need, either. If you're trying to lose weight, cut back on the fat at the next meal or over the entire day instead of this particular self-denial. Eat an ice cream cone instead of butter on your bread or choose a bagel instead of a croissant for breakfast, then enjoy your ice cream and call it even.

Keep your freezer stocked with a supply of good basic flavors—coffee, vanilla, and deep chocolate—to fit your mood. It's like having a great white shirt in your closet: You can dress it up or down to suit any occasion. Go one step farther than you normally do and dress it up with liqueur (make a sundae with vanilla ice cream and Kahlua, sloe gin, or Creme de Menthe). Or make a champagne float, a fabulous and creative use of leftover champagne. Top ice cream with shaved chocolate, fruit, cookies, or cereal (I like Rice Krispies). If you're afraid of overeating, one way to control yourself so that you can have your cake—or ice cream—and eat it too is to buy the ice cream (or cake) that you like—but buy a pint instead of a gallon.

One of the reasons we have trouble with intimate relationships is because we have lost our inner female. Recall it every day, if only for yourself.

～

Cooking by feel is like adding love, because you do it with your senses. Measure with your eyes and season by taste, as your grandmother did before there were cookbooks. Add a bit of honey and spices such as cinnamon or nutmeg, or vanilla if you like, to this hot fruit topping. Taking the time to feel your way through cooking (or solving a problem, washing dishes, making love) grounds you and makes it more real. (If you don't want to cook anything at all, you might open up a can of cherry, blueberry, or apple pie filling and spoon that over ice cream.)

Piña Colada Sundae

1 (8-ounce) can crushed pineapple in juice
1 tablespoon water
1 tablespoon cornstarch
¼ cup rum
3 cups light vanilla ice cream
¼ flaked sweetened coconut

Drain pineapple, reserving juice in a 2-cup glass measure. Add enough water to reserved liquid to yield ¾ cup. Add cornstarch to liquid and whisk until smooth.

Microwave cornstarch mixture, uncovered, on high for 3 minutes or until thickened and bubbly, stirring after 1½ minutes. Stir in rum and microwave on high for 30 seconds. Stir in pineapple and microwave on high for 30 seconds. Serve sauce over ice cream. Garnish with flaked coconut. Makes 6 servings.

Per serving: 173 calories; 3 grams protein; 28 grams carbohydrate; 3 grams fat; 1 gram saturated fat; 10 mg cholesterol; 71 mg sodium; .5 gram fiber.

Eat all you want of this hot fudge sundae sauce without worry of fat. Or substitute whipping cream for the light creamer and add a dab of unsalted butter if you've decided that calories don't count today.

Rich Hot Fudge Sauce

⅓ cup plus 2 tablespoons sugar
¼ cup unsweetened cocoa
1 tablespoon plus 1 teaspoon cornstarch
½ cup light cream or evaporated milk
2 teaspoons vanilla

In small saucepan, stir together sugar, cocoa, and cornstarch; stir in cream.

Cook over low heat, stirring constantly with wire whisk, until mixture boils; continue cooking and stirring until thickened and smooth. Remove from heat; stir in vanilla.

Serve as warm or cold sauce over ice cream or frozen yogurt or with fresh fruits and cake. Makes 4 servings.

Per serving: 75 calories; >1 gram protein; 15 grams carbohydrate; >1 gram fat; 0 gram saturated fat; 0 mg cholesterol; 5 mg sodium; .01 gram fiber.

Because we are estrogen-based creatures, women must waste one hour a day. (Lay around, listen to music, read a trashy novel, etc.) If we don't go off duty once a day for at least an hour, we'll be too much invested in our intellectual side and not be emotionally or spiritually grounded. It is imperative for us to feel good to do good.
—PAT ALLEN, PH.D.

Picnic at the Beach

Plan at least one late-night beach rendezvous; a midnight picnic under the stars. Bring a quilt; throw pillows; plus something to cover up with; soft cheese; baguettes; salami; chocolate cake; champagne; fruit juice; candles; a long dress; and a camera with a flash.

What? You haven't time to picnic at the beach? Just how do you spend your time? This coming week, write down at the end of the day what you accomplished. Then evaluate if these activities were your priorities. What did you spend too much time doing? How much was for you and how much was for others? What activities did you do that were important to you? Little by little, alter what you say yes to according to what's really important to you.

～

It's spiked with vodka and coffee liqueur (add a bit more if you like). Everyone will remember this. My sister, Carol Hulka, won a recipe contest for this recipe.

White Russian Parfait Cake

1 ounce vodka
⅓ cup coffee liqueur such as Kahlua
1 package devil's food cake with pudding,
    baked and allowed to cool
1 large or 2 small packages instant fat-free pudding,
    prepared with skim milk
1 (16-ounce) tub light whipped topping
3 chocolate-covered toffee bars, crushed (freeze and hammer),
    or buy toffee bits in a bag

Combine vodka and Kahlua. Crumble ⅓ of cake in bottom of a very large brandy snifter or glass bowl. Drizzle ⅓ of combined alcohol over crumbs. Neatly spread ⅓ pudding over cake, then ⅓ topping and ⅓ candy bar bits. Repeat twice more. Spoon cake into serving bowls. This cake is pretty garnished with mounds of whipped cream with cherries in the center of each mound, or use your imagination. I like to garnish the center with flowers, raspberries, or strawberries. Makes 20 servings.

Per serving: 274 calories; 3 grams protein; 40 grams carbohydrate; 30 grams fat; 3 grams saturated fat; 49 mg cholesterol; 386 mg sodium; 0 gram fiber.

BAKE SOME MEMORIES!

The aroma, the velvety textures, and the fact that someone cares enough to do it in itself feels good.

⁓

I get vicarious pleasure simply in the act of preparing a sinful dessert so when I am invited to a potluck, I make something decadent to share—like this trifle. In this way I enjoy it vicariously through the making of it, then give it away to pleasure others; the perfect win-win situation.

A Trifle Sinful

1 (.9-ounce) box instant pudding (you choose the flavor)
2 cups currants
1 (18-ounce) can unsweetened applesauce
1 box of your favorite cookies
1 half-gallon carton vanilla ice cream
  Mint leaves to garnish

Plan to live young, even when you think you're old.

❦

Make pudding as directed, and set aside. Mix currants and applesauce together and set aside. Line the bottom of a large bowl with cookies. Begin a successive layer of cookies, applesauce mixture, ice cream, then pudding. Make three layers, ending with pudding. Sprinkle with currants and chill in freezer for 30 minutes before serving. Garnish with mint leaves. Makes 10 servings.

Using lowfat ice cream and 20 chocolate chip cookies: 455 calories; 6 grams protein; 86 grams carbohydrate; 11 grams fat; 2 grams saturated fat; 16 mg cholesterol; 385 mg sodium; 3.6 grams fiber.

Good combinations

Pecan sandies and toasted nut ice cream (substitute coconut for currants)

Oreos and chocolate chip ice cream (substitute nuts for currants)

Beer and cake go together, several of my ex-husband's friends tell me—particularly on a sizzling hot summer's day. Living in Phoenix, where it's so hot that tubes of lipstick melt in your purse when left in the car or where you can get burned shifting a five-speed if the knob is black, sure, cake does go well with beer, weird as it sounds. If beer tastes bitter to you, mix it half and half with 7UP. You may get a few stares because it's not the macho way to drink it, but then maybe that's a positive. At any rate, try it for yourself with poke cake. It's a fun cake to make (you get to poke the cake layers with a fork and pour gelatin over it) and we can now choose from several gelatin flavors that weren't available in the 1960s when the recipe first appeared, such as mango, blueberry, cranberry, and watermelon.

Luscious Lemon-Lime Poke Cake

1 (18.5-ounce) package lemon cake mix
2 cups boiling water
1 (8-serving size) package or 2 packages (4-serving size)
    lime gelatin (or your choice of flavors)
1 (16-ounce) can vanilla frosting or
    1 (8-ounce) container whipped topping

Preheat oven to 350 degrees.

Prepare, bake, and cool cake as directed on package for two 9-inch round cake layers. Place cake layers, top sides up, in two clean 9-inch round cake pans. Pierce cake with large fork at ½-inch intervals.

Stir boiling water into gelatin in medium bowl 2 minutes or until dissolved. Carefully pour half the gelatin over each cake layer. Refrigerate 3 hours. Dip the bottom of one cake pan in warm water 10 seconds; unmold onto serving plate. Spread top with about 1 cup of frosting or whipped topping. Unmold second cake layer and carefully place on first cake layer. Frost top and sides of cake with remaining frosting.

Refrigerate at least 1 hour or until ready to serve. Decorate as desired. Store leftover cake in refrigerator. Makes 12 servings.

> **Per serving using sugar-free gelatin with icing: 343 calories; 5 grams protein; 42 grams carbohydrate; 12 grams fat; 2 grams saturated fat; 69 mg cholesterol; 18 mg sodium; 0 gram fiber.**

Guy Marshall created his own "light as air" goddess food to woo his women with "foods they love." Sounds like a good idea to me.

Guy's Super Tap

5 egg whites
½ cup sugar, divided
3 tablespoons tapioca
2 cups lowfat milk
1 egg yolk
1 teaspoon vanilla

When I was growing up, my neighbors, the Maciejewskis, would bake Christmas cookies in the heat of summer to remind them of Christmas, their most joyful holiday. Isn't that a charming idea?

～

Beat egg whites in a large nongreasy metal bowl (don't use plastic) with electric mixer on high speed until foamy. Keep beating until peaks form, gradually add ½ of the sugar. Mix together tapioca, remaining sugar, milk, and egg yolk in medium saucepan. Let stand 5 minutes. Stirring constantly, cook on medium heat until mixture comes to full boil. Wait a moment and feel if it's cooked enough. Guy says, "You have to know that it knows it's done." Boil for half a minute and remove from heat. Quickly stir egg white mixture into hot tapioca in saucepan until well blended. Stir in vanilla. Cool 20 minutes; stir. Spoon into dishes. Serve warm or chilled. Makes 6 servings.

Per serving: 290 calories; 36 grams protein; 28 grams carbohydrate; 2 grams fat; 1 gram saturated fat; 41 mg cholesterol; 558 mg sodium; 0 gram fiber.

Gelatin and whipped cream seem the perfect pair, but please try it the way Aunt Lucille still serves it—with ice cream. Chewy gelatin resists ice cream's cool creaminess, then gives into sensuousness, which is always healthy.

Quick-Setting Gelatin

1 (3-ounce) package sugar-free gelatin, any flavor

¾ cup boiling water

½ cup cold water plus ice cubes to make 1¼ cups

1 medium banana, sliced, optional

Completely dissolve gelatin in boiling water. Stir in cold water and ice cubes until slightly thickened. Remove any unmelted ice. Add banana slices. Chill. Gelatin will be soft-set and ready to eat in about 30 minutes. Makes about 4 servings.

> Per serving using sugar-free gelatin: 10 calories; 1 gram protein; 1 grams carbohydrate; 0 gram fat; 0 gram saturated fat; 0 mg cholesterol; 60 mg sodium; 0 gram fiber.

> Per serving using regular gelatin: 70 calories; 2 grams protein; 17 grams carbohydrate; 0 gram fat; 0 gram saturated fat; 0 mg cholesterol; 110 mg sodium; 0 gram fiber.

Instant Desserts

Prepare these instant packaged mixes at home. They take less than fifteen minutes to set up!

Tapioca

Ask your mother over for some (even if she is 1,000 miles or more away, like mine). It's always nice to be asked. Add ice cream, whipped cream, or pour milk over it.

Pudding

Available in sugar-free, you can also use lowfat or nonfat milk, and save the calories for whipped cream or cream. Spoon into parfait glasses and keep a few in the refrigerator for emergencies.

Also the perfect ending to a sensual meal. Begin the main course, maybe a grilled T-bone and baked potato, with a glass of Merlot, and culminate the experience with this spicy dessert nipped with bourbon-doused whipping cream. Gingerbread emits such a strong, intense, enticing fragrance that it is a stimulant by itself.

Upside-Down Apple Gingerbread

¼ cup shortening
¼ cup brown sugar, packed
1 beaten egg
⅞ cup molasses
1 teaspoon grated lemon peel
½ cup boiling water, buttermilk, or sour milk
1¼ cups flour
¼ teaspoon salt
¾ teaspoon ginger
½ teaspoon cinnamon
¾ teaspoon soda

Apple filling

2 tablespoons butter
3–4 tart apples, sliced thin
½ cup brown sugar, packed
1 teaspoon cinnamon

Cream shortening until soft. Gradually add sugar and continue creaming until smooth. Add the egg, molasses, and grated lemon peel and beat until light. Add the water or milk alternately with the flour, which has been sifted with the salt, spices, and soda, mixing thoroughly after each addition; set aside.

Melt butter in a heavy 9 by 9-inch baking pan. Arrange the apples in the pan overlapping layers. Sprinkle the brown sugar and cinnamon over the apples. Pour the batter over it.

Bake in a moderate oven (350 degrees) 30 to 40 minutes. When cool, sift with confectioners' sugar. Serve with whipping cream with a bit of bourbon folded in. Makes 8 servings.

> Per serving: 314 calories; 3 grams protein; 87 grams carbohydrate; 13 grams fat; 8 grams saturated fat; 66 mg cholesterol; 438 mg sodium; 4.8 grams fiber.

If it's true that you are what you eat, you're about to become irresistible! Vary pie to match your favorite kind of drink; for example, substitute frozen margarita mix for strawberry daiquiri mix. Preparation time is a few minutes; freeze and serve. I get many requests for this recipe.

Strawberry Daiquiri Pie

  1 8-inch graham cracker pie shell (prepared)
  1 (6-ounce) can frozen strawberry daiquiri mix
1–2 shots rum, optional
  1 (14-ounce) can sweetened condensed milk (do not
     use lowfat condensed milk)
  1 (8-ounce) tub frozen whipped topping, thawed
     Strawberries, whipped cream, and mint leaves to garnish

Combine mix, rum, and milk and fold into whipped topping; freeze. Garnish with strawberries, whipped cream, and mint leaves. Makes 8 servings.

> Per serving: 440 delicious calories; 6 grams protein; 63 grams carbohydrate; 73 grams fat; 5 grams saturated fat; 37 mg cholesterol; 85 mg sodium; 0 gram fiber.

For the ultimate in physical gratification . . .
Visit a Spa

Stay overnight, or just go for the day. The cost of facilities can be as little as six to ten dollars a day for use of the heated swimming pool, or ten dollars per hour, per person for a hot tub or hot mineral bath. Mud baths, blanket wraps, and massage may be available (especially in California). Many spas have excellent restaurants, offering vegetarian buffets or juice bars. On-premises gift shops may sell clay masks from the Dead Sea (reputed to be loaded with minerals), body butters, and other hard-to-find beauty supplies, all in a healing, peaceful environment.

Bring bathing suit, beauty supplies, shampoo, conditioner, tanning lotion, and towel.

Hot tubs may be clothing-optional; a nice getaway for the two of you. Take along or possibly buy on the premises bottled water, beer, or champagne.

Get a massage: A back, neck, facial, or whole body at half or full hour rates.

Pamper your "pore self" with a facial. They will cleanse, exfoliate (clean deep into the pores), treat for skin problems and protect the skin with a sealant. Expect to pay anywhere from thirty-five dollars for a thirty-minute facial upward to one hundred and twenty-five dollars. Best of all is the after-glow; it's soul-satisfying.

～

A woman can have it all and do it all, but not at the same time.
—ERMA BOMBECK

❧

The sensual pleasures of
Eating Fruit Au Naturel

Fruit is sensual, low in calories, high in fiber, and naturally comforting. When you're about to eat an apple, don't just bite into it! Instead, take a paring knife and carefully peel it first; carve off each piece and feed it to yourself, or someone else, which of course is also very sensual (as is feeding grapes, orange sections, or wedding cake, for that matter). Speaking of sensual, one can communicate much about their sexual appetite in their attitude toward and style of eating. It's just hunger of a different order.

Rip open an orange with your hands. Separate each section, piece by piece, and eat it or dip into sour cream, then sweetened cocoa powder.

When frozen, grapes taste like candy and persimmons taste like French vanilla ice cream. Sweet cherries, watermelon, and cantaloupe balls are also scrumptious frozen.

Make an entire meal out of fruit: Shortcake, cobbler, fruit salad, fruit soup. Include lowfat sour cream or yogurt for a protein boost.

Eat cold cereal for dinner with sliced bananas, strawberries, and a few blueberries. Add a scoop of vanilla ice cream and sprinkle with wheat germ or chocolate sauce.

Eat an entire meal without the help of utensils. Use only your hands, as is done in most African countries, particularly Ethiopia. If this feels squeamish, start with a simple pancake: Tear it apart, dip it and drag it through a pool of syrup.

Perfectionism is self-abuse of the highest order.

—ANN WILSON, "MEDITATIONS FOR WOMEN WHO DO TOO MUCH"

Exercises in Creating Your Reality

What we can envision we can create, by drawing it to us. Here are a few ideas to practice on. Visualize, then create:

A wooden bowl full of fresh raspberries and cream.

The perfect way to spend a weekend (money is no object; there are no restrictions whatsoever).

A red earthenware bowl full of fresh blackberries and cream.

Crushed pineapple over melting vanilla ice cream.

The perfect job. What is it you are doing?

How you would like to see yourself after a weekend of pampering at a spa.

The perfect mate.

Making a cake does not necessarily mean baking, it can be creating. Here are some marvelous tricks for making angel food cake appear that you slaved all day (or are terribly clever).

Pick up an angel food cake and a bunch of fresh flowers (or pick your own blossoms or borrow a few roses from the neighbors). This is a good project for the children. They will delight in how creative they are and be inspired to produce more creative works.

Flower Cake

5 drops yellow food coloring
½ teaspoon lemon extract
1 (12-ounce) container frozen light whipped cream, thawed
1 ready-made 8-ounce angel food tube cake
1 small bunch fresh flowers, such as: Sweet peas, miniature roses, carnations, Bachelor's buttons, nasturtiums, daisies, camellias, gardenias, and marigolds

We have so very few days
Treasure
Treasure
Treasure
—REV. DOREEN RING

Fold food coloring and extract into whipped cream. Set angel food cake on a cake plate with pedestal or the prettiest plate you have. Cover cake with whipped cream.

Find a thin vase or other container that will fit in the center of the cake tube and fill vase ¾ of the way full of water. Place your vase in the middle of the cake. Insert a few stems of flowers in the vase. Arrange remaining flowers around the cakes' base. Use leaves, cut flowers from the stems, whatever you like. Makes 8 servings.

Per serving: 167 calories; 2 grams protein; 27 grams carbohydrate; 6 grams fat; 0 gram saturated fat; 1 mg cholesterol; 243 mg sodium; 0 gram fiber.

This perfect summer cake forms a custard on the bottom while the batter bakes. Serve covered with fresh berries and a scoop of ice cream.

Old-Fashioned Lemon Pudding Cake

- ¼ cup all-purpose flour
- 1 cup sugar
- ¼ teaspoon salt
- 1½ teaspoons grated lemon rind
- ¼ cup lemon juice
- 2 eggs, separated
- 1 cup lowfat milk

In mixing bowl, sift together flour, sugar, and salt. Stir in lemon rind, lemon juice, beaten egg yolks, and milk. Whip egg whites until stiff and fold into batter. Turn batter into 1-quart casserole or 6 custard cups. Set casserole or cups in a large pan filled with 1 inch of water.

Bake in preheated 350-degree oven 50 minutes. Makes 6 servings.

Per serving: 193 calories; 4 grams protein; 40 grams carbohydrate; 3 grams fat; 1 gram saturated fat; 73 mg cholesterol; 33 mg sodium; .18 gram fiber.

⁓

How To Tell If You're a Perfectionist

If you find yourself frequently saying, "I should," "I must," or "I have to."

Solution: Prioritize your perfectionism. Pick two or three things in your job or your life and focus your perfectionism on them. Then you may constantly remind yourself that it is fine to do other things in a less-than-perfect manner. Or you can tell yourself that being perfect at everything isn't the perfect things to do.

Long-term stress increases your need for calcium, magnesium, potassium, zinc, and several B vitamins. Also, blood levels of vitamin A, vitamin C, iron, and zinc can drop below normal when you're stressed out. Eat a variety of foods for health insurance.

A favorite at church gatherings and potlucks.

Easy Banana Cream Pie

1 (3⅜-ounce) package vanilla instant pudding and pie filling
1¾ cups milk
3 large bananas, peeled and sliced
1 (9-ounce) ready-made graham cracker pie crust
1 (8-ounce) container frozen nondairy whipped
　　topping, thawed
Cherries for garnish

Prepare pudding as package directs for pie filling using milk. Arrange banana slices evenly over bottom of crust. Top with prepared pudding. Cover with thawed whipped topping, sealing edges. Refrigerate 2 hours or longer before serving. Just before serving, garnish with cherries. Makes 6 servings.

Per serving: 394 calories; 5 grams protein; 68 grams carbohydrate; 10 grams fat; 3 grams saturated fat; 5 mg cholesterol; 463 mg sodium; .56 gram fiber.

ENJOYING THE BEACH

Put together your own personal Beach Survival Kit. You might want to include a delicious novel, lots of suntan lotion (with a sunscreen of SPF 15 or more), a huge straw hat, music, mineral water, a cooler filled with plenty of good cold drinks and ice, lip balm, sunglasses, a big T-shirt or cover-up, a shade umbrella, the camera, and a bag big enough to hold it all.

Serve over whole strawberries, ice cream, or frozen yogurt. Or serve in a fruit cloud: Spoon out a huge dollop of whipped cream. Make a bowl shape by scooping out some of the whipped cream with a spoon. Spoon strawberries and sauce into cloud. Just do it!

Soused Strawberries on a Cloud

2 pints fresh strawberries

2 tablespoons sugar

1 tablespoon Kirsch or other fruit liqueur

Wash and hull the strawberries. Select one cup of the softer berries and purée them in food processor or blender with sugar and liqueur. Makes 4 servings.

Per serving: 83 calories; 1 gram protein; 19 grams carbohydrate; less than 1 gram fat; 0 gram saturated fat; 0 mg cholesterol; 1 mg sodium; 3.9 grams fiber.

SUMMER WATER RITUALS

Swim swim, swim:
In the river, the lake,
the ocean, or the pool.

Go skinny dipping.

To whomever taught
you how to swim, thank
them, now!

Take a tepid bubble
bath and float flowers
in the suds.

Toss coins into the river
and make wishes.

Protect Your Skin Against Premature Wrinkles

CRANBERRY JUICE

Keep cranberry juice stocked in your pantry to drink year-round, but especially in summer if you tend to not drink enough water.

In a recent study, women who drank ten ounces a day of cranberry juice for six months were less than half as likely to have urinary tract infections as women who drank an identical-tasting placebo.

Reason: Cranberry juice may keep bacteria from attaching themselves to the lining of the bladder.

—JERRY AVORN, MD, ASSOCIATE PROFESSOR OF MEDICINE, HARVARD MEDICAL SCHOOL, AND LEADER OF A STUDY OF MORE THAN 150 WOMEN, QUOTED IN HARVARD HEALTH LETTER (164 LONGWOOD AVE., BOSTON, MA 02115)

Warmth is wonderful, wrinkles are not—so use some discretion (we in our forties know this, but try to tell women in their twenties and they don't get it—yet). Use some discretion and protect your skin—use a sunscreen with an SPF (sun protection factor) of at least 15, and limit your exposure to the sun while the sun's rays are at their strongest, between 10:00 A.M. and 2:00 P.M. (Perhaps the smartest thing to do is to buy some sun-less tanning cream and look great without the sun!)

If you are going to be on a beach, in Phoenix, on a boat, in a tropical climate, or won't be able to reapply sunscreen, go for an SPF in the 20s or 30s—if some wears off, you'll have more protection left. And sunscreen takes about fifteen minutes to penetrate the top layer of skin, so apply it at last thirty minutes before you go into the sun. And don't skimp. When companies test their products for effectiveness, the sunscreen is applied very liberally. You should do the same.

You need high SPF sunscreen protection (at least SPF 20, preferably SPF 30+) and good cover-ups if you have very fair skin that burns easily; are prone to "sun bumps;" are at a high altitude; are taking certain prescription drugs (some tetracyclines, sulfa drugs or medications for kidney or heart disease); or if you've had skin cancer or have a family history of skin cancer.

Treat the sting of sunburn immediately by dabbing with vinegar or slicing open the leaf of an aloe vera plant. Acetaminophen and ibuprofen can help relieve sunburn pain. Moisturize your skin with a good water-based moisturizer to keep it from drying out and tightening.

Protect your eyes with sunglasses that screen out both UV and glare. Wraparound sunglasses offer the most protection from the sun. If sunglasses do not fit closely, almost three times as much UV radiation reaches eyes.

It ought to be a crime how much this tastes like iced tea.

Long Island Iced Tea

½ ounce vodka
½ ounce gin
½ ounce rum
½ ounce tequila
    Splash of sweet and sour mix
    Splash of orange juice
    Cola
    Lemon twist

Fill your largest, tallest glass with the above ingredients. Fill with cola, stir, and add lemon twist.

Float through summer on this version that tastes just like a root beer float!

Faux Root Beer Float

1 ounce vodka
1 ounce Kahlua
1 ounce Galliano
    Cola

Fill a long, tall glass with ice cubes and pour in the above ingredients.

A GOOD DRINK

Moderate drinking can raise good cholesterol, lower bad cholesterol, and cut the risk of heart disease.

According to a study of 35,709 women at Brigham and Women's Hospital, the greatest health benefits were found in women who drank one to three drinks a week.

Didn't you love root beer drive-ins when you were a kid? Instead of ordering a root beer, being the experimenter that I am, I was told about the "half and half," which is half orange and half root beer. At home on Sunday afternoons we would either have this drink or the good old root beer float, although Aunt Lucille called it a "Black Cow."

Root Beer Float (or Black Cow)

- 1 can or bottle of sugar-free root beer
- 1 or more scoops vanilla ice cream or ice milk
- 1 glass mug, frosted

When you look into a mirror, do you look for flaws? Instead, when you catch your reflection in a mirror or a window, look for what's right, what is beautiful!

Should you keep glasses in the freezer, you're all set. Pour root beer into glass; add the scoop of ice cream or ice milk. Insert straw, if you have one, into glass.

Use white, dark, spiced, or 151 rum—whatever you fancy—or make these without alcohol.

Berry Daiquiri

- 1 ounce light rum
- 1½ ounces sweet and sour mix, sugar syrup, or honey
- ½ cup strawberries, raspberries, or cut-up peaches, nectarines, apricots, or plums
- 1 cup crushed ice

Into blender, pour the above ingredients and process until blended. Pour into a fancy cocktail glass.

Drop one or several berries or pieces of fruit into a glass of champagne or make a champagne cocktail.

Champagne Cocktail

1 cube of sugar
3 drops of bitters
  Champagne
  Lemon twist

Into a champagne glass, add the sugar and bitters, and fill with champagne. Add lemon twist.

~

Water Will Improve Your Mood!

A long, tall glass of water is insurance against fatigue and will make you feel better.

When I was young, my brother-in-law told me to drink water when I didn't feel well. It sounds too simple—but, then, so are most answers. Since our bodies are composed of approximately eighty percent water, it makes sense that to feel good, we need it—and lots of it. If you're mildly dehydrated, even by one percent of your body weight, you can feel fatigued. Dehydration is a precursor to many symptoms, including headaches, lower back pain, and rapid aging. Drinking plenty of liquids primes the blood flow to the organs, including the brain. And women may need more fluid than men because they have more subcutaneous fat, which acts as a body insulator and increases body temperature and fluid loss.

We need a minimum of sixty-four ounces each day to replenish the amount lost every twenty-four hours. Make your diet sixty percent water-rich and you'll feel lighter and have more energy. (You'll also probably eat less!) Do this by drinking as much liquid as your thirst dictates and eating foods naturally rich in water, which are fruit, vegetables, and sprouts.

Tap water may contain contaminants. Choose, instead, purified water, sparkling water, mineral water, spring, seltzer, and flavored water as well as herbal tea.

Fill your refrigerator full of sodas (buy caffeine-free if you're over-stressed), juice, and mineral waters. Bring nonfat milk to work and keep it in the refrigerator.

Alcohol Alert

Too much alcohol can interfere with a well-functioning body and mind. It can (and probably will):

Rob your body of B vitamins.

Slow down your metabolism.

Add calories and contribute to weight gain.

Lower serotonin levels, causing carbohydrate cravings, another contributor to weight gain.

Dehydrate your system.

Cause birth defects in pregnant women.

In excess, it will interfere with sleep patterns, cause premature aging, and probably set you back a day or two!

Hangover Prevention

Rehydrate yourself. Alcohol dehydrates the body, heightening sensitivity in the blood vessels of the brain, leading to a pounding headache. Drink as much water as you can during the day, or at least an hour before you drink alcohol. All too often I forget that alcohol is going to hurt if I don't take care of myself beforehand. If you do drink, compensate.

Pace your drinking. Alternate a nonalcoholic drink with any alcoholic one. Water is the best pacer because it replaces the body fluids that are lost when you drink.

Dilute alcohol with plenty of ice cubes, water, or nonalcoholic mixers.

Drink a glass of water along with the alcohol and eat as you drink, particularly foods with fat. Because fat stays in the stomach longer, it slows alcohol absorption that much more.

Sip, don't gulp. The slower you drink, the more time you give the liver enzymes to break down the alcohol.

Take a B complex vitamin and two glasses of water before retiring.

Hangover relief

My idea of a great night is feeling happy the next morning—and I won't be happy if I'm in pain. What does work is swallowing as much water as I can before going to sleep—and taking aspirin or ibuprofen may stave off a headache. The next morning, replace B vitamins with a good breakfast (eat protein—eggs, a rare steak, and so on) and perhaps a multivitamin, or a therapeutic dose of B complex vitamins (how about some wheat germ?).

To soothe your stomach, take several magnesium or aluminum-based antacids (calcium-based antacids may increase stomach acid overnight).

If necessary, a hair of the dog that bit you, with a bare minimum of alcohol, such as a red dog (recipe below). And always, if you have a history of liver damage, avoid alcohol altogether.

~

Best on a hot summer's day: This refreshes and supplies vitamin C and a genteel kick.

ed Dog

    Bloody Mary mix
    Beer

Pour beer glass half full of Bloody Mary mix. Fill glass up with beer (your choice: Light or regular).

Tastes just like its name. Most women I know love this. It can't help but revive your flagging spirits.

Strawberry Shortcake Colada

Handful of crushed ice
½ ounce rum
½ ounce Creme de Banana
1½ ounces cream
⅓ cup crushed strawberries
1 (4-inch) fresh banana
Wedge of lime and superfine sugar

Add to blender and process until blended. Wipe rim of glass with a wedge of lime and dip into superfine sugar before pouring into glass.

～

Chapter 6

Winter is a natural time to go within

❧

Cold Weather Comforts

Dig deeply into the quieter pleasures

*W*omen must have a container for their energy, a way of thinking, a way of moving from one place to another that is contained. This is one way that women sustain their energy. It is their center—the center of their life. And, as fall overtakes summer, now is the perfect time to come to that center of peace and balance. Happiness is a form of courage, I think, and even more so in the cold of winter. Winter is a natural time to go within.

Where is the center of your life? Is it in your journal or in your creative art? Or is it at the computer, on a hill . . . or at the office? For my girl-friend Sharon, it's in the bathtub, where she'll often eat a blueberry bagel with cream cheese. For me it is in writing, in my home, and even in my car. These places I keep cozy and immaculate to make me feel good about myself. Where are you fed?

It's the perfect season for digging deep into the quieter pleasures—such as drawing, reading, watching movies, dreaming, or writing. What are your pleasures?

With the kids back in school and a chill in the night air, turn on the oven (if only to get warm)! While you're at it, bake a ready-made frozen pie, turnovers, cobbler, or brownies. Fill your home with heavenly aromas

*W*hen you're feeling down just think to yourself: What would I say to myself were I my own mother?
—REV. DOREEN RING

❧

201

and the down-to-earth feeling that home-baked food (yours or someone else's) always brings.

Winterize your car, your house, and particularly yourself. Invest in a supply of soft, cozy sweaters, warm gloves, insulated underwear, and perhaps a down jacket—anything and everything to stay warm. Take long, lingering steamy baths, drink hot cocoa, and do what you love to give yourself a self-directed passion that warms the coldest days—and a down comforter or an electric blanket and a good, loving man (or a big dog!) to warm the long, cold nights.

Live an extraordinary ordinary life simply by enjoying the joys within your reach at any given moment. Take on some of these autumn pleasures . . .

Simplify the holidays with meaningful old-fashioned rituals, or create new ones if need be. Enjoy all the home-baked goodies you would like—without the stress and strain—by being smart about it, and wind up the year on a fulfilling (not just a filling) note.

Invite yourself on an old-fashioned hayride.

Listen to crickets at night.

Walk through the woods.

Sit by a fireplace on a cold fall afternoon.

Take a moonlight walk on a beach.

Rock in a rocking chair.

Play monopoly or Chinese checkers on a cool night.

Bob for apples.

Decorate a bare mantel with an armful of colored leaves.

Carve a Halloween pumpkin.

Master that killer chili recipe.

Plant sweet peas.

Make hot chocolate and spike it with brandy.

Take a long, hot bath; light a candle.

Invest in a pair of flannel sheets.

Buy a bottle of cream liqueur, such as Baileys or a generic brand, and pour it into coffee, skim milk, or on the rocks.

Find your own way to make love to each day.

∼

This makes a lovely instant breakfast on the run, as it is filling, warm, full of caffeine and protein, and there's lots of it.

Spiced Hot Mocha Chocolate

1 envelope sugarless hot cocoa mix
1 teaspoon instant coffee granules
1 cup boiling water
1 cup milk, heated
1 stick cinnamon

Combine cocoa mix and coffee in a large 16-ounce mug or glass (I use a jelly glass). Add water and milk, stir with cinnamon stick. Makes 1 serving.

Per serving: 179 calories; 256 mg sodium; 3.3 mg cholesterol; 8 grams fat; 5 grams saturated fat; 16 grams carbohydrate; 10 grams protein; 1 gram fiber.

～

Find your own way to make love to each day.

A Practical Feel-Good Exercise

Make and keep a list of twenty things that give you pleasure—whether it's road trips on Route 66 or savoring a piece of strawberry cheesecake.

After you've finished that, make another list of all the things, projects, and experiences you wish to have, do, and experience before you die. Really!

Input them into your computer, print them out, and insert them into a 3-ring notebook. You might call it your "Inspiration Book," a book that will illustrate your goals and dreams. Now, day by day, weave these experiences you crave into your daily life. Refer to these lists often, especially when you get so caught up in chores, duties, and "have-to's" that you don't remember who you are or what you want to do.

～

Thick and creamy, and with traditional baked potato toppings garnishing the top, this soup is perfectly comforting. It's also a great way to get more calcium! Bone loss increases in winter, when people tend to exercise less, catch less sunlight, and eat fewer green leafy vegetables. Increase your intake of calcium (lowfat dairy products, dark leafy greens, canned sardines, salmon, and tofu). Or find a weight-bearing exercise that you like to do, such as exercising (or dancing) with weights, cross-country skiing, or shoveling snow!

Rosie's Baked Potato Soup

The best way to serve soup is to ladle it at the table right out of the pot or soup tureen and into warmed bowls. To warm the bowls, place them in a 200-degree oven for 10 minutes.

2 cups chicken stock
2 cups milk
4 tablespoons butter
¼ cup flour
3 bay leaves
¼ teaspoon black pepper
1 large baking potato, peeled and finely diced
½ teaspoon salt

Toppings

1 cup sour cream
1 cup shredded cheddar cheese
½ cup green onion, finely sliced
½ cup bacon bits

Heat chicken stock and milk in large saucepan over medium-high heat to almost boiling. Remove from heat and set aside. Reduce heat to low. In large soup pot, melt butter. Add flour, stirring constantly for 3 minutes to cook flour and make a roux. Gradually add milk mixture to roux, pouring in a slow steady stream while stirring vigorously to blend and eliminate lumps. Add bay leaves, pepper, diced potato, and salt and continue to simmer over low heat 15 to 20 minutes or until potatoes are tender and soup thickens. Lightly mash potatoes in soup, and stir to blend well. Pour soup into ovenproof soup crocks and top with sour cream, cheddar cheese, green onion, and bacon bits. Bake in oven to melt cheese. Makes 4 cups, serving 2 to 4 people.

Substitute low-sodium chicken broth and reduce sodium to 464 milligrams.

> Per cup: 265 calories; 836 mg sodium; 40 mg cholesterol; 14 grams fat; 9 grams saturated fat; 25 grams carbohydrate; 9 grams protein; 1.3 grams fiber.

〜

How To Keep Your Summer Body

Most of us increase our food intake by 200 calories a day during winter. To make up for the lack of sunlight, women tend to crave more carbohydrates, which stimulates the brain's production of serotonin, a mood-elevating chemical. Keeping this in mind, you may want to counteract possible weight gain by flying to Hawaii every other weekend, by staying busy in the evenings with projects and people instead of food, and by eating your comfort foods with less fat! You might:

Use nonfat milk and diet margarine when preparing instant mashed potatoes and macaroni and cheese.

Sooth yourself with soups that are broth-based with plenty of vegetables.

Enjoy lots of popcorn, fat-free chips, warm teas, coffees, and calorie-free sodas.

〜

BAKE SOMETHING!

It takes minutes to bake refrigerator cookies, crescent rolls, or to heat up sourdough bread—and the house will smell so good!

What? Afraid you'll eat it? Don't be! You can always bring it to work, give it to the lady next door, or freeze it for company instead of eating it all yourself.

I've tested half a dozen recipes for banana bread, and Aunt Lucille's mother's recipe is still the best I've tried! Be sure the bananas are good and ripe and that you pull it out of the oven just before it's perfectly done. Moistness makes the difference between just so-so and bread you're really proud to serve or give away.

My Favorite Banana Bread

2 cups sifted all-purpose flour (or up to 1 cup
    whole wheat flour may be substituted)
1 teaspoon baking powder
½ teaspoon baking soda
¼ teaspoon salt
½ cup butter
1 cup sugar
2 eggs
3 large ripe bananas or 1 cup mashed
½ cup chopped nuts, optional

To keep your skin moist in winter: Take warm showers, then apply a moisturizer while your skin is still wet; use a humidifier in your home.

～

Sift flour with baking powder, baking soda, and salt into a bowl. Beat butter, sugar, and egg in a large bowl until smooth. Mash bananas to make 1 cup. Add flour mixture and mix just until well blended. Turn into greased 9 by 5 by 3-inch pan that has been sprayed with vegetable spray. Push batter into corners of pan, leaving center slightly hollow. Let batter sit 20 minutes before baking for a nice rounded top.

Bake in lower third of a 350-degree oven for 55 minutes or until center springs back when lightly touched with fingertip. Cool in pan on wire rack 10 minutes; turn out and allow to cool completely. If freezing, allow bread to set a day or two first (covered in foil) for the banana flavor to mature. Makes 15 slices.

Per slice with nuts: 234 calories; 143 mg sodium; 58 mg cholesterol; 8 grams fat; .4 gram saturated fat; 35 grams carbohydrate; 4 grams protein; .8 gram fiber.

Pork chops are much leaner today than when your mother cooked for you, and require special care to keep them tender. This recipe will have you baking them slowly with a creamy mushroom gravy made with beer. Sure it takes time, but there's always other things to do while it bakes—and when everyone is that hungry, you know that the food will taste even better!

Mom's Breaded Pork Chops

    1   egg
    ½   cup milk or light cream
  2–4   center-cut pork chops, cut 1-inch thick
        Finely crushed cracker or bread crumbs
        Vegetable oil
    1   can beer
    1   can cream of mushroom soup
    1   (4-ounce) can sliced mushrooms, optional

In a bowl, combine egg and milk and beat until smooth. Dip chops in this mixture. Roll in crumbs until thoroughly coated on both sides.

Heat just enough vegetable oil to coat the bottom of a heavy frying pan. Over medium-high heat, brown chops quickly in oil. Turn carefully, making sure not to break the breading. This locks in the juices. Place chops in layers in the bottom of a roasting pan. Combine beer and condensed soup, stirring well with a wire whisk. Stir in mushrooms, then pour evenly over chops. Bake, covered, in 275-degree oven for 1 hour and 15 minutes.

Per chop: 469 calories; 752 mg sodium; 186 mg cholesterol; 31 grams fat; 11 grams saturated fat; 18 grams carbohydrate; 27 grams protein; .25 gram fiber.

When the world is spinning too fast . . .
Soothe Your Soul with Music

Music is powerful, as you know. It has the power to heal the body, strengthen the mind (even increase IQ!), and unlock the creative spirit. Many a midnight Phoebe Snow has soothed my soul. *I say a little prayer for you:* The gentle beat of Aretha Franklin has helped me through days of tortuous unresolved meetings and paperwork. Use music wherever you can as an emotional tool to cheer you, to energize you, or to bring out your emotions so they can heal. For fast stress relief, choose music you know well that has positive memories—sounds of nature or meditative music such as Gregorian chants. Bluegrass and Cajun music are joyful; hard rock blasts intense energy; classical music brings a elevated sense of calm (yet too much drives me crazy); and so on. Then there is the power of melody to bring back a memory and its associated emotions. Old tunes can light a candle to your soul. But beware of emotional tunes, especially after a breakup. Doug Stone says it well with the song, "They ought to put warning labels on those sad country songs."

> Turn off all the lights, lie on the couch, and listen, really listen, to your favorite music.

> Listen to a tape of nature sounds: The roar of the ocean waves or the fall of spring rain. Allow the natural rhythm to synchronize with your heartbeat.

> Get rhythm when you get the blues! Dance. Dance alone, or in a crowd. Dance like nobody is watching. They really don't care, you know, how you dance. Most people are concerned with how they look to others, so get out there and enjoy *you!*

> Take a couple of hours some evening (this is enjoyable to do while cleaning) and make a tape of all your favorite songs. Dub it and give to a friend.

TAKE ZINC

When everyone is sneezing around you . . . take zinc!

Zinc ions interfere with the viral integration of the cell. Doctors prescribe a 13.3 milligram zinc gluconate lozenge every two hours while awake.

～

On your day off, plan a day hike. Pack a blanket, a small camera to record the fall colors, a pad to draw or write on, maybe some granola, apples, hot chocolate, brandy, or schnapps, and this stew packed in a thermos, to keep you warm.

Also consider luxuriating some dreary weekend with this easy-to-make stew. There's no chopping required and you could make a potpie with the leftovers.

Luxuriating Stew

1	pound stew meat
¼	cup flour
1	package onion soup mix
1	can beef consommé
1	(16-ounce) can Italian-style tomatoes, undrained
1	can potatoes, sliced
1	jar beef gravy
1	(16-ounce) package frozen corn, broccoli, and red peppers
½	teaspoon Worcestershire sauce

Spray Dutch oven with nonstick cooking spray. Heat over medium-high heat until hot. Add beef, flour, and onion soup mix; cook, stirring occasionally, until beef is browned. Add consommé, tomatoes, and potatoes. Simmer for 30 minutes on low heat.

Add gravy and frozen vegetables to meat mixture. Bring to a boil, stirring frequently. Reduce heat to medium-low and cook for about 6 minutes or until vegetables are tender. Add Worcestershire sauce. Makes 6 servings.

Per serving: 311 calories; 847 mg sodium; 55 mg cholesterol; 5 grams fat; 2 grams saturated fat; 30 grams carbohydrate; 28 grams protein; 3.6 grams fiber.

Here is my favorite winter casserole, substantial with corn meal and lean ground meat. Olives, raisins, tomatoes, and chili powder keep it interesting. Make two and freeze one.

Tamale Pie

2½ cups water
1¼ cups yellow cornmeal
 ½ teaspoon salt
  1 large onion, chopped
  1 clove garlic, minced
  1 pound lean ground round, chicken, or turkey
  3 tablespoons flour
  1 teaspoons salt
  2 teaspoons chili powder
  1 (16-ounce) can whole tomatoes
  1 (6-ounce) can tomato paste
  1 (4-ounce) can mushroom stems and pieces, drained
 ½ cup pimento-stuffed olives, sliced
 ½ cup raisins, optional

Combine water, cornmeal, and salt in a medium-sized saucepan. Bring to boil; cook over medium heat until mixture thickens, about 5 minutes, stirring frequently. Turn mixture into a lightly oiled 8-cup deep casserole. Press cornmeal mixture on bottom and sides of casserole to form shell.

Coat a 9 or 10-inch sauté pan with cooking spray and sauté onion and garlic until lightly browned over low heat. Add ground meat. Cook and stir until meat loses its redness. Add remaining ingredients; mix thoroughly, bring to boiling, and spoon into casserole.

Bake in a slow (325-degree) oven for 40 minutes, or until mixture is bubbly-hot. Serve garnished with lowfat cheddar cheese and pimentos, if you wish! Serves 8.

Per serving: 281 calories; 991 mg sodium; 47 mg cholesterol; 11 grams fat; 4 grams saturated fat; 27 grams carbohydrate; 17 grams protein; 3.5 grams fiber.

How to Put More Joy Into Thanksgiving
(and less pressure on you)

Friends, relatives, and leftovers (not necessarily in that order) are the most comforting elements of Thanksgiving. How much work you choose to do is strictly up to you. A good old-fashioned roasted turkey dinner can be purchased from a restaurant, deli, or grocery store. Consider giving yourself a little extra time to get grateful. If making the dinner yourself, pare down the number of dishes, purchase prepared salads from the local delicatessen, cook as much of it as possible ahead of time, or buy frozen or already-prepared pies and slip them into a regular metal pie tin. (Another option is to celebrate Thanksgiving in a restaurant and prearrange for extra turkey to bring home.)

Life is supposed to be fun!
How to Have a Romantic Country Thanksgiving

Before you buckle, remember— the food can be ordered!

~

For the romantic rebel in you: Celebrate Thanksgiving nontraditionally with a feast out-of-doors, under a golden birch tree or in an open meadow. Candles, flowers, and, of course, the turkey, cranberries, and all the essentials might adorn a white linen-covered table. All it takes is a sense of adventure and romance, people you care about—and a truck or van for transporting.

Suggested Menu

Hickory smoked turkey.

Blueberry walnut stuffing.

Cranberry orange relish.

Squash margarita puff.

Waldorf salad.

Hot rolls.

Pumpkin walnut pie.

Your favorite champagne.

Note: If dishes are prepared ahead, to be reheated later, undercook them a bit so that they come out to the perfect doneness.

Order a roasted turkey from a deli, a restaurant, or bake it yourself using a cooking bag (it turns out extra moist that way and shaves about an hour off the roasting time). Or have your significant other smoke it on a smoker, which is basically a closed-in barbecue grill.

Hickory smoked turkey: Use mesquite or other flavored chips, and be careful not to overcook: The insides will look naturally red because it is smoked, thus it is not an indicator of its state of doneness! Call a turkey talk-line, sponsored by major companies that sell turkeys, such as Butterball, for more exacting cooking times.

Blueberry walnut stuffing: Prepare stuffing mix and add a few handfuls of frozen, thawed blueberries, chopped walnuts, and raisins. (If you prefer, substitute 2 chopped apples for the blueberries with a few dashes of cinnamon.)

Cranberry orange relish: Buy the best from a local quality delicatessen to give you a break! Quickly pour it into your own crystal bowl so that it looks as though you made it.

Squash margarita puff: Squash baked in its own skin is attractive and rather fun to make. Bake a 1½ to 3-pound Buttercup or Kabocho squash until done, 45 minutes to 1 hour. (But don't overcook the body of the squash, it will hold up better.) Spoon out inside and mash, stir in butter or margarine and add ¼ cup sugar. Stir in ¼ cup tequila and 2 tablespoons lime juice, season with salt and pepper. Return to 350-degree oven and bake until warmed through, about 30 minutes.

Waldorf salad: Make your traditional recipe, which is chopped apples combined with chopped walnuts and celery. For the dressing, simply mix half mayonnaise with half whipped cream. Add a handful of grapes.

Pumpkin walnut pie: You may as well make two. They are so good for breakfast! Buy a deep-dish frozen pie crust or refrigerated pie crust and fold out, fitting it into your own deep-dish pie pan. Follow the recipe for pumpkin pie on the side of a can of pumpkin, and double the amount of spices (this gives the filling greater depth and is not too spicy)! Also, be sure to use regular or lowfat evaporated milk. I sprinkle walnuts over the top like my mother always does.

On making gravy, use a mix or make it yourself. What stumps most of us is getting rid of the lumps. This can be done by using Wondra flour, a finer flour designed for making gravy, or by making a roux, or gravy base of flour and either fat drippings or water, that is stirred together until smooth. Well, the secret is, when the lumps are worked out in the roux before the gravy is made, you don't have to keep stirring to get the lumps out in the final gravy. (And if all else fails, whirl gravy in the blender until smooth.)

~

Now don't forget the best:
Your favorite champagne!

~

Packing the Picnic

Arrange ahead of time to get three or more large cardboard boxes.

Load largest items into van or truck first (table and chairs). Remember blankets (optional), candle holders and candles, flowers and vases, glasses, plates, flatware, napkins, and tablecloth.

Tuck glasses and plates between towels in a box. Wrap hot casserole dishes in newspaper to keep them good and warm. Pack champagne and cold drinks in ice, in a tub or plastic food containers.

With the willing hands and hearts of your guests, the table will be placed and set up in no time. Your food and the entire day will be appreciated like no other. Yes, this time, the time and energy you spend preparing food and creating atmosphere will be well worth it.

SAFE DRIVING IN SNOW AND ICE

For an up-to-date weather report and current road conditions, call the highway patrol or the American Automobile Association (AAA). Membership in motor clubs is good safety insurance. Annual fees usually cover towing and unlocking cars that have their keys left in them.

Sure, you can make chili from scratch, but canned chili is remarkably good, and is available in a variety of combinations: Turkey, beans, or no beans, to name a few. In the time you ordinarily would spend on preparation, spice it up the way you like it with extra chili powder, cilantro, or perhaps oregano, then line up some delightful condiments. Be sure to tell them it took you hours to prepare it.

Learn to get in touch with silence within yourself and know that everything in this life has a purpose. There are no mistakes, no coincidences; all events are blessings given to us to learn from. There is no need to go to India or anywhere else to find peace. You will find that deep place of silence right in your room, your garden, or even your bathtub.

—ELIZABETH
KÜBLER-ROSS

Canned Chili You Could Love

Chili garnishes

Sour cream
Grated cheese
Chopped onion or green onion
Sliced avocado
Salsa, a squeeze of lime juice, and a sprinkling of cilantro
    (popular in the West)
Hot sauce

Simple to make, custard is beautiful topped with fresh fruits, canned cherry pie filling, or whatever else blows your skirt up.

Pour into a 9-inch pie crust and bake as a pie, or simply make it crustless and pour into a 9-inch glass pie pan. Or you can pour custard into an oven-proof cup so that it becomes a pot de crème. Or you can sprinkle the surface of a baked custard with sugar, then brown it under a flame, to make crème brûlée. Another reason to make custard is to use it as part of an assembly, layered in a bowl with cake, fruit, and liqueur, for a trifle.

Warm Custard

    4 eggs (or 1 cup egg substitute)
  2⅔ cups milk
    ½ cup sugar
    ¼ teaspoon salt
    ¼ teaspoon nutmeg
    1 teaspoon vanilla
    1 (9-inch) unbaked pie shell (for pie)

Directions for custard

Heat oven to 450 degrees. Beat eggs slightly with rotary beater, then beat in rest of ingredients. Pour into 6 custard cups or a 1½-quart baking dish and set in pan of hot water (1-inch deep). Sprinkle a little nutmeg over the tops. Bake 45 to 50 minutes, or just until a knife inserted 1 inch from the edge comes out clean. Remove from oven. Serve cool or well chilled with fruit or whipped cream.

Directions for pie

Heat oven to 425 degrees. Pour into pastry-lined pan. Bake 25 to 30 minutes, until pie tests done or when a knife inserted one inch from the edge comes out clean. The center may still look soft but will set later.

For custard, per serving: 98 calories; 173 mg sodium; 11 mg cholesterol; 16 grams fat; 2 grams saturated fat; 16 grams carbohydrate; 3 grams protein; 0 gram fiber.

For pie, per slice: 375 calories; 515 mg sodium; 126 mg cholesterol; 19 grams fat; 2 grams saturated fat; 40 grams carbohydrate; 8 grams protein; 0 gram fiber.

Inherently comforting: Milk and eggs gently baked until they are set—could anything be more soothing to the palate, or to the soul?

Smooth, creamy, and easy. And who said what's sinful isn't good for you, too? Like most recipes, this one can be low or high in fat, depending on whether you choose cream, nonfat milk, or somewhere in between. Rice pudding has been a favorite with our family as early as I can remember—we first ate hot cooked rice as a breakfast cereal, naked in a bowl of milk with little else than a pat of butter. Now I fix it with dried cherries, blueberries, or cranberries if we have them, or if not, currants or raisins.

Do you remember what it was like when your mother left for a few hours and you had the run of the kitchen? I remember how thrilled I was knowing I could cook whatever I wanted! Usually I would make rice pudding. Make it tonight, but first, put on some Bonnie Raitt or a Tanya Tucker CD for good measure, then take a warm cup to your favorite chair (or the computer) and nourish yourself. You're worth it.

It tastes like
Your Grandmother's Rice Pudding

- 2 eggs, beaten
- ½ cup sugar
- ¼ teaspoon salt
- 2 cups milk (any octane you prefer, but the richer the milk, the richer the end result)
- 2 cups cooked rice
- ½ cup raisins
- 1 teaspoon vanilla
- Nutmeg

Beat eggs, sugar, and salt together. Scald milk until a film forms on top and pour into egg mixture. Add rice, raisins, and vanilla. Stir to combine. Set a pan in the oven large enough to hold 1 inch of water and 6 custard cups or a 1½-quart casserole. Set cups or casserole in pan and fill with hot water. Sprinkle with nutmeg and bake 1 hour and 15 minutes, just until set and knife inserted into center comes out clean. Serve warm or chilled. Makes 6 servings.

Per serving using 1% milk: 192 calories; 136 mg sodium; 3 mg cholesterol; 1 gram fat; .6 gram saturated fat; 43 grams carbohydrate; 4 grams protein; 1.7 grams fiber.

A cozy project to start on a blustery winter's day
Your Family Cookbook

Keep your family roots alive with a cookbook of your family's recipes. Ask your mother for her favorite recipes (and be sure to include the ones you love most). Notify relatives of your plans and give them a deadline for contributing their favorites. Also ask for a history of the recipes—where they came from and how they were first served. Input these into your computer. Add stories, personal anecdotes, familiar phrases, even songs and quotations that members of the family are famous for. If you can wait with this, build on this data as years go by. You'll have a treasure in the making. When the time is right, print the book. Duplicate it yourself at a copy shop, and staple it or put the pages in three-ring binders.

I began this project fifteen years ago and have been adding to these computer files ever since. My mother has written her story, which I've included; favorite recipes of my favorite aunt who has since passed away are preserved; and I've found that most of my sisters' favorite recipes change, and to keep track of them is like a record book of their lives at a very personal yet rarely considered angle. It will undoubtedly be my most important cookbook!

～

The earliest moment of ecstasy I can remember was running across a grassy field with my eyes closed, eating a peanut butter cookie. The Girl Scouts called them "Savannahs." To this day, I remember that intense pleasure and intend to find more of them that no one can take from me!

Patrice's mother sprinkles cinnamon sugar over these before baking. Rather nutritious besides delicious with a glass of fat-free milk.

Old-Fashioned Peanut Butter Cookies

- 1 cup (2 sticks) unsalted butter, softened
- 1 cup granulated sugar
- 1 cup (packed) brown sugar
- 1 cup peanut butter, smooth or crunchy
- 2 eggs
- 1 teaspoon vanilla extract
- 3 cups all-purpose flour
- 1 teaspoon baking powder
- 1 teaspoon baking soda

Preheat oven to 350 degrees. Lightly spray 2 cookie sheets with vegetable spray.

Cream together butter, granulated and brown sugar. Stir in peanut butter until smooth. Add eggs and vanilla. Mix until well combined.

In another bowl, mix together flour, baking powder, and baking soda. Add to peanut butter mixture and stir just until flour disappears. Spoon about 1 tablespoon batter each for small cookies and 3 tablespoons each for jumbos on prepared cookie sheets. Dip the tines of a fork into flour and score each cookie in a traditional crisscross pattern. Bake about 15 minutes for small cookies and 20 minutes for jumbos. The edges should just begin to turn golden. Set aside to cool on racks. Makes 50 small cookies or 18 jumbos.

Note: Substitute lowfat peanut butter for 130 calories and 6 grams of fat per cookie!

Per cookie: 170 calories; 79 mg sodium; 13 mg cholesterol; 10 grams fat; 2 grams saturated fat; 20 grams carbohydrate; 3 grams protein; .47 gram fiber.

Make Your Home a Winter Refuge

Make your home a little more intimate, to help you feel more balanced and in harmony with the season. Add more patterns, more texture, and more color after the spareness of summer. Perhaps some of the following suggestions might help!

Replace white lampshades with craft paper or parchment shades in warm browns—or boost the wattage of the lightbulbs.

Cluster photographs with artful frames.

Shape your environment to reflect your feelings about the season. If you love sledding, put up pictures of fun times you had in the past or display an antique sled in plain view. If your favorite winter activity is taking a hot bath, fill your bathroom with pine-scented candles and winter greenery.

If you're sensitive to less light during the longer days, set up more lamps and paint rooms white or yellow to brighten up the indoors (this helps to modify one's mood to a more positive one all year long).

～

Passions

What are your everyday passions? What is it you do that stirs up a fierce creative urge or that yearns to nurture, to care for our children, to watch them grow to be the best they can be? Or do you feel that you have a mission to help the needy, build a company, change laws, or make a difference in your community? These are all forms of passion, our life force that directs our actions through what it is that gives our lives meaning. Focusing on your passions more often is being true to yourself—and more of it will show up in your life. Bless what blesses you.

Desirée's passions

A cup of raspberry cocoa

Anything French Country

Fresh strawberry pie

A hot, sultry summer's day

Men who ask how I feel

Others who are passionate

Now list yours . . .

List your favorite passions here

Passion is the love of turning being into action. It fuels the engine of creation. It changes concepts to experience. Passion is the fire that drives us to express who we really are. Never deny passion, for that is to deny Who You Are and Who You Truly Want to Be.

—NEALE DONALD WALSCH, "CONVERSATIONS WITH GOD, BOOK 1"

A hot toddy is what your grandmother might have made for a sore throat or a cold. Like modern-day nighttime cold medicines, they contain alcohol. Make your own with this recipe. It will help you to fall into a deep sleep so that your body can repair itself.

Hot Toddy

1–2 teaspoons lemon juice
  Brandy or whiskey
  Honey

Combine a couple teaspoons of lemon juice in a mug of hot water; add a shot of brandy or whiskey and honey to taste.

～

There can be no healing that doesn't first start with love of self.

～

Please Yourself for Good Health

Happiness, joy, and pleasure keep our spirit alive, contribute to good health, and make a long worthwhile life possible. A study of people who enjoyed especially robust health, described by Robert Ornstein, Ph.D., and David Sobel, M.D., in their book *Healthy Pleasures* (Addison-Wesley, 1989), revealed that these people shared an expectation that what they did would offer them pleasure. Learning to love life actually repays in a healthier life.

～

Drug interactions can lead to problems. Check with your pharmacist about any over-the-counter drugs you buy, particularly if you are using two or more drugs from different doctors or dentists!

Have a Soup and Sandwich

On a blustery day, make yourself what your mother may have made for you: Chicken noodle soup and a sandwich, or grilled cheese and cream of tomato soup. Warm your tummy and your heart.

~

THINGS TO DO IN FRONT OF A FIREPLACE

Unwind and eat dinner. Fire has an allure that mystifies and allows you to dream.

Experience the quiet delight of toasting marshmallows.

Pretend you're a kid and roast hot dogs (the lowfat ones are great)! Enjoy them with all the trimmings: Relishes, pickles, chopped onions, ketchup, various mustards, and so on.

Drink cognac and eat popcorn.

Make love.

Use your imagination and do it again.

Make S'mores.

As yummy now as it was when you were a little girl. Could you could use a gooey, chocolaty, marshmallowy lift right now?

S'mores

8 whole graham crackers
16 marshmallows, snipped in half horizontally with kitchen shears
1 chocolate bar or ¼ cup semisweet chocolate chips

Oven method: Place 4 graham crackers in single layer on baking sheet. Space 8 marshmallow halves evenly over each cracker. Break chocolate bar to fit or sprinkle chocolate chips over top (if using). Cover each with graham cracker to make sandwich. Cover S'mores with a tent of foil.

Bake on center oven rack at 400 degrees until marshmallows just start to ooze, about 10 minutes. Serve warm. Makes 4 S'mores.

Fireplace method: Roast marshmallows over fire until brown as you like them. Place between 2 graham crackers and cover with chocolate bar, pieced to fit, or sprinkle with chocolate chips. Press top graham cracker over melted marshmallows, which kiss the chocolate, and let it melt—if you can wait—a minute or two.

Variations: Add sliced bananas, sliced strawberries, preserves or spread second graham cracker half with peanut butter.

Per S'more: 267 calories; 2 grams protein; 50 grams carbohydrate; 6 grams fat; .2 gram saturated fat; 3 grams cholesterol; 20 mg sodium; .5 gram fiber.

The sun always shines. We just don't always see it.

The Winter Blues Remedy: Get Some Sun!

Living near Lake Michigan, when the winters are long and dreary, I felt like a canary with a towel over my cage. When I finally made it to eighteen, I moved to sunny Phoenix where February could be June as far as the weather is concerned—and voilá! I didn't get depressed for months at a time anymore! All I needed was sunlight. That's because the less daylight there is, the more melatonin is secreted by the pineal gland. When melatonin is high, the neurotransmitter serotonin is low, and some of us tend to experience more sleepiness, fatigue, a decrease in sex drive, carbohydrate cravings, and depression. In other words, we're in really bad moods. To remedy this, I would take a walk in the sunshine, taking advantage of the reflection on the snow or spend a few minutes under the sun lamp.

For more severe cases, artificial therapy may be needed. It's called Seasonal Affective Disorder (SAD) and women are six times more likely to experience it. Since lack of sunlight is the cause, increasing environmental light is the answer. Extra light in the home or the workplace may be helpful by installing more lights on the ceiling or placing more lamps in the room. Or you may simply increase indoor light levels by trimming hedges around the windows, or go as far as constructing skylights. I know a waitress from Cloverville, Michigan, who painted her ironing room yellow. The bright color was so uplifting that she found a reason to spend most of her time there. Increase your natural light intake. It is naturally healing—both chemically and emotionally.

> Head south. Take your vacations during the winter. Two weeks in Florida or the Bahamas will do you a world of good.
>
> Turn on lots of light when you wake up in the morning and when you get home in the afternoon.
>
> Watch your weight. Aerobic activity combined with a carbohydrate-rich diet will stave off winter weight gain and help elevate spirits.

Don't forget cozy fireside meals, ice skates, snow angels, and hot cocoa with marshmallows. When we focus on the good aspects of anything, our attention to it brings it to us—and even freezing weather can be enjoyable!

Spend part of your lunch break on a chair in the sun or on a blanket in a park. Grass feels wonderful even through nylons.

Anything you would do inside, do outside in the sun: Read the paper, write memos, notes, and so on.

Discover the simple joy of snowshoeing. (You can rent snowshoes at any sporting goods store.)

For severe depression, obtain the help of a qualified professional. Healthy people know when to get help! A popular treatment is to increase light. Controlled "light therapy" is accomplished by buying or building a light box, in which you can increase your exposure to light up to two to three hours each day. For more reading on this subject, I recommend *Seasons of the Mind—Why You Get The Winter Blues and What You Can Do About It* by Norman E. Rosenthal, M.D.

～

Children learn twenty percent more from rooms flooded with natural light. Shoppers buy forty percent more when surrounded with natural light, such as from a skylight, according to a recent study.

Probably the most soul-satisfying vegetable soup in the world. It's the best I've tasted and though the ingredient list is long, it's a cinch to prepare and a good use of time. (You can eat it all week and it just gets better.) Freeze leftovers in individual containers so that you can bring a bowl to work.

Serve with a glass of Cabernet, a fresh green salad, and toasted garlic bread, or impress them by serving the minestrone in bread bowls. This is how to make them: Buy small round unsliced loaves of bread (8 ounces each), cut off the top with a serrated knife, and scoop out the insides with a fork. Tear off pieces of bread to dip as you eat.

Perfect Minestrone

2 tablespoons olive oil

2 onions, thinly sliced

6 cups low-sodium chicken broth

1 (16-ounce) can Italian plum tomatoes, drained and cut up

1 (10-ounce) package frozen mixed vegetables

1 (10-ounce) package frozen green beans, thawed

1 (10-ounce) package frozen spinach, thawed

1 (15-ounce) can kidney beans, drained

1 cup uncooked pasta, any style*

½ cup red wine

Toppings: Parmesan, pesto, chopped green onions

A CALMING RITUAL

When I'm feeling lonely or scattered, I'll light a candle and keep it burning all evening long.

I might also light a stick of rose-scented incense—then my mood changes, and everything changes.

～

Heat the oil in a very large pot over medium heat. Cook the onions 2 minutes. Add the chicken broth and tomatoes, then let it cook over a low flame for 30 minutes.

Add the mixed vegetables, green beans, spinach, beans, pasta, and wine, and cook for 2 minutes; turn off the heat and cover the pan. Let it sit 10 minutes (the heat will cook the pasta). Serve hot, topped with grated Parmesan, pesto, and chopped green onion. Add more water if soup gets too thick. Makes 10 servings.

*If you will be reheating this more than twice, cook pasta separately and add cold pasta to the hot minestrone.

Per serving: 244 calories; 871 mg sodium; 9 mg cholesterol; 5 grams fat; 1 gram saturated fat; 41 grams carbohydrate; 10 grams protein; 5.9 grams fiber.

Here is a delicious antidote for too many restaurant meals. Some people simply call it corned beef and cabbage. Cooked ham can be substituted for the corned beef which will cut cooking time down to thirty minutes or less. Some nice bread or rolls fresh from a nearby bakery will complete dinner— or make dumplings (see page 228) and cook them, covered, the final ten minutes.

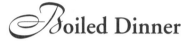

Boiled Dinner

1 (3–3½-pound) corned beef brisket
½ teaspoon salt
¼ teaspoon pepper
1 medium cabbage, cut into chunks
6 turnips, quartered
6 small potatoes
6 small carrots
3 medium onions, cut in quarters

In a 4-quart saucepan, cover beef with cold water and slowly bring to a boil, skimming off the fat as it accumulates. Reduce heat. Season with salt and pepper; cover and simmer 3 hours, or until beef is tender. Add vegetables; simmer an additional 45 minutes, or until tender. Arrange beef in the center of a serving platter surrounded by vegetables. Makes 10 servings.

Per serving: 407 calories; 372 mg sodium; 86 mg cholesterol; 24 grams fat; 8 grams saturated fat; 22 grams carbohydrate; 26 grams protein; 4.43 grams fiber.

How to Save Time to Do the Things You Want to Do
(Get work out of the way—quick!)

Do whatever chore you are avoiding, or dislike the most, first.

Portion out chores during the week, doing a little each day: wash on Monday, iron on Tuesday, and so on.

Use the first half-hour after coming home as transition time and complete one of your chores.

Begin with the end in mind. Don't let chores take up a full day. Set a limit on the amount of time it will take to do a particular job—then stop!

⁓

We tend to feel more order when our environment is in order. Winter is a good time to organize closets and drawers.

⁓

Women who can be in uncomfortable environments can also be in uncomfortable bodies.

—PAT ALLEN, PH.D.

Showier than an apple pie, and easier. And you know, this gorgeous work of art is even more edible with a side of ice cream!

Apple Dumplings

1 package (about 15 ounces) refrigerated fold-out pie crust
8 medium tart apples, peeled and cored
7 tablespoons sugar
1 teaspoon ground cinnamon
8 teaspoons butter
2 cups water
Ice cream or whipping cream, optional

Keep pastry between plastic and roll out pastry circles to a square as thin as possible. Cut each round into 4 sections. Place an apple in center of each square. Combine sugar and cinnamon; fill apple cavities with cinnamon mixture. Dot each with 1 tablespoon butter. Fold pastry around each apple, pinching to smooth and seal. At this point I like to cut a couple of leaves from the dough with a sharp-pointed knife and press them on the apple with a bit of water. Then make a stem by rolling a tiny piece of dough between your fingers and gently securing it in place with a bit of pressure and a dab of water. Place in a baking dish.

Bake in preheated 425-degree oven 40 to 45 minutes, or until browned. Serve with ice cream or whipping cream. Makes 8 apple dumplings.

Per dumpling: 474 calories; 1 gram protein; 73 grams carbohydrate; 24 grams fat; 34 grams cholesterol; 6 grams saturated fat; 302 mg sodium; 5.4 grams fiber.

Take two hugs and call me in the morning
Feeling Under the Weather?

The word "disease" breaks down into the words "dis-ease." Your body is telling you to slow down and get back on-line with yourself.

> Pamper thyself. Prepare whatever food or drink you were served as a child—chicken soup, tea, or red pop, for example.

> Sit in the sun, if only for a few minutes.

> Be patient—you may as well enjoy the time your body needs to heal itself.

> Drink plenty of liquids—make them warm, soothing liquid if you're stuffed up, such as hot tea, hot lemonade, hot chicken soup, or a hot toddy (page 221).

> Take aspirin or ibuprofen for fever, minor aches, pains, and headaches. Make an appointment to see a physician if the malady lasts more than a couple of days.

> Go to bed—and preferably, not alone. Love is the best painkiller.

Cold Remedies

Reduce stress by taking better control of your life, talking to a therapist, or by simply treating yourself better. People under a lot of stress develop nearly twice as many colds as those who aren't.

If you already have a cold, minimize the symptoms with some chicken soup, perhaps a tea called Gypsy Cold Remedy (I heard it really works), the cold and flu herb echinacea (ask a helpful clerk at your health food store), a massage, vitamin C, and some good loving. (Before trying any herb for medicinal purposes, consult your doctor.)

～

Chase the chill from the house this weekend with a simmering pot of chicken soup. My former boss Rick Tobin would add a dash or two of lemon juice. Good served with a basket of hot garlic bread and grilled cheese sandwiches.

Mama's Chicken Soup

1 (3-pound) plump chicken, rinsed
3 quarts cold water
3 stalks celery, leaves and all, cut in thirds
1 medium-sized onion, halved
3 carrots, peeled and cut in thirds
⅓ cup chopped fresh parsley
1 teaspoon salt
2 bay leaves
1 bunch celery, chopped course
1 cup fresh or frozen peas
1 cup fresh or frozen corn

Place chicken and water in large soup pot and bring to a boil. Skim foam from surface, reduce heat to medium-low, and add 3 stalks of celery, the onion, carrots, and remaining ingredients. Simmer, with lid ajar, for at least 1½ hours or until chicken is very tender. Allow the chicken to cool completely before deboning the chicken (this allows the juices to be reabsorbed). Remove chicken from bones; cut into bite-size pieces and return chicken to broth. Refrigerate overnight. When you're ready to prepare the soup for serving, add the rest of the celery and carrots, the peas and the corn, and adjust the seasoning. Serves 8.

Chicken Dumpling Soup: Add dumpling batter. Combine 1 cup Bisquick, ⅓ cup milk, and 2 tablespoons fresh chopped parsley or other favorite herbs, and blend well. Spoon dumpling dough on top of boiling soup. Reduce heat and simmer, covered, 10 minutes. Simmer, uncovered, 10 minutes longer.

Chicken Noodle Soup: Follow the recipe for Mama's chicken soup and add noodles before adding the cooked chicken.

> Per serving using original recipe: 397 calories; 422 mg sodium; 164 mg cholesterol; 7 grams fat; 4 grams saturated fat; 164 grams carbohydrate; 42 grams protein; 1.5 grams fiber.

～

Should you wish to live a rich life, being reasonable is not always preferable behavior. Sometimes what feels right is what will pay back in passion and meaning.

～

If I Had My Life To Live Over . . .

I'd dare to make more mistakes next time. I'd relax, I would limber up. I would be sillier than I have been this trip. I would take fewer things seriously. I would take more chances. I would climb more mountains and swim more rivers. I would eat more ice cream and less beans. I would perhaps have more actual troubles, but I'd have fewer imaginary ones.

You see, I'm one of those people who live sensibly and sanely hour after hour, day after day. Oh, I've had my moments, and if I had it to do over again, I'd have more of them. In fact, I'd try to have nothing else. Just moments, one after another, instead of living so many years ahead of each day. I've been one of those persons who never goes anywhere without a thermometer, a hot water bottle, a raincoat, and a parachute. If I had to do it again, I would travel lighter than I have.

If I had my life to live over, I would start barefoot earlier in the spring and stay that way later in the fall. I would go to more dances. I would ride more merry-go-rounds. I would pick more daisies.

—NADINE STRAIN, 85 YEARS OLD,
LOUISVILLE, KY.

～

A lovely soup: Classic, earthy, and sensual. Have it with a glass of white wine and some opera. Maybe Nina Simone and Shirley Horne—or a soothing Gordon Lightfoot.

French Onion Soup

3 tablespoons butter or margarine
1 tablespoon olive oil
4 cups thinly sliced onions
1 teaspoon sugar
¼ cup flour
7 cups beef broth*
½ cup dry sherry or white wine
½ teaspoon pepper
3 tablespoons brandy
16 thin slices French bread
2 cups grated Swiss cheese

IMPROVING ON A MOVIE AT THE THEATER

Get off work a half hour early and take in a twilight show.

Take a big comfortable coat that will double as a throw to make you cozy and feel at home.

～

Melt butter or margarine with oil in large heavy saucepan. Add onions and toss until coated. Cover and cook over medium heat 15 minutes. Uncover and stir in sugar. Cook, stirring frequently, until onions are evenly browned. Blend in flour and cook 5 minutes more. Add broth, sherry, and pepper. Heat to boiling over high heat. Reduce heat to medium and simmer, partially covered, 40 minutes. Ladle soup into ovenproof bowls, and add brandy. Preheat oven to 400 degrees. Lightly toast slices of French bread and float 2 slices in each bowl. Sprinkle Swiss cheese over bowls. Bake for 10 minutes or until puffed and browned. Makes 8 servings.

*Use low-sodium beef broth for a reduced 591 milligrams sodium per serving instead of 1,255 milligrams for regular beef broth.

Per serving: 313 calories; 1,255 mg sodium; 34 mg cholesterol; 13 grams fat; 7 grams saturated fat; 31 grams carbohydrate; 13 grams protein; 1.9 grams fiber.

Playtime!

A clinical psychologist I know runs seminars on learning how to play, and it is designed by his six-year-old daughter. He asked her what she would do if she wanted to have fun, and that's exactly the participants do. Playing in the mud, jumping rope, and cutting out paper dolls are activities still included as part of the weekend participants actually pay to experience!

Playing with your child is a natural way to get in touch with your own playful spirit. Here are some activities to share:

Jump rope.

Hopscotch.

Jacks.

Chinese jump rope (double).

Play pick-up sticks.

Put together a Mr. Potato Head.

Play Cootie.

Cut out paper dolls.

Papier-mâché.

Finger paint.

Keep disposable cameras located throughout your house to catch your kid's smiles and poses.

Play is creativity. Re-creating oneself with one's children through play can create a bonding that puts all of life in perspective.

ingerpaint

2 cups cold water
¼ cup cornstarch
   Food coloring

Boil water and cornstarch together in a saucepan, stirring, until thick. Pour into smaller containers and stir in food coloring.

Improving on a Movie at Home

Rent a video. (Cut costs by borrowing movies, books on tape, and CDs from the library.)

Pop some popcorn, snuggle under your coziest blanket with, if possible, a warm body next to you (a man, child, dog, or cat will do). Call a friend and invite him or her over to see it with you.

Throw something frozen or an easy quiche or casserole in the oven to eat midway through. Pop popcorn. Make hot cocoa or iced coffee or serve wine.

Play with dough—create Christmas ornaments, beads, or letters to spell out your name. They will last for years.

Play Dough

2 cups flour
1 cup salt
   Water

Combine flour and salt together in a bowl. Add just enough water to make a rubbery and soft-feeling mixture. Store in a plastic container with a tight-fitting lid to prevent drying out.

You can eat this one and it's delicious.

Peanut Butter Play Dough

Large jar peanut butter
Few spoonfuls honey
Powdered milk (instant or non-instant)
Cocoa to flavor, optional
Raisins and nuts, optional

Spoon out big globs of peanut butter into bowl. Then pour in a few spoonfuls of honey. Now add some powdered milk. Start mixing it all up with your hands. Keep adding the powdered milk until it makes a good dough. For chocolate flavor, you can add some cocoa powder. Now mold into any shape or roll out and cut with cookie cutters. Make designs with nuts and raisins.

Remember these?

Paper Dolls

Cut a piece of typing paper in half. Fold this in half (to 4¼ by 5½ inches), then in half again. Fold in half once more. Place the paper with its folded edge to your right.

Draw in half a person on the folded edge. The arm is the connecting link and must reach the opposite edge. Cut out through all the layers of paper and unfold.

Build a city, zoo, or farm with papier-mâché. Dip newspaper strips into a flour and water mixture and layer over molds. Make a house using a small beverage carton as a mold. When dry, paint on windows, the roof, and a door.

Papier-Mâché

      2 cups cold water
1½–1¾ cups all-purpose flour
          Newspaper, cut into strips that measure about
              1 inch by 15 inches

Mix water and flour in large bowl with wire whisk until smooth. Mixture should be the same thickness as heavy cream.

Coat a mold (molded clay or an inflated balloon work well) with one layer of newspaper strips that have been dipped in water. Then dip strips in flour mixture and lay over first layer of strips until mold is well coated.

Let stand until strips on mold are dry and had. (This may take several hours.) Paint over the strips if you like.

Apple crisp is my all-time favorite dessert. It's like apple pie but cozier (and easier). Apples are at their best served warm in pastry, as in apple dumplings or in the traditional heart-warming spoon pies, so called because they lack a bottom crust; a Brown Betty or a crumble in New England; or a buckle in the Pacific Northwest. Pandowdy is the same as cobbler, except that the biscuit dough is always rolled out like a pie crust. A grunt is a steamed cobbler with a thick biscuit topping, and the steaming gives it a moist, cake-like texture. Grunts are often served upside-down, which makes them look like cake.

A crisp is a baked dessert with layers of sugared and spiced fruit and buttered bread crumbs or sweetened oatmeal. These are wonderful for breakfast or as a heartier main dish sprinkled with a little cheese then microwaved.

A former boyfriend of mine would say to substitute dark brown sugar for the light because it's sexier!

pple Crisp

4 cups thinly sliced baking apples, such as pippin or Granny Smith
1 tablespoon lemon juice

Crisp topping

⅓ cup flour
1 cup quick or old-fashioned oats
½ cup brown sugar
½ teaspoon salt, optional
1 teaspoon cinnamon
½ cup chopped pecans or walnuts, optional
1 cup lowfat cheddar cheese, optional
⅓ cup melted butter

Preheat oven to 350 degrees. Coat an 8 by 8-inch baking dish with vegetable spray and toss in apples; sprinkle with lemon juice. Make the topping by combining dry ingredients and tossing with melted butter until mixture is crumbly. Spread topping over apples. Bake 30 to 35 minutes, or until apples are tender and topping is golden brown. Serve hot (or cold) with a scoop of ice cream. Makes 6 servings.

Time-saving tip: Keep a batch of crisp topping in the freezer so, if unexpected guests drop in, you can open a can of canned fruit or slice fresh fruit into a casserole, sprinkle with topping, and bake.

Per serving: 323 calories; 292 mg sodium; 27 mg cholesterol; 12 grams fat; 7 grams saturated fat; 52 grams carbohydrate; 3 grams protein; 3.6 grams fiber.

More sensual than corn bread, our pioneer foremothers called it "Indian pudding." I'm sure they would have loved to eat it with ice cream, if they had been born a little later. It's also good to serve overly active children a meal containing complex carbohydrates such as pasta, potatoes, or a grain, such as this delicious spoon bread, for it will eventually calm them. You will have a wonderful, satisfying meal if you serve a generous serving of hot spoon bread on each plate with a spoonful or two of salsa or stewed tomatoes.

Custard Cornbread
or Spoon Bread

> 1 cup yellow cornmeal
> 1½ cups lowfat milk
> ½ cup light sour cream
> ½ teaspoon salt, or to taste
> ¼ cup grated onion
> 2 tablespoons butter, melted
> 4 large eggs, separated

Preheat oven to 350 degrees and butter a 6-cup soufflé dish.

In a large metal bowl set over simmering water, whisk together cornmeal and milk until thickened and smooth. Remove from heat and whisk in sour cream, salt, onion, butter, and yolks. Set aside to cool.

In a large bowl beat egg whites until they just hold stiff peaks. Fold one third of whites into cornmeal mixture to lighten it and fold in remaining whites gently but thoroughly.

Pour batter into prepared dish and bake in middle of oven 40 to 45 minutes, or until puffed, golden brown, and just set in middle. Serves 6.

Per serving: 173 calories; 9 grams protein; 18 grams carbohydrate; 7 grams fat; 4 grams saturated fat; 150 mg cholesterol; 300 mg sodium; .89 gram fiber.

Transform the Blues

Feeling sad and blue is quite normal—not fun, but normal—as are other cantankerous feelings: Cranky, miserable, dissatisfied, pessimistic, negative, and generally rotten. And our power, the power to be passionate, also emotes from this well—so honor them! But know that one thing is for certain: Feelings change. And so will these. Try to identify what is causing these feelings, so that you can eventually deal with it. An advantage (yes, advantage) of being depressed is that when we walk through it with ourselves, when we *feel* feelings rather than stuff them, we feel more "at one" with ourselves, and know we can take care of ourselves through good and bad. It's a nice security to have.

A workshop teacher at Elysium Fields in Topanga Canyon shared the following technique. She said it was the "best thing I learned from EST."

When you're feeling an uncomfortable emotion, such as jealousy, anger, or you just feel "like crap" (as she put it), sit down, look into a mirror, and tell yourself what is bothering you. Don't give yourself a scapegoat. See what happens.

Are You Getting Enough Iron and Folic Acid?

Women who menstruate tend to be iron deficiency-prone, which will cause depression-like symptoms of tiredness and apathy. We need almost twice that of men: eighteen milligrams, which is four and a half cups of cooked spinach, nine ounces of liver, or four and a half cups of cooked beans, if the iron is absorbed. For optimal iron intake, use meat, vitamin C, and other iron sources together, or take an iron supplement. Tea, milk, and fiber interfere with iron absorption.

Men and women tend to be low in folic acid, which will cause depression, dementia, and mood changes—but who would think of eating broccoli when depressed? Other good sources include fortified grains, beans, oranges, and legumes. The recommended daily intake is 400 milligrams.

Be Smart About Bs

Marginal deficiencies of B vitamins, especially B6, have been linked to depression. It appears that with lower B levels the nerves cannot manufacture enough serotonin and other nerve chemicals which could result in insomnia, depression, irritability and nervousness. B vitamins can be depleted with the use of medications (such as birth control pills) and alcohol. If you try to enrich your diet with good dietary sources of B complex (enriched breads and grains), B6 (bananas, potatoes with the skin, avocados, skinless chicken, and salmon) and take a daily multivitamin supplement that supplies the RDAs also of B12 and folic acid, you'll be taking good care of yourself.

Working From the Inside Out, The Outside In

Make yourself more beautiful than you were yesterday. Maybe it's time for a haircut or a new perfume.

Change your physiology. Stand up straight if you're depressed. Pretend: Smile! Fake it till you make it. It takes as much energy to be miserable as it does to be happy. Transform the energy.

⁓

Expect something wonderful to happen!
(It will.)

⁓

Use These Depression-Reliever Visualizations

For depression: Visualize yourself behind the lines of a marathon. See the people who pass by as "depression" and watch them go by. Be with it: Feel it, then watch it pass. Remember that sad feelings come in waves, just as other emotions do, so if you just wait long enough, depression, like all feelings, will pass.

For letting go: Lay down in the sunshine—or completely relax wherever you are. Visualize the person, place, or thing that you wish to let go of and put it in a brown paper bag. Now picture yourself rolling the bag up and burying it.

If you are depressed, just for now, call or visit someone you laugh with a lot. Laughing is the most direct way out of depression. This is my favorite way out. I like to drop in on my friend John and within minutes I start laughing at myself. Life is simply a matter of perspective, so do whatever you can to find it.

Distract yourself. Fresh stimulus produces endorphins so even though it's the last thing you want to do, do something new and slightly challenging, such as begin a new project or buy a new book on your favorite subject.

Never Underestimate the Power of Love

The sun is always shining behind the clouds—we just don't always see it! Allow yourself to come to a quiet place within you, then say with every inhalation, "I choose love here, I choose love." Your mind may not understand how you pushed the clouds away, but it will work.

⌒

Life is simply a matter of perspective, so do whatever you can to find it.

Tools for Emotional Health Maintenance

When we've been denying our feelings, we may have to dig a little to know what's eating us. Here is an exercise that can help. Do it with a close friend or do it alone—with a pen and paper or your computer—for when you're not feeling quite right and don't know your underlying feelings.

I call this technique "Mad, sad, scared, glad." Ask your partner (or, if alone, write your answers on paper, or go to your computer):

Q.   What are you mad about?

A.   Work, my boss, etc., etc.

Interviewer says "thank you" after each response. Then he or she continues with the next three emotions:

Q.   What are you sad about?

A.

Q.   What are you scared about?

A.

Q.   What are you glad about? (Glad is last because
         it leaves you with energy.)

A:

Let your answers tell you how you really are.

∼

Bake (or Microwave)
Away the Blues

Record your favorite goodie recipe here:

Recipe Title: ....

Ingredients:

....

....

....

....

....

....

....

....

Method: ....

....

....

....

....

....

....

....

....

....

Bake by feel
Design Your Own Cookies

Release tension (and abandon) making cookies without a recipe. I know it sounds crazy, and it's not for everybody because it won't guarantee "perfect" cookies every time, but it sure makes me feel better to choose ingredients as I go along. It makes you the authority! (Which you are anyway.) So next time, find the nerve to get in there and throw ingredients together. Drop cookies such as oatmeal or chocolate chip are a pretty safe choice (you can always turn the batter into a bread if it doesn't turn out). Start with your favorite recipe and take off from there, adding or subtracting spices, nuts, chocolate chips, and the like, to fit your mood. Now personalize them. Name them after yourself or someone you love, such as Bob's Cowpies, Katie's Snowballs, Carol's Peanut Butter Surprises, or simply Sara's Sugar Cookies.

Record your favorite designer cookie recipes here:

Make a Christmas breakfast ritual of Kahlua pancakes. Though they're terrific served simply with whipped butter and a sifting of confectioners' sugar, I like to add whipped cream laced with more Kahlua, after which we spend the afternoon opening gifts, lounging, and snacking. Or, if it's just my boyfriend and me, we'll spend it unwrapping the gift of each other.

Kahlua Pancakes

1¾ cup complete pancake mix
2 tablespoons unsweetened cocoa
3 tablespoons brown sugar
1 teaspoon vanilla extract
2 tablespoons Kahlua or coffee liqueur
1 cup lowfat milk
⅓ cup chopped almonds or peanuts, optional

Stir together pancake mix, cocoa, and brown sugar. Add vanilla and Kahlua to milk and combine with dry ingredients, stirring well to eliminate most of the lumps.

Spray a nonstick skillet with vegetable spray and set over medium-low heat. Test pan to see if it is hot enough with a few drops of water (if droplets dance across skillet, it's ready).

Pour ¼-cup batter into pan and cook until bubbles around edge rise to the surface and pop; sprinkle over a few chopped almonds, then flip and cook until done. Makes about twelve 4-inch pancakes.

Per pancake: 128 calories; 4 grams protein; 22 grams carbohydrate; 2 grams fat; 1.5 grams cholesterol; .5 gram saturated fat; 369 mg sodium; .03 gram fiber.

Give yourself what you want for Christmas
How to Survive the Holidays—Well

It's impossible to create the type of holiday we see represented in magazines. The pressure is great, causing many of us to overwork and completely forget what is important: Being together and enjoying each other. Rise above holiday expectations and design a holiday that works for you! Have a meeting with the family. Ask them to make a list of what they like and don't like to do in celebrating Christmas. Compile their answers then do only those rituals that matter to everyone. Deal with the guilt of what you have to let go of. A little guilt is still better than overworking yourself and missing the whole reason for the season.

Women do the work creating the magic of Christmas. Perhaps your husband could help handle some of it! Why not share the load?

Plan the season around the idea of winter and less around the idea of holiday. Enjoy the cooler weather by enjoying winter recreational sports such as skiing, snowmobiling, ice skating, and so on. This will help to avoid the postholiday letdown.

Rethink gift-giving. People need your presence not presents. Set limits with money. Stick to a budget. Don't allow yourself to get caught up in the last-minute buying frenzy. Just say no to unwanted obligation (always) in the form of gifts or parties. It is a healthy way to avoid the anger that can come from letting yourself down while trying to make everyone else happy. A family I know has an agreement with each other to give only gifts without a dollar value. Typical gifts might be seashells, beautiful rocks, photos, drawings, or gifts of services, which tend to carry more sentimental value than pricey presents.

Set limits with food. You don't have to look like Santa after the holidays, but there is no sense in ruining the good spirit by getting too serious about it either. Bring your own lowfat dishes to a party. Enjoy lots of fruit and vegetables, then take a small amount of whatever else looks good. If you're entertaining, center it around an event, like a tree trimming or caroling, then serve snacks so everyone's minds aren't just on the food.

Rise above holiday expectations and design a holiday that works for you! ⁓

Be realistic. Plan events that you can realistically accomplish—no six-course dinners followed by two nights of caroling and two parties. Plan on using your energy and money well, and . . .

Pamper yourself. Maintain your routine. Your eating and sleeping routine should be maintained more often than not. Take time out from the business of your day to read, watch a special movie, or just unwind. Relearn how to play. Ask for toys for Christmas.

Focus on the people who matter. People are important, not spending money. This includes only those whom you love. If you feel there is no one, create a substitute family. Be with friends.

Develop new traditions that feel good to you. Remember what this season is for and take charge of what you do. If you can't go home, develop your own rituals.

～

It's party season, so buy a new dress (how about sequins and rhinestones?) and enjoy yourself! Unless you have a firm commitment from him, keep your options open and broaden your horizons.

One of the world's most delectable comfort foods, sweet potatoes were considered an aphrodisiac, according to Henry VIII, and they most definitely are when you think they are. Or experience their distinctive earthiness by simply baking them as you would a baked potato. Cover with sweet butter or horseradish and whipped cream. (Oh, by the way, women—and more feminine men—tend to fall in love with their ears, so be sure and tell whoever is eating it that this pie is an aphrodisiac.)

weet Potato Pie

3 large eggs
¾ cup sugar
  Dash of salt
1 teaspoon cinnamon
½ teaspoon allspice
¼ teaspoon nutmeg
1 cup lowfat evaporated milk
3 cups cooked mashed sweet potatoes
1 unbaked 10-inch pie shell

Beat eggs well, add sugar, salt, and spices, and mix thoroughly. Add milk and stir. Add mashed potatoes and mix thoroughly. Turn into pie shell and bake in a preheated 350-degree oven for 1 hour or until firm. Makes 8 servings.

Per serving: 339 calories; 125 mg sodium; 79 mg cholesterol; 8 grams fat; 61 grams carbohydrate; 5 grams protein; 3.6 grams fiber.

⁓

*Take something ordinary and turn it
into something special . . .*

Take a Great Bath!

As I mentioned, my girlfriend Sharon eats in the bathtub. Yes, she *eats*. So of course I had to try it too: A small dish of chocolate ice cream within a hot bath. And it's true, they really do go together, like hot fudge and ice cream!

If this is a bit too nontraditional for your taste, find your own bath ritual. Perhaps it might be a hot oil bath, or bathing with a candle, a rubber ducky, and one of your favorite CDs. Bathe while you read at least one chapter in a book you've been wanting to start. Or . . .

To keep your skin moist in winter: Take a warm bath or shower, then apply a moisturizer while your skin is still wet; drink lots of water; and use a mask for dry skin.

❦

Fill the bathtub with steamy hot water almost to the top; add bubble bath, bath beads or a fragrant bath oil. Close the bathroom door and let the room become a sauna. Set out a fluffy towel. Dim the lights.

Set one or several candles next to the tub and light them. Invest in a permanent candleholder for the bath. Place other objects you enjoy gazing at, such as a print, plants, flowers, or a treasured object. Meanwhile, make yourself a cup of mint tea or pour yourself a glass of wine.

For a French Herbal Bath, insert sprigs of French lavender and rosemary into an old pair of nylon stockings or wrap in a piece of cheesecloth. Run hot water over the herbs to release the oils into the water.

Or make your own bath oil by filling a pretty jar with baby oil and a spritz of two of cologne. Float a few flower petals in the tub or, if you're feeling playful, fill up the tub with the kids' inflatable toys—a boat, rubber duck, inflated dinosaur, and so on.

Put up your hair. Using baby oil, massage your neck, shoulders, and upper chest, which often holds the most tension; massage your feet and legs, too.

Pat dry lightly with a towel, leaving some of the oil on your skin to moisturize.

～

Soak away tension and reduce rheumatism and arthritis-like pains with your own private mineral bath. All you need is lots of water and this easy-to-make mixture of medicated minerals.

Private Mineral Bath Salts

2 cups ordinary Epsom salts (magnesium sulfate)
1 cup water softener, like Calgon
1 teaspoon eucalyptus oil
1 teaspoon menthol, 10 percent solution
1 teaspoon liquid iodine

Place salt and water softener in a mixing bowl. Add eucalyptus oil, menthol solution, and iodine, and mix with a spoon. This makes a pale-yellow mineral bath combination second to none. Use ½ cup to 1 cup in a tub of pleasantly warm water. Relax and luxuriate for at least 15 minutes.

Healing, pretty, and aromatic are reasons to draw yourself an herb bath.

Healing Herb Bath

3 tablespoons dried chamomile
3 tablespoons dried rosebuds
2 tablespoons dried rosemary or lavender or
   your favorite herbal tea bags*

Combine herbs or tea bags in a bowl. Pour 4 cups of hot water over the herbs and let the mixture steep, covered, for at least 15 minutes. Strain the herbs and pour the liquid into the bath right under the running water. Strew a few fresh herb sprigs and flower petals into the tub.

  *Or simply hold tea bags (or dried herbs tucked into cheesecloth) under running water.

HOW TO HANDLE STRESS (WITH A SENSE OF HUMOR!)

When someone says, "Have a nice day," tell them you have other plans.

Make a list of things you have already done.

Dance naked in front of your pets.

Bill your doctor for the time you spent in his waiting room.

∼

How to Make Flowers Last Longer

There is no better cure for winter doldrums than flowers. They liven up a room like nothing else. In the late fall, buy winter bouquets of everlasting flowers such as statice, cornflowers, love-in-a-mist, and baby's breath, as they dry naturally and last for months, even years.

Or tie a ribbon around the stems of flower bouquets just before they've lost their bloom for a ready-made natural arrangement. Hang this upside-down from a doorway, a rafter, a doorknob, or on the wall. The bouquet will be almost as beautiful for a week as if they were fresh—and when they're dry, they'll last. I always have flowers around me because I take advantage of the fresh bouquets and transform them into dried bouquets, which are much too beautiful to dispose of. It's economical yet beautiful and classy.

When roses are past their prime, collect them and show them off in an attractive bowl. When the snow comes, as it always does for most of us, they'll be most welcome decoratively scattered on the fireplace, in the bathtub, or wherever you want a touch of summer. Not all flowers retain their original color, but all are still beautiful. Do try this!

~

This is an easy and classy dessert.

Old-Fashioned Bottom-Crust Apple Tart

　1　package (about 15 ounces) refrigerated fold-out pie crust
　¼　cup oatmeal
　1　large egg beaten with 1 teaspoon water
　3　tart apples, peeled, cored, and thinly sliced
　1　tablespoon of bourbon, optional
　¼　cup raisins
　⅓　cup brown sugar, packed
　⅓　cup granulated sugar
　½　teaspoon cinnamon
　　　Mace
　　　Nutmeg
　2　tablespoons margarine or butter
　2　teaspoons granulated sugar (raw is best), for topping

Unfold pie crust and place on a surface lightly sprinkled with raw oatmeal; transfer to a (non-oiled) cookie sheet. Beat together the egg and water. Using a pastry brush, brush the inside of the crust with the egg wash. Reserve leftover egg mixture.

Preheat oven to 375 degrees. Combine the apples, bourbon, raisins, sugars, cinnamon, mace, nutmeg, and toss. Pile into center of dough. Dot with margarine or butter, then fold pastry over the apples. Brush the top of the crust with the egg wash. Sprinkle with granulated sugar.

Bake for about 50 minutes or until pastry is golden and apples are tender. Serve warm or cold with ice cream or whipped cream. Makes one 9-inch tart.

Per serving: 285 calories; 2 grams protein; 45 grams carbohydrate; 11 grams fat; 2 grams saturated fat; 39 mg cholesterol; 143 mg sodium; 2.2 grams fiber.

Have a Serene, Happy, and Joyful Christmas!

It's not what you do but how you do it, and this includes celebrating Christmas. Many of us go completely overboard, only to find ourselves frazzled, a few pounds heavier, and with a serious deficit in the checkbook. Don't postpone joy—plan for it to get the most from it with the least stress. Do only what you have the time to enjoy and can be mentally and emotionally present.

We Do Have Choices

Don't postpone joy—expect it!

Of course there will always be pressure to do what others prefer us to do, but to not choose and do it anyway is to choose to be a victim. How we spend our time is our option. Christmas can be a month of meeting deadlines—just like work—or we can pick and choose what gives us pleasure. We can choose to send Christmas cards—or not. We can spend Christmas in a ski resort or go to Mexico or to Grandma's house. We can expect resistance to any change we make concerning others, so let them know in advance if you are cutting back in gifts, parties, or any other hullabaloo. Remember that what is good for us is ultimately best for everyone else because we will be happier and others will benefit from that as well. Stress comes from overcommitting. This year, take on only what is comfortable—and this time, enjoy it all.

Shop Smart

Pick up gifts for Christmas, birthdays, and other occasions throughout the year when you see something they would love at the price you want to pay. Scout flea markets for one-of-a-kind, quality second-hand gifts.

For those gifts you didn't buy, around Thanksgiving, make a list around of everyone you wish to buy gifts for and two or three items you might think might be appropriate for each to save hours of endless browsing. Carry the list in your purse so that when you shop you can check off the person's name after you've bought the gift.

Enlarge summer photos and put them on T-shirts, on posters, or surprise a loved one with a wallet-sized picture of her and her boyfriend.

A Gift For Yourself

Not only does giving yourself time to "make over yourself" make you feel better, but somehow others treat you better as well. Before the party, take time to get a natural glow with a mask, a hot steamy bath, or a leisurely session of making love. Concentrate on feeling good. Odds are no one will steal your rainbow.

Take advantage of the free turkey given away by grocery stores and employers. Cook it in a cooking bag for the best tasting, moistest turkey without fuss. And make Christmas cookies a snap with a little help from premade cookie dough.

Homemade Christmas Cookies for Creative Women with Little Time

Use refrigerated sugar cookie dough from the grocery store. To make sugar cookies, using cookie cutters, start with the special Christmas refrigerated sugar cookie dough, and follow directions for rolled cookies.

Decorate unbaked cookies by sprinkling with colored decorator sugar or candy sprinkles and then bake as directed, or place frosting in a heavy plastic sandwich bag. Cut a small hole in one corner, close top, and squeeze frosting gently through hole to make thin lines.

Dress Up Store-Bought Cookies

Another time-saving method for making really beautiful Christmas cookies is to ice plain sugar or shortbread cookies with icing through decorating tips. Purchased icing, cinnamon candies, and shiny silver balls turn plain cookies into wreaths or pretty packages. Use round chocolate cookies, round sugar cookies, or square shortbread cookies with purchased red and green decorating icing and silver balls.

Using a small leaf tip, pipe green icing onto each cookie to resemble a ribbon, making the cookie look like a package wrapped up in ribbon. Using a small writing tip, pipe red icing onto each cookie to resemble a poinsettia.

Buy a selection of cookies, pretzels, and candies. Dip to ice with the following dark and white chocolate dipping recipes. You can also dip lollipops, fortune cookies, and dried fruit—use your imagination!

Chocolate Cookie-Dipping Recipe

1 pound white or dark chocolate
   Candies to sprinkle over icing:
      Chocolate and other cookie sprinkles
      Shredded coconut
      Silver balls
      Butterscotch candies

In a double boiler, melt chocolate over hot (not boiling) water. Once water is hot, turn flame off as chocolate burns easily. Stir until smooth. For dipping: Dip part or all of your favorite cookies or pretzels in melted chocolate, and place on a foil-covered cookie tray. Refrigerate until chocolate hardens.

Pipe white icing on purchased gingerbread, vanilla wafers, or plain chocolate cookies.

White Icing

2¼ cups sifted confectioners' sugar
 2 egg whites
¼ teaspoon cream of tartar

In a large bowl, mix all icing ingredients with a hand mixer on medium speed for 2 minutes. Using a double boiler, heat mixture until just warm. Remove from heat. Transfer mixture to a large bowl and beat with a hand mixer at high speed for 5 or 6 minutes, until icing stands in peaks.

Using a pastry bag, follow manufacturer's instructions to create desired designs, or coat cookies with a thin layer of icing using a knife or spatula.

A party favorite everyone reaches for.

Chex Party Mix

½ cup butter or margarine
1¼ teaspoons seasoned salt
1½ tablespoons Worcestershire sauce
2 cups Wheat Chex cereal
2 cups Rice Chex cereal
2 cups Corn Chex cereal
2 cups Bran Chex cereal
1 cup salted mixed nuts

Preheat oven to 350 degrees. Heat butter or margarine in 13 by 9 by 2-inch baking pan in oven until melted. Remove. Stir in seasoned salt and Worcestershire sauce. Add Chex and nuts. Mix until all pieces are coated. Heat in oven 1 hour. Stir every 15 minutes. Spread on absorbent paper to cool. Makes eight ½-cup servings.

Per ½ cup: 130 calories; 4 grams protein; 16 grams carbohydrate; 7 grams fat; 2 grams saturated fat; 7 mg cholesterol; 306 mg sodium; 1.8 grams fiber.

Keep packets of instant cider at work and make the real thing at home.

Hot Mulled Vino (or Spicy Cider, depending on what you use)

1 cup red table wine, apple cider, or apple juice
2 whole cloves
Juice of half an orange
1 cinnamon stick

Heat wine or cider, cloves, and orange juice together in a small saucepan slowly over low to medium heat. Use cinnamon stick as garnish. Makes 1 serving.

> Per serving: 106 calories; 1 grams protein; 7 grams carbohydrate; 0 gram fat; 0 mg cholesterol; 11 mg sodium; .05 gram fiber.

This is also called Norfolk Punch.

Hot Spiced Vino

1 quart red table wine apple cider or apple juice
¼ cup lemon juice
1 teaspoon cloves
1 teaspoon ground nutmeg
3 cinnamon sticks

Combine apple juice or cider and lemon juice in saucepan. Cut square of cheesecloth, about 5 by 5 inches. Place the cloves, nutmeg and cinnamon sticks, broken into smaller pieces, in the square. Tie ends together, making a pouch. Place saucepan over low heat; bring to a boil, add bag of spices, and simmer 5 to 10 minutes. Remove bag of spices. Makes eight ½-cup servings.

> Using red wine: 90 calories; 1 gram protein; 9 grams carbohydrate; 0 gram fat; 0 gram saturated fat; 0 mg cholesterol; 82 mg sodium; .09 gram fiber.

Cloudy, dreary winter's days used to send me to my favorite restaurant for a Keokee Coffee. Find a friend to share with.

*K*eokee Coffee

1 ounce (2 tablespoons) brandy
½ ounce Kahlua
Fill with hot coffee

Pour into a fine glass or other fancy coffee cup. Add sugar, cream, and whipped cream to taste. Garnish with a cherry.

Without sugar, cream, or whipped cream, 1 serving: 127 calories; 0 mg sodium; 0 mg cholesterol; 0 gram fat; 0 gram saturated fat; 8 grams carbohydrate; 0 gram protein; 0 gram fiber.

Faith in a Higher Power

Having faith in a higher power is security.

I was raised a Catholic and have followed the religious regimen over twenty years without ever really feeling close to God. The trouble with most organized religions is that in order for people to put faith in something else, they must first lose faith in themselves. Most religions have to make people believe they need it. To need anything is to fear it because without it we can lose it. The truth is we can never lose God.

Higher power, God, the source Allah, Jehovah, or the Great Spirit . . . all are within.

A woman has, as her source, her feelings and intuitions. Your feelings are your truth and no one knows what is true for you more than you do. Having faith in yourself is one and the same as having faith in God, for we are in unison. Therein lies our true power.

If you're having difficulty finding or feeling God or your source, start with intention. Get quiet and ask to feel a sense of his presence. (It's good practice. And we humans often forget to ask.) Trust that you know the way (you do). It matters not the method of finding your higher power. Often I

Call on Me, therefore, wherever and whenever you are separate from the peace that I am.

—NEALE DONALD
WALSCH,
"CONVERSATIONS
WITH GOD, BOOK I"

commune while ironing, listening to jazz, reading spiritual literature, chanting, or exercising. Meditating is a struggle for me, yet these diversions still busy a part of me, leaving another part totally at peace. Your relationship with God is as personal as the relationship you have with yourself.

We may also hear our answers from the outside world in any form whatsoever: An offhand conversation with a stranger to a rowdy country-western video. Neale Donald Walsch writes in *Conversations with God: An Uncommon Dialogue (Book I),*

> Listen to Me in the truth of your soul. Listen to Me in the feelings of your heart. Listen to Me in the quiet of your mind. Hear Me, everywhere. Whenever you have a question, simply know that I have answered it already. Then open your eyes to your world. My response could be in an article already published. In the sermon already written and about to be delivered.

Knock and the door shall be opened . . . .

The feeling of love is your experience of God.

NEALE DONALD WALSCH, "CONVERSATIONS WITH GOD, BOOK I"

When you get more secure in asking for answers, you can even set the rules for a sign. When I was a little girl, I would ride my bike three miles from my sister's house to my aunt's house. One day it was particularly cloudy and I asked for a sign to know if it was safe to ride my bike. I requested that if it was going to rain, it would show me by the time I got up to the big Colonial-style house up ahead. I rode up to it and there was no rain, so I knew it would be all right, and it was.

Within the past year I asked for a particular sign to know if a man I was seeing was the one for me. I told God that if he was, he would go out and purchase my first book. He never did. In fact, he told me, "I wanted to, but don't know why—I just didn't. Maybe it's because I just didn't need a cookbook?" I understood even though he didn't.

Another time I felt such a love for a man whom I knew I wouldn't see again for a long time. When he left, he gave me a bouquet of flowers. I prayed that they would live until I saw him again. The last flower dropped six and a half weeks later at ten in the morning. He knocked on the door just before midnight. Cross my heart, it's true!

To act on Spirit takes trust but, with each time, the knowing, the surety, the connection, will become stronger—and you will have invested in your greatest wealth.

So take that weight off your shoulders. Give up fear in the form of not having enough, not doing enough, or of fearing your kids or your man doing without you. Find God yourself and you won't need to hang onto those things. Now that's security!

∿

Have the faith of a mustard seed.

∿

Recommended Reading

Conversations with God: An Uncommon Dialogue, Books 1, 2, and 3, by Neale Donald Walsch.

Jonathon Robinson, author of *The Experience of God: How Well-Known Seekers Encounter the Sacred,* interviewed forty of the world's top spiritual leaders on how to find and keep the kingdom of God within. The following were their general consensus:

God isn't in the plowing of the field or the washing of the dishes—God is in the joy, the love, and the passion behind it.

1. We need a method that works for us in five minutes or less to feel we are in touch with God, whether it be through meditation, literature, or nature. We need to find a practical way to bring ourselves there.

2. We must have the faith and act on what our feelings, our intuitions tell us.

3. We need a sense of urgency in keeping God a priority. We need to consult with God before we do the laundry, clean up the kitchen, and so on.

4. We must be disciplined in keeping God a priority on a daily basis.

5. We need to do God's will with a sense of service, to be one with all of God's creation (not for our own selfish ends).

Make a "God Box"

Let go of your worries. They don't help one bit! Make this release seem more real through symbolically "giving it to God" by making a box and putting the worry inside. Write each worry—problems with your boss, your boyfriend, or his "ex," and so on—on a strip of paper, then put it in the special box you have ordained a God Box. Make over a shoe box, an old jewelry box, or whatever box that can represent a kind of "God's mail box" to you. Remember that every time you want to worry about these problems, God has them. This makes a nice gift for others, too!

Dressing Warm

**WARM-UP
QUICK TIP**

When your hands
and feet are cold,
your whole body
is cold.

For temporary relief,
run your hands
and wrists under
warm water.

～

Women are more likely to feel cold than men—up to five times more. When your hands and feet are cold, your whole body feels cold, and if it continues our body becomes tense, then sore, from tense muscles. I find that I work much better and feel more together when I'm warm. If you're the same, dress warmly in layers and bring an extra sweater to work with you. I've also found that if the top half of my body is warm (with sweaters and jackets), as well as my hands and feet, I tend to be warm even if I am wearing shorts.

A holiday ritual with a feeling of intimacy
Bathtub Luminaria

Luminaria is the name given to a Spanish Christmas ritual and decoration. They are small brown paper bags with a votive candle inside, and when lit, they make a lovely nighttime decoration.

Make your own bathtub luminaria this way: Place five to ten votive candles around your bathtub and light them. Fire danger is minimal and melted wax is a breeze to chip off! So what are you waiting for? Bring a bottle of champagne and your lover to the bathtub with you.

～

Instead of fruit cake, make a liquored cake that you know everyone will like. Made popular twenty years ago by the Bacardi rum people, this is a pound cake with a nice, fine texture. You can add some chopped dates, apricots, candied cherries, raisins, and chopped nuts if you care to. Or be a purist and simply decorate by outlining the edges with a border of whipped cream from an aerosol can and garnish with seedless green grapes dusted with confectioners' sugar.

um Cake

Cake

1   cup chopped pecans or walnuts
1   package yellow cake mix (spice is also good)
1   (3¾-ounce) package instant vanilla pudding mix
4   eggs
¼   cup cold water
½   cup oil
1   cup dark rum

Glaze

¼   pound butter
¼   cup water
1   cup sugar
½   cup dark rum

Next time you go grocery shopping, buy bite-size Oreos or a Moon Pie. Eat them, filling first, with milk or ice cream.

~

Preheat oven to 325 degrees. Grease and flour 10-inch tube or bundt pan. Sprinkle nuts over bottom of pan. Mix all cake ingredients together.

Pour batter over nuts in pan. Bake one hour. Set on rack to cool. Invert on serving plate. Prick top.

For glaze, melt butter in saucepan. Stir in water and sugar. Boil 5 minutes, stirring constantly. Stir in rum. Drizzle and brush glaze evenly over top and sides of cake. Makes 12 servings.

Per serving: 528 calories; 6 grams protein; 61 grams carbohydrate; 61 grams fat; 80 mg cholesterol; 405 mg sodium; .38 gram fiber.

Home-Cooking for the Holidays

It wouldn't be Christmas without your family's favorite foods, but you come first. Plan ahead to buy them or juggle a few hours here and there for advance baking and freeze them—or choose breads and desserts that improve with time, such as fruit cakes, plum pudding, and bourbon balls. Remember what is most important and don't compromise your health—physical or emotional—unless you will be enjoying it as well.

Be traditional. Keep it simple, keep it easy, and keep it familiar. Christmas is steeped in history and tradition and celebrating it as we always have evokes security.

Planning Ahead Is the Key

Shop early and buy everything you need. (You'll eliminate a great deal of stress if you can avoid last-minute dashes to the store.) Buy any relishes, chutneys, or conserves the week before. Yams, stuffing, and pie filling can also be prepared two days ahead, covered, and refrigerated (though we'll never tell if you take the frozen pie out of the freezer and follow directions). Simply reheat and garnish just before serving.

Work Smart, Not Hard

Early on the big day, fill the pie shell (if you're baking pies) and begin baking while you prepare your meat dish for cooking. When the pie is done, raise the oven temperature and cook the meat. Get others to help. Relax and smile. If things go wrong, laugh them off because they really do not matter. People matter.

Baked with Love, or No-Fuss Baked Goods

Baked items are a practical, easy way to add zest to your holiday table. Here are some ideas that take little time. Make yeast nut breads and fruit breads using automatic bread makers, or doctor up quick breads in the following ways:

Add nuts and dried fruit to gingerbread cake mix.

Mix chocolate chunks, chopped marshmallows, and walnuts with chocolate cake mix.

Sometimes it's nice to live in a messy house or cook in a messy kitchen, knowing whatever else you do isn't going to make a hill of difference—you can just enjoy it.

—AUTHOR REMAINS ANONYMOUS

With several of the high-quality mixes available, bake quick breads or yeast breads in tin cans for unusual, giftable shapes. Save up all sizes of tin cans a month before baking; wash, dry, and spray with nonstick spray before filling.

Take advantage of neighborhood bake sales. Buy handmade gifts of food and put your ribbon and label on it.

Buy refrigerated cookie dough, which lasts indefinitely because you can freeze it. The great thing about refrigerator cookie dough (originally called icebox cookies) is the fact that you can serve a plate of freshly baked cookies in just fifteen minutes!

～

Make everyday routines festive. Play Christmas tapes in the car; fill a vase at work with evergreens; light holiday candles at dinner; ice skate at noon.

～

Christmas Time Savers

Instead of decorating the entire house, make a major event out of one activity, such as trimming the tree.

Sacrifice one of the "big" things—gift wrapping, elaborate cooking, and cleaning—since it is impossible to do everything perfectly and still have time to celebrate the true meaning of Christmas. Wrap gifts quickly, using few bows, or buy fabric gift bags in different sizes and use them every year.

Announce your independence. Make life easier for yourself and tell your family that this year you'll be giving a general gift for the whole family instead of individual gifts. This year, casually and sweetly tell them anything you want to. This year, find ways to do less and enjoy it more.

Here is an easy-to-make, desirable homemade Christmas gift. Package in a pretty container.

Microwave Peanut Brittle

¾ cup sugar
½ cup light corn syrup
¼ teaspoon salt
1½ cups unsalted, dry roasted peanuts
   Butter
1 tablespoon vanilla
1 teaspoon baking soda

Combine sugar, corn syrup, and salt in 8-cup glass measure or bowl. Microwave on high power 5 minutes. Stir in peanuts. Microwave 2 to 6 minutes or until syrup and peanuts are light brown, stirring every 2 minutes. Add butter, vanilla, and baking soda; stir until light and foamy. Working quickly, spread ¼-inch thick on buttered cookie sheet. Let stand until cool, 40 to 60 minutes. Break into pieces. Store in airtight container in a cool place. Makes 8 servings.

Green Chile Peanut Brittle: Drain 4 ounces chopped green chiles and pat with a paper towel, and add along with peanuts.

Red Chile Peanut Brittle: Add ⅛ to ¼ cup red chile flakes, depending on your taste.

Almond Brittle: Substitute almonds for the peanuts.

Per serving using original recipe: 316 calories; 341 mg sodium; 0 mg cholesterol; 3 grams fat; 2 grams saturated fat; 46 grams carbohydrate; 7 grams protein; 1.8 grams fiber.

A jar of buttered rum makes a nice gift. It is also the perfect blend for stirring into a bowl of oatmeal, Cream of Wheat, or hot couscous in the morning.

Hot Buttered Rum

1   ounce light or dark rum
1   teaspoon hot buttered rum mix, below
    Hot water
    Cinnamon stick

Combine rum and mix in a mug and fill with hot water. Stir with cinnamon stick until dissolved. Settle down in front of a fire or with a good book.

75 calories; 0 mg sodium; 0 mg cholesterol; 0 gram fat; 0 gram saturated fat; 3 grams carbohydrate; 0 gram protein; 0 gram fiber.

Hot Buttered Rum Mix

1   teaspoon cinnamon
¼   teaspoon ground cloves
¼   teaspoon allspice
⅛   teaspoon ground nutmeg
½   teaspoon vanilla extract
½   cup dark brown sugar
2   tablespoons butter

Mix all ingredients together and store, covered, in refrigerator.

A little fudge goes a long way. It's perfect for cutting and wrapping, first in plastic wrap, then foiled paper, and giving it away. Even a couple of pieces tastes like a lot (they won't overindulge and hate you for it). You feel good. They feel good. And no one but you knows how easy it was to make.

What a nice Christmas or Valentine's gift this would make! Marshmallows make fudge creamier.

Heavenly Hash Fudge

2 cups sugar
⅔ cup evaporated milk
12 regular marshmallows
½ cup butter or margarine
   Dash of salt
6 ounces (1 cup) semisweet chocolate pieces
1 cup nuts, chopped
1 teaspoon vanilla

Cook first five ingredients, stirring constantly, over medium heat until it boils (mixture will be bubbling all over the top). Boil and stir 5 minutes more. Take off heat.

Stir in chocolate pieces until completely melted. Stir in nuts and vanilla. Spread fudge in a buttered 8-inch square pan. Cool. Cut into 30 pieces.

Per piece: 110 calories; 43 mg sodium; 10 mg cholesterol; 6 grams fat; 3 grams saturated fat; 3 grams saturated fat; 12 grams carbohydrate; 2 grams protein; .48 gram fiber.

You don't have to look like Santa after the holidays. Lighten up emotionally by preparing desserts that are festive but without unnecessary fat and calories.

This dessert has everything: It is sensuous, easy, inexpensive, gorgeous, readily available, and contains no fat apart from the filling. Microwave meringue is a billowy puff of white meringue, piled high, and an ideal dessert served plain or used as a backdrop for fruits, sauces, or liqueurs.

Microwave Meringue

4 large egg whites
¼ teaspoon cream of tartar
1 teaspoon vanilla
2 tablespoons sugar

Filling (optional)

½ cup sliced strawberries
A handful of chocolate chips
1 tablespoon toasted chopped nuts
Confectioners' sugar

In a large, clean bowl, combine egg whites and cream of tartar. Beat at high speed with an electric mixer until whites are foamy. Add vanilla and continue beating at high speed and add sugar, about 1 tablespoon at a time, until whites hold stiff peaks.

On a shallow-rimmed, microwave-safe platter, pile spoonfuls of the meringue into a tall mound. Insert strawberry slices and chocolate chips throughout. Cook, uncovered, in a microwave oven on half power until meringue is soft set when touched lightly and center is 140 degrees, about 1 to 2 minutes; if overcooked, meringue condenses in the center and gets tough. Serve immediately with confectioners' sugar sprinkled over the top. Makes 2 servings.

> Per serving using strawberries and 2 tablespoons chocolate chips: 272 calories; 9 grams protein; 37 grams carbohydrate; 11 grams fat; 2 grams saturated fat; 4 mg cholesterol; 131 mg sodium; .9 gram fiber.

It's not fattening, illegal, or expensive
Ladies Don't Talk
Like That

Only those who dare go against proper behavior know the subtle joy of profanity.

As Barbara Holland writes in her book *Endangered Pleasures,* it brings a "lightening of the accumulated load, a stimulating explosion in the cylinder head of the spirit."

One doesn't have to use it in front of one's boss or mother-in-law—you can cuss to yourself, to your cat, to your best friend, or to anyone at all if you're secure enough. Bad words bring a sense of release, when not overdone. Occasionally, it is fun to shock: "Horse feathers!" just doesn't carry the potency of "damn it!"

"Damnation" was the strongest word my grandmother ever used, and if my own mother ever said "damn," we would all faint. Words are just words . . . why, hell's bells, we could talk dirty, Victorian-style, by commenting on what we bought today. The word "spending" was the Victorian word for "orgasm." Perhaps this is how they—and we—enjoy a bit of our own power. (And men *hate* to hear women cuss!)

∼

Traditionally delicious.

Candied Brandied Yams

1 (29-ounce) can yams, drained
⅓ cup dark brown sugar, firmly packed
½ teaspoon salt
½ cup chopped pecans
½ cup orange juice
½ cup brandy, optional
1 cup miniature marshmallows, optional

Preheat oven to 375 degrees. Place yams into buttered shallow baking dish. Sprinkle with brown sugar, salt, and pecans. Combine orange juice and brandy; pour over yams. Cover and bake for 30 minutes or until glazed. If desired, sprinkle marshmallows over potatoes and broil until golden. Makes 6 servings.

Per serving: 291 calories; 231 mg sodium; 0 mg cholesterol; 7 grams fat; .2 gram saturated fat; 52 grams carbohydrate; 3 grams protein; 2.9 grams fiber.

To Toast Nuts

Place in single layer on baking sheet. Place in preheated 350-degree oven for about 5 minutes or until lightly browned.

Watch nuts carefully; they can burn easily. Cool.

Toasted nuts can be stored in an airtight container in the freezer.

~

Find quality time for yourself. It's as easy as stopping for tea at an elegant hotel, or making this scrumptious pie.

Pecan Pie

3 eggs
1 cup dark corn syrup
1 cup sugar
¼ teaspoon salt
2½ tablespoons melted butter
1½ cups pecans
1 tablespoon milk
1 teaspoon vanilla
1 (9-inch) unbaked pastry shell
   Pecan halves

Beat eggs until thick and fluffy. Add syrup, sugar, salt, butter, pecans, milk, and vanilla. Mix together and pour into pastry shell. Bake for 15 to 20 minutes or until filling is set and toothpick inserted in center comes out clean. Cool before serving.

Per serving: 522 calories; 293 mg sodium; 88mg cholesterol; 27 grams fat; 6 grams saturated fat; 69 gram carbohydrate; 5 gram protein; 1.9 grams fiber.

Will You Be My Valentine?

Years ago, I began what I considered a most loving tradition—really celebrating Valentine's Day. Now I lean on it to take the pressure off of Christmas. I mail Valentine cards instead of Christmas cards, make heart-shaped cookies and give ready-to-plant pansies and primroses. I love to give mushy cards (the one time of year you can get away with it), sexy nighties, and silk boxer shorts. Being that these gifts are unexpected, they're appreciated more, and somehow it feels better to give out of love than the duty often associated with Christmas.

～

Chapter 7

❦

Making Yourself at Home at Work

Put passion into your work day

"Y ou have to make love to each day," he softly extolled to the rock-and-roll audience. The guitar player was telling his secret. He glowed. Whenever I see a person brimming over with happiness, I always stop and listen. What is it they know? What do they do differently? I still think about what he said and look at my day and what it is I make love to. It may be poetry, or discovering great lyrics to a song, or finding one helluva of a recipe, or a beautiful person. These are my passions—what gives meaning to what I do, to my life. When you experience it through your work for very long, you'll find that working with love, with passion for what you are doing, is the only way to live.

One never "works" a day in their life if they do what they love or love what they do. To do this, find a passion and follow it.

It is never too late to change what you want to be when you grow up. What do you love? What do you do the best? What gives you the greatest fulfillment? If time and money were no object, how would you spend your time? You can always tell if you're on the right path because it feels so very good to be there. These are the clues to uncovering your path, your career in life.

When we are not in an environment that is supportive of our femininity, our productivity goes down.

—PAT ALLEN, PH.D.

Finding your passion is finding your task in life.
If you find something that fills you
and thrills you, please go after it
with everything you've got!

～

If you asked me
what I wanted to be,
my first answer was
to be six feet tall.
My second answer was
to be a veterinarian.
And if I had a third
answer, it is to be
joyous and radiate it
outward. My instinct
just led me, blindly
and naively, to the
thing where I felt
I could find and
create the most joy.
—Julia Roberts

Have you converted a passion for building treehouses into a talent for designing grown-up sanctuaries? Everyone has a passion or a dream, but too often it's squelched by family and other societal pressures. If you're not sure anymore what your passion is, just look at what you like to do naturally and the things you fantasize about. Your family or others may tell you that following what you love is not practical. In reality, it's the most practical thing you can do. Because if you don't love it, you won't have the concentration, enthusiasm, and stick-to-it-iveness to do the work required to be an expert. And even if you did, it wouldn't be enough.

Doing what you love also makes your world more manageable. Too many people look at everything around them and try to fit themselves in. When you operate from your soul out, you can concentrate instead on your part of the world that's important to you.

I've always craved the time to simply enjoy the seasons, celebrating holidays, having picnics daily, and just being, like when I was a kid. That's what I wanted most of all. Today I live next to a river and most of my windows look out onto a rolling green meadow under a Persian blue mountain range. And, most importantly, I have time to spend as I wish, as I need to, and it all began with a layoff, then the decision to get off the hamster wheel and lead a slower, more meaningful life where I could feel what I wanted. I told myself that even if I had to be a waitress in a truck stop, I didn't care—just no more impersonal office jobs!

Commitment is what allows grace (some call it miracles) to happen. First I was paid unemployment, then I tried housecleaning, and then I did astrology readings. Then I met a man I lived with who wanted to pay all my bills. I let him. I was taken care of until he left. Shortly thereafter a friend called, offering me the perfect part-time cooking job. She was offered it, but couldn't accept it and thought of me immediately. This job was my ticket to writing! And it all began with a promise to myself that I knew I would keep. The rest came—and will come for you, if you want it badly enough. When you ask, you do receive. Have faith.

Good morning!
Getting Ready for Work

On the seventh day, God made coffee. There's little better than the aroma of freshly brewed coffee and you can use it to be your alarm clock if you buy a coffeepot with a built-in timer.

Then, if you set the radio alarm to go off five minutes earlier, it's like being coddled and entertained before you get out of bed. My girlfriend has an alarm clock shaped like a rooster with "cock-a-doodle-doo" alarm. Or maybe a clock that plays reveille is more your style. These types of novelty clocks can get us up on the right side of the bed—with a smile! They're available in the children's sections of some department stores. One thing's for sure: Toss out the clock with the horrible buzzer, or use it just to keep time. Waking up gently is better.

Revving up your metabolism with some type of physical exercise and a good breakfast strengthens the mind and body. Try getting up a half hour early and riding your bicycle, taking a walk, jogging, or lifting weights. After you've reached a natural metabolic high, you'll be more likely to stay there with intermittent physical activity throughout the day.

And for heaven's sake, eat!

A good breakfast has so many important benefits: It helps you to maintain a balanced food intake over the course of a day, which keeps energy levels steady and helps keep weight down. Good, comforting food (see chapter 3) is a simple psychological lift—we perform (think) better and are more pleasant to be around when we're balanced and satisfied.

~

BEGIN THE DAY IN PEACE

Every morning I take some time to find that place of peace within.

Sometimes I read from an inspiring book, do a walking meditation, or pray. It's worth the time to build an inner foundation for the day.

I've also noticed that beginning the day in peace tends to make it go that way.

WHAT TO EAT TO PERFORM AND FEEL GREAT FOR A JOB INTERVIEW OR AN IMPORTANT MEETING

Speaking before a staff meeting or a crowd can be nerve-wracking, but a light snack before you go on can help. If you need some extra zip, try protein. The jitters can be calmed with carbohydrates. Avoid alcohol, and never step out on an empty stomach.

When you want to remain alert and in complete control, eat a breakfast rich in protein and low in carbohydrates about two hours before your appointment, such as an omelet; scrambled eggs, lowfat sausage, and mushrooms with toast; or a light breakfast sandwich.

When you haven't time to eat, Swiss coffee can give you the protein boost you need to sustain your blood sugar level for a few hours and the calcium to help keep you calm. Drink it while you're getting ready. Also try this method with herbal tea!

Swiss Coffee

1 cup milk
  Coffee
  Sugar, optional

Microwave 1 cup milk on high for 1 minute. (The milk will heat up without burning.) Fill a tall cup halfway with coffee and top with heated milk. Add sugar to sweeten, if desired. Makes 2 cups.

Per 2-cup serving, using whole milk: 150 calories; 8 grams protein; 11 grams carbohydrate; 11 grams fat; 2 grams saturated fat; 5 mg cholesterol; 120 mg sodium; 0 gram fiber.

~

Dressing for Work

No other business skill is as visible as your image. Statistics have it that image comprises fifty-five percent of what is believed about us in business. So dress as if you're heading for the next rung on the career ladder.

Quality, well-chosen clothing is one of the most important investments you can make. A practical approach would be to see clothing as a powerful tool. And, like valuable tools, buy quality. My ex-husband would always buy the pricey Snap-On tools instead of cheap tools at the hardware store because they were precise, did exactly what he wanted them to, and had a lifetime guarantee. They made him feel confident. Wearing an attractive $200 blouse (and knowing it's a $200 blouse) will do the same thing for you. A gorgeous, stylish piece of clothing can make you feel like God's gift to the world—contrast it with how you would feel in a dowdy, faded article that's now at the back of your closet. Not to mention that quality clothing lasts much, much longer.

Whenever I feel like I need new clothes, I'll do an inventory and go through my closet and give away everything that doesn't fit right or make me feel wonderful. Quantity is less important than quality. Women in Europe are not afraid to wear the same skirt several times in the same week (and guys do it all the time)!

When your wardrobe, for whatever reason, is no longer working, make a list and inventory each item by color, fabric, and style. You will then have a working list of what you need to complete your work wardrobe.

When I need to get a tighter sense of control in my life, I'll choose my clothes for the next work day, then lay them out the night before. It tends to streamline the morning, paving the way to a smoother day.

If you want to convey credibility, dress in brown. If you want to appear self-confident, wear navy blue or red. If it's inspiration you need, or if you're searching for that great new idea, wear bright colors. They'll boost your brainstorming powers.

Choose Quality Undergarments

And just because we cannot see underwear (most of the time) doesn't mean we should skimp on quality whatsoever, because we know! They should fit well, look well, and remind you that you're a desirable, sexy woman. What you know about yourself is always projected by you to others. Wearing a black bra, a red slip, or lacy thong underwear, for example, will give a girl that knowing sense of assurance that says, "I know I'm powerful, worthwhile, and sexy," even and especially under a business suit. Throw out all underwear that doesn't do this for you. Dress only with undergarments that give you the message of how important you are, because you are.

∼

Wear a lace slip under everything for a week,
as if you're a sexy forties movie star.

∼

STUBBORN ZIPPER?

Rib candle wax or soap on both sides, then unzip and rub more on the unopened teeth.

Comfortable Feet Equal Good Attitude

Looking good stems from feeling good, and you can't be pretty when your feet hurt. Toes crammed into spiked heals will eventually be reflected on your face and attitude. Replace stressful, uncomfortable shoes with lower-height, good-fitting shoes or boots like Easy Spirit or other pumps that are designed for comfort. If you must wear heels, wear heels of different heights at different times of the day to stretch muscles and tendons.

COMMUTING WITH SCENTS

Sitting in a beautifully scented car can lift your spirits the entire drive.

Set a stick of incense, a twig of flowers or herbs, or scented sachet on the dashboard of your car. The warm sun will activate its scent and infuse the car's interior with its heavenly scent.

Or, to begin the commute peacefully, imagine a tranquil scene, like a relaxing day at the beach.

Giving your space a heart
Making Yourself At Home At Work

To the extent that you can, personalize your physical environment at work so that it gives you what you need for you to feel at home and in command of your area. Your essence is like a container that needs a place to be, and this includes your work environment. Bring "you" to your workplace by first determining the type of environment you need to feel productive. Is it efficient and orderly or creatively eclectic? Would you prefer a homey atmosphere or one that is elegant? Determine what brings you pleasure and translate that feeling into an object or way of decorating so as to empower you with these happy associations. Most of us like a combination.

For example, photographs and prints of adobes and soft Santa Fe sunsets adorn my office because I love the spirituality and earthiness of New Mexico. When I managed a print shop in Phoenix, I missed the countryside and yearned for the oak trees I grew up with in Michigan—so I painted one wall in the shop a brilliant grass green, and painted a mural of a tree on the adjacent wall.

Move the furniture around your office until they feel right and function the best. Add furniture, if possible, that reflects you and what you need: Perhaps an antique desk, an upholstered chair, or even a small sofa. Have you considered bringing in your own lamp or desk clock?

An estimated fifty-eight percent of American white-collar workers sit in cubicles, yet we can do the little things that make the difference. Bring in momentos of your personal life that bring you pleasure, such as photographs of your family, framed prints, posters, a drawing from your child, birthday cards, scenes from vacation spots you want to visit, scenic prints, an enlarged photograph of your dream home, philosophical sayings, or quotations of your own personal philosophy.

~

Buy flowers or a blooming plant. There's always room to tuck in a rose, even on an assembly line.

~

Work with a view. Recent research suggests that expansive views of trees, lawns, flowers, and weather promotes healing by capturing one's attention and, in so doing, alters one's perspective, reducing tension. So arrange to get a view, or find one during breaks. Focusing on a far-away object is also restful to the eyes.

Bring your own porcelain mug from home. Or buy one with the image of a woman enjoying herself!

If the job permits, bring your radio and favorite tapes. My girlfriend swears that praise music cuts her workload in half! Music can lift your consciousness above the mundane and make work easier. Capitalize on it with your favorite style of music—with headphones while cleaning a house or working in a warehouse to just having a tune play in your head!

A spritz of your favorite scent does more than freshen the air, it can also boost your mood.

Goethe once said that when the brain reaches its limits and feels restricted, music and color release us. Use color to dynamically affect you for the better. Choose your favorite color or colors to soothe, such as blue and green, or yellow to cheer. Coordinate desk accessories, file colors, picture frames, and so on.

Bring some cut-up vegetables or fruit from home to munch on. Eating a light, high-fiber carbohydrate snack at midafternoon break will help to focus your energies and give an energy boost that can take you smoothly into the evening. It's also a good idea to keep a box of fat-free crackers, cookies, and some lowfat milk in the refrigerator for those times you can't get out to get nourishment.

To stir your imagination, think back to places where you've been that warmed your heart. What qualities and features did each place have? Can you translate any of these into your present surroundings? Can you introduce something—perhaps as simple as a photograph or an object—that will remind you of that place and induce in you its peace and happiness?

—CAROL VENOLIA, "HEALING ENVIRONMENTS"

For ten to twelve-hour workdays, you need more to make yourself at home. Bring in some office emergency kits:

Health Maintenance Kit: Vitamin C tablets, Rolaids, allergy pills, throat lozenges, tea tree oil (for paper cuts).

Mood-booster Kit: Favorite vacation photo, joke book, a love letter, a favorite toy (such as a dog magnet that says "woof, woof!"), body and room mists.

The more in control you feel, the less stress you feel
Boosting Efficiency and Productivity at Work and At Home

Eat a nourishing breakfast. We cannot focus on getting things done when we keep thinking about food or are low-energy or irritable. A balanced breakfast improves mental acuity and is a good investment in your time.

Have a good system for scheduling, whether it be a Day Runner or other system. Streamline and organize.

Do one thing at a time. Pick your priority and do just that. When doing more than one thing, neither gets full attention, nor are we enjoying our "center," which robs your satisfaction. Notice which tasks give you satisfaction—whether it be using the computer or organizing your desk—and then don't rush through them. Allow yourself to take pleasure in it.

Gain cooperation from others. Develop a support system at work.

Boost energy with short breaks. Take mini breaks. Before you start a new task or go off to a meeting, pause for a moment. This will allow you to become more peaceful. Keep aware of how you are feeling.

In everything you do, begin with the end in mind. Before beginning anything—the day, a project, a vacation, or an important phone call—visualize first how you want it to go or what you want from the situation. Picture the kitchen clean before you clean it. Visualize *all* the chocolate chip cookie dough on the baking sheets, not half in your mouth! Seeing the end tends to trim away the scattering of your energy. Instead, ones energy is streamlined toward the goal, your desired end result.

Take full advantage of your breaks. Each state has its own labor laws requiring that a break be taken every so many hours. California labor laws, for instance, require a ten-minute break every four hours or fraction thereof and a half-hour lunch break after five consecutive hours of work.

Use your break for what it was meant to be—a break—even if no one else is! I used to get up and take a walk every morning and afternoon break, even though no one else in the office would move from their desks. After one month, they were doing it too. Be assertive with your needs and the time you are given by simply using your time to refresh yourself. It is unlawful not to take a break! It is your time. It's treating yourself well. Think of it as the adult version of recess and use it to regenerate. The quality of your work will stay constant or improve, and you'll last longer, too. Some of the following ideas are from *You Don't Have to Go Home From Work Exhausted!* by Ann McGee-Cooper (Bantam, 1990).

Ways to Have Fun in a Few Minutes

Do some simple stretching exercises, or give your neck or your hands and wrists a self-massage.

Listen to your favorite music.

Close your eyes and visualize yourself performing your favorite sport perfectly.

Plan to see movie later in the day.

Close your eyes and visualize yourself driving home from work happy and energized.

Call a friend for a quick chat.

The task, for me, is to care, daily, for myself and my life . . . to love and to nurture, within myself, moment by moment, the quality of quiet presence quietly being present to my life, which sanctifies it . . . to live as if the candle is lighted.

—JUDITH DUERK, "CIRCLE OF STONES: WOMAN'S JOURNEY TO HERSELF"

TIME MANAGEMENT

The number one work-related stressor is too much work and too little time—and that is because we do not tend to take the time to control it.

Time management is thought management. Try prioritizing your thoughts and you'll automatically prioritize your actions. If you're still overworked, talk to your boss and explain the situation. Maybe he or she doesn't appreciate the fact that you're overloaded.

At the very least, your boss will know what you're trying to accomplish and can help prioritize. You might even have a co-worker who could handle a little more responsibility. Just don't be afraid to let it go.

Refresh your face with a spritz of water; reapply lipstick and blush. Spritz on cologne.

Keep toys at your desk to play with.

Take a walk around the block or around the office.

Work on a crossword puzzle.

Tell someone a joke.

Read an inspirational poem.

Call someone just to say, "I love you."

Test-drive a car you would like to own someday.

Lose yourself in a romance novel.

Learn another language on tape.

Read an magazine article.

Lay back in your car seat and take a fifteen-minute nap (tell yourself to wake up in fifteen minutes).

Plan a picnic lunch during the week.

Stop by a bookstore to browse, or browse a magazine that fuels a passion, like a trip to Europe.

Do a crossword puzzle.

Plan a surprise for someone you love or appreciate.

Go home from work on a different route, stopping to walk in a beautiful neighborhood, to sit by a pond, to shop at a rural produce stand, or simply to drive through the countryside with your windows down.

∼

Quick Food Fix

It's smart to have healthy food on hand everywhere as a preference to high-fat snack foods. Keep fresh fruit, cut-up veggies, and lowfat milk in the office refrigerator. Keep nonperishable food, such as crackers and pretzels, in your desk drawer.

If you didn't have time for breakfast, opt for a snack that will make you feel good longer—such as a bagel, lowfat milk, or Swiss coffee (page 274). If appropriate, keep a toaster in the lunchroom and toast a bagel (they also make mini bagels). They're so good spread with whipped cream cheese and jelly.

Sip warm water or herbal tea throughout the day to normalize metabolic rate and eliminate toxins. Fill a thermos with warm water and keep it on your desk. Take a few sips every half hour.

Take Tea

Although it's not always easy getting sympathy at work, I find that tea soothes my frazzled nerves more than coffee does. And professional or no, it's important to me to get hugs at work too. Find a pretty little tin for tea bags and keep them in your purse.

A wise woman doesn't let her work rule her life.

Chamomile relaxes tension in both mind and body.

Mint will refresh and renew; helps you to feel whole.

Rosemary relieves nervous palpitations and lifts the spirits.

Linden flower quiets the nerves and promotes sleep.

Fragrant jasmine will lift you up then set you down, gently, within its fragrance. Available in Asian markets or any oriental restaurant.

Peppermint stimulates the taste buds and spirits.

Ginseng and Gotu Kola restore, much like a tonic.

Fruit flavors—strawberry, lemon, peach, apple, cherry, and blackberry—are cheery and aromatic.

You're the Boss
How to Say "No" to Your Boss

When your boss wants to give you more work, first you must have a written weekly schedule. Show this to your boss and ask which project to let go of so that you can do it. Asking a boss to set priorities protects you and makes your boss' expectations more realistic.

Ditto for a life plan. When you have a good idea of what you want to accomplish, it's easier to say no to things that aren't consistent with your long-term goals.

How to Protect Yourself From a Passive-Aggressive Boss

"Let me see if I understand you correctly." Rephrase directions even when you think you understand them perfectly.

Share Household Chores

Being in charge of your home life brings peace of mind at work. If you're married or something like it, each of you (including any children) need to be in harmony and balance by sharing the household tasks so that you can be a partner, not a maid. For instance, when each of you have heavy schedules, whoever had the easier day or is home first can prepare dinner, and the other can clean up. If you eat separately, find ways to spend quality time later in the evening.

Consider hiring a housekeeper, if only for a few hours a week or twice a month, to take care of major chores. It is surprising how much pressure this can take off your shoulders.

Getting More Satisfaction On the Job

Eliminate the busywork by prioritizing before you start work, then don't do anything unless it is on your list.

Involve your family in your work life. If you can swing it, this brings love, connectedness, familiarity, and comfort into your work and the resulting happiness cannot help but affect the quality of your work. Bringing children, friends, or other family members into the job environment can bring the staff closer. It may not be possible to bring children into the

---

How to Do Nothing

One of the best uses of time!

During your next break, try something earth-shattering—something more challenging than not telling a co-worker off. What is it?
Do nothing.

Then do it twice.

I learned how to do this from an old boyfriend who ran a take-out restaurant that was absolutely dead after 2 P.M. He sat around until 6 P.M. and it didn't phase him at all. Being a workaholic, this was incomprehensible to me! But he thought of it as productive, and rest certainly is.

Emulate a co-worker if you have to. Sit and look out a window, or relax at your desk.

～

workplace during the week, but consider weekends or after hours. The children and your husband or significant other will have a better understanding of what you do and be more willing to work within your needs.

Resign From Those Meetings You Dread

Yup, that's what I said. And I wouldn't say it if I hadn't done it and loved the results. Elaine St. James agrees in her book, *Simplify Your Life; 100 Ways to Slow Down and Enjoy the Things That Really Matter.* She suggests taking all your membership cards and making two stacks: the smaller (maybe nonexistent) pile may consist of organizations that meet at least two of three criteria:

1. Membership is a professional imperative.

2. You actually look forward to their meetings.

3. You never find yourself apologizing for being a member.

She recommends keeping these organizations and letting the other ones lapse. You won't find yourself dreading the meetings, which will free you up for what satisfies you, professional or not.

Have a Support System at Work

This is a powerful way to reduce stress on the job. Having a pal is like having family. Sure, work friendships take time, effort, and planning, but hey, they're always there! You're in the trenches together, under the same pressure, and combining work and friendship may be the only way to wedge personal relationships into our crowded modern lives.

Christine A. Leatz, in her book *Career Stress/Personal Stress: How to Stay Healthy in a High-Stress Environment,* points out the advantages of building alliances and networks in your job. They can

> tie you into the grapevine and provide you with information you might not otherwise be privy to; foster the development of a 'mutual aid society' of people to commiserate with (especially during reorganizations, mergers, and reductions in force); act as a reality check when stressful situations develop on the job; increase your pool of ideas on how to handle a crisis or stressful situations; link you into wider networks of colleagues and friends outside your company; and sometimes, if you're lucky, even develop into close friendships.

Lunchtime Escapes

Get away, if you can. The change of environment will renew, and you'll feel better, be more productive. If you can't get away every day, do it at least every other day. Don't squeeze all your errands into your lunch period. You need some time to be you.

Take a stroll through a gourmet food shop. Instead of the standard fast food or coffee shop, enjoy a ripe pear and blue cheese; new tastes and a different environment can stimulate new thoughts as well as new approaches to problems.

Be a tourist. Get out and discover something. Make it your mission to search the specialty shops and find the best of everything. Make it your business to find (through sampling, of course) the best coffee, cheese, frozen yogurt, and so on.

Go to the gym or the pool. Or walk around the neighborhood. Energize yourself both physically and mentally. While you're at it, get to know what is around you; people and businesses within walking distance. They may also be useful to you!

Amuse yourself. Drive to where you can hear rushing water, perhaps a fountain, a park, stream, waterfall, or the pounding of the surf at the ocean. Walk barefoot in the water if you're not wearing nylons (and bring a towel to wipe the sand off your feet).

Have an art attack—go to a gallery or notice the architecture on the street. Walk through a museum or the library and take in the latest art exhibits, then catch up on the latest magazines.

On a particularly trying day I used to spend my lunch hour at a Mexican restaurant nearby and sip one of their keokee coffees (page 257), which help me relax enough to enjoy the rest of the day. Just knowing I had such an escape made me feel I had a private secret—like wearing a red bra might do!

Visit a nursery; buy a plant for your desk, or visit the botanical gardens, or go to the farmer's market. Ask a friendly farmer how to cook a vegetable you're not familiar with.

Visit the zoo. You eat the peanuts. Let the elephants get their own.

Shop at a card shop, read the funny cards . . . and laugh!

Take lunch to a park. Walk barefoot in nylons on the grass. Swing on a swing. Lie on a blanket and pretend you're far away—perhaps on the banks of the French Riviera or lying on a hillside in the Mediterranean. This doesn't cost a dime and you will have packed hours, even days, into your lunch break.

$\sim$

Comfort Foods from Home

Whether you eat at home or out in the world, choose your food well because what we eat largely determines how we think and feel. Think of lunch as an opportunity to get more of the nutrients you need. Don't rush. If you have only ten minutes to eat, eat only ten minutes' worth of food. Try not to eat at your desk. You're more likely to eat in a hurry if you do. You'll also be tempted to do some work. If at all possible, leave work and other business behind and get away. Find a quiet spot out-of-doors or at least in another room. Eat with friends when possible. Talk about things other than work—relax! The time you take will double work productivity and a clear mind is its own reward.

Foods to Make You More Productive

The key to maintaining high performance levels is to eat foods that are energizing when your biological rhythms are beginning to slow down. Your midday meal will either sustain your morning alertness or accelerate the drop in your energy level. Your best bet is a high-protein, low-fat, alcohol-free meal. Here are some examples.

Build nutrient-packed sandwiches with whole-wheat bread, a couple of ounces of lean meat or poultry, a slice of reduced-fat cheese for added calcium, extra lettuce, and tomato. Make salads substantial with cheese, shredded chicken, chickpeas, other vegetables, and dark-green lettuce. Accompany them with a whole-grain roll or crackers. Drink juice or lowfat milk instead of diet soda. Get an extra vegetable in there somewhere—a baked potato, vegetable soup, or vegetable sticks.

Have you noticed how "instant" and low protein lunches such as meal-in-a-bars, pasta, frozen yogurt, ramen noodles, garden salads, and light vegetable soups make you feel? Be wary of these foods as complete meals because eaten alone, they are primarily carbohydrates and will most likely leave you feeling lethargic or even drowsy later in the afternoon. Pasta has the reputation for being an energy food because athletes load up on carbohydrate foods before a race. However, carbohydrates fuel the muscles with the carbohydrate glycogen, but not the brain. Pasta, being a carbohydrate, is a food that relaxes your moods—which is good when you're anxious or need to relax, which is not normally in the middle of a working day.

Without protein at lunch, most people are going to feel hungry and tired in an hour or two. Therefore, fortify salads with legumes, cottage cheese, lean meats, or cheese; and soups with parmesan cheese or a slice of lowfat cheese. Supplement a half sandwich with frozen yogurt (my weakness). And a glass of fat-free milk provides eight grams of protein and rounds out any meal.

Eating Well on Fast Food

Choose grilled chicken breast sandwiches, single hamburgers without cheese, grilled chicken salad, garden salad, lowfat or nonfat yogurt, fat-free muffin, cereal, and lowfat milk.

Bringing Your Own Lunch

Soups, Stews, and Chili: Wide-mouth thermos containers are great for keeping thick soup, stew, and chili hot. Warm thermos first by filling with hot water. Or pour soup into a microwave-safe bowl and warm up in the microwave. Bring a baggy full of chopped tomatoes, cilantro leaves, grated cheese, and crackers or a slice of good whole-wheat bread.

Ramen: Choose the lowfat variety and save yourself almost eighteen grams of fat. For added protein, bring a baggy full of chopped meat, shrimp, other fish, and vegetables and drop into cup of ramen before adding hot water.

Chef salad: Bring a nice bowl and bag of prewashed greens and cut-up vegetables, strips of cheese, meat, poultry, fish (a three-ounce can of tuna), and bottled or packaged dressing.

Pick Up Your Lunch from the Market Deli

Pick up a tossed salad or hot soup from the salad bar, barbecued chicken and a roll from the deli section, and some juice and a lowfat yogurt from the dairy case. Or buy lowfat cottage cheese with pineapple and a box of whole-grain crackers.

Making Sandwiches Interesting

Vary the type of breads, spreads, and ingredients. Instead of bread, roll out refrigerator biscuits and enclose a filling. Substitute buns, pita bread, flour tortillas, bagels, English muffins, or crisp taco shells. Cut off the top of a hard roll, hollow it out by scooping out the insides with a fork, and fill with tuna, egg salad, or leftovers.

Sliced cucumbers, mushrooms, radishes, carrots, and spinach are a refreshing alternative to lettuce. Give sandwiches an extra kick with horse-radish, chutney, or fresh herbs. Mix chopped fruit or vegetables into peanut butter.

Develop a repertoire of totable sandwich fillings you love. Here are some comforting basics—we all love familiarity—with interesting twists.

Life would be much nicer if one could carry the smells and tastes of the material home wherever one pleases.

—LAURA ESQUIVAL,
"LIKE WATER FOR
CHOCOLATE"

Cheese Sandwiches

Try jalapeño or smoked cheese, or add a touch of blue cheese to lowfat cheese slices.

Add Dijon mustard, slices of tomato, salsa, chopped vegetables, spinach, sprouts, or chiles.

Use rye bread, cheese bread, or make a quesadilla by sprinkling shredded cheese over tortillas and microwaving just until cheese melts; serve with salsa.

Peanut Butter and Jelly

Add low-sugar jam or jelly, apple butter, honey, sliced bananas, or chopped vegetables.

Spread over rice cakes, in apples, or stuff into celery sticks.

Sliced Lunchmeats
(ham, turkey, bologna, beef)

Make a plain sandwich using light breads, whipped butter, mayonnaise, and mustard, or make your sandwich exotic by adding horseradish, salsa, chutney, flavored mustards, or coleslaw. Make yourself a club sandwich and use whipped cream cheese mixed with chutney or salsa on the second layer, for instance.

Egg Salad

Make regular egg salad using mayonnaise, and mustard, then add one or more of the following: Fresh or dried herbs, flavored rice vinegar, chopped black olives, and sun-dried tomatoes.

Tuna Salad

Make a tuna salad the usual way with mayonnaise, a bit of mustard, chopped onion, celery, pickle relish, and cucumbers, or spice it up with green or black chopped olives, change it to a whole new flavor slant with Hawaiian tuna (add grated coconut, crushed drained pineapple, chopped green pepper, lowfat sour cream, and a dash of rum or rum extract), or Chinese tuna (add mandarin oranges, bean sprouts, water chestnuts, soy sauce, and lowfat sour cream), or maybe a tuna Waldorf sandwich (add chopped apples, celery, and walnuts to tuna, and moisten with plain yogurt).

～

Remember the fifties' tradition of cream cheese and olives stuffed into celery sticks? Make it into a lowfat sandwich.

Fifties' Cream Cheese Sandwich

¼ cup finely chopped celery
¼ cup finely chopped green onion
¾ cup finely chopped carrots
¼ cup diced green pepper
¼ cup shredded seeded cucumber
⅓ cup sliced green olives with pimentos
1 (8-ounce) package light cream cheese
1 tablespoon lemon juice
  Dash Worcestershire sauce
½ cup crumbled bacon or chopped ham, optional

Place vegetables and olives in a small colander or strainer; drain well. In a bowl, cream together cream cheese, lemon juice, and Worcestershire sauce until smooth. Stir in vegetables and optional bacon or ham. Cover and refrigerate. Makes enough filling for 3 sandwiches.

Filling per sandwich: 151 calories; 7 grams protein; 10 grams fat; 6 grams saturated fat; 11 grams carbohydrate; 20 cholesterol; 347 mg sodium; .96 gram fiber.

Here's a sandwich you can't buy at the deli. Buy preshredded coleslaw mix to simplify this low-calorie sandwich that provides fifty percent of the RDA for fiber.

Peanut Butter Chow Chow

¼ cup apple juice
3 tablespoons reduced-fat crunchy peanut butter
3 tablespoons raisins
½ cup chopped apple
1 cup shredded cabbage
⅓ cup shredded carrot
3 whole-wheat hamburger buns

Combine apple juice, peanut butter, raisins, and chopped apple. Stir in cabbage and shredded carrots. Makes 3 sandwiches.

Per sandwich: 431 calories; 12 grams protein; 14 grams fat; 2.5 grams saturated fat; 64 grams carbohydrate; 0 gram cholesterol; 469 mg sodium; 10 grams fiber.

Drink plenty of fluids throughout the day, such as water, flavored seltzers, decaffeinated iced tea, or coffee. We often feel hungry when what we really need is water.

Crock-Pot meals are a delight as a communal meal. Everyone brings in one item, throws it into the Crock-Pot, stirs all items together, and by noon dinner is ready. My dear friend Elaine shared this idea with me.

Elaine's Creamed Tuna with Noodles

  1 (5-ounce) package egg noodles, cooked
  2 (6½-ounce) cans tuna in water, drained
  1 (4-ounce) can mushrooms, optional
  1 (10-ounce) can peas, drained, optional
  1 tablespoon dried minced onion
  1 (10¼-ounce) can mushroom soup
     Seasoning salt to taste

Cook noodles until just barely done. Rinse with cold water. Combine all ingredients in Crock-Pot and cook on low 1 hour. Makes 6 servings.

Per serving: 224 calories; 21 grams protein; 5 grams fat; 1.3 grams saturated fat; 24 grams carbohydrate; 44 grams cholesterol; 555 mg sodium; 1.04 grams fiber.

SHARING WITH OTHERS AT WORK

Since most workplaces have refrigerators and microwaves, if all are so inclined, have a potluck!

Each person can bring a dish to pass once or twice a month to get closer to home cooking and a sense of togetherness.

Another option is the Crock-Pot.

∼

It takes only a moment to be on vacation
Create a Scene

At a stop light, while standing at the copier, or whenever you get a breather, infuse your body with short, effective visualizations.

One-Minute Mental Vacations

To balance yourself, imagine building blocks stacked one on top of the other and see them as representing your present emotional needs.

To revitalize, see/feel yourself as a rag doll with entirely loose and floppy joints, or as a limp sock. Then fantasize about how you'd spend a year's leave from work (then later find a way to fit some of that stuff in now).

Or picture a peaceful river. See it sparkle in the sunlight. You can hear the sound of the water. Put your hand in it. How does it feel?

Be the branch of a bush blowing in the wind, or seaweed in the ocean going back and forth with the waves. Identifying yourself as a particular thing gives your mind something to focus on and take on the qualities of that object.

Twenty-Minute Mental Vacations

Find a comfortable place to sit where you can avoid distractions.

Choose a mental image of a place that is relaxing to you, one that is vivid and real—perhaps a favorite serene vacation spot.

Completely let go of the world around you. Close your eyes and start breathing slowly and smoothly. Concentrate on your breathing for a few minutes; feel your body becoming heavier. Imagine tension leaving your body with each exhalation.

Visualization to Shrink Your Problems

Mentally removing a problem has very real physical effects. Visualize that you're on a deserted beach in Tahiti and the sun is hot and beating down all around you. Your physical tensions and problems melt away. Take care of any problems by digging a hole, visualizing the problem (your boss? your significant other?), then burying it with beach sand. Now the problem is gone. Poof! Or simply let a wave roll over it and let it wash away.

DON'T FIGHT FATIGUE

Look at your energy dips positively, as a time to rest, reflect, or listen to others.

Don't fight fatigue if you're really bushed. Give into it and take a nap. They're called "power naps" because you feel so darn good with just a little bit of rest.

Picture yourself at the river's edge. Nearby is an inflated rubber raft. You take your shoes off and step into the water. You push the dinghy a little way out, then climb in. The gentle current catches the raft while you lie down and get comfortable. The sounds of the water surround you soothingly. You drift along without effort. The sun shines warmly on your face, and a breeze brings the clean smell of the river to you. Your problem sneaks into the picture. Shrink it down, smaller, smaller yet. Now mentally drop it into a paper bag, then fold down the bag and throw it into the air, where the heat melts it and it disappears. It's gone!

〜

A high-carbohydrate lunch tends to calm anxiety. Make this pasta salad when you know you're going to have a hectic week.

All-Week Pasta Salad

2 cups lean ham, cut into julienne strips
2 cups pasta bow ties or shells, cooked according
      to package directions
8 ounces frozen vegetables, thawed
5 cherry tomatoes, cut in half
¾ cup of your favorite bottled dressing, or combine ½ cup
      lowfat mayonnaise with 2 tablespoons sugar and cider
      vinegar and mix well
4 cups prepackaged mixed greens

Combine ham, pasta, vegetables, tomatoes, and salad dressing in large bowl; toss to coat well, cover, and refrigerate. To serve, bring to work in plastic containers, with lettuce on the side in a baggy. Makes 4 servings.

Without dressing, per cup: 230 calories; 23 grams protein; 5 grams fat; 1.5 grams saturated fat; 24 grams carbohydrate; 57 grams cholesterol; 960 mg sodium; 3.1 grams fiber.

HOW TO POWER NAP

Find a private place (a doctor friend of mine uses his car during lunch break) or find a quiet break room and close your eyes. If you cannot sleep, simply close your eyes and rest. Imagine turning your inner dial from high to very low. Picture yourself going through the process of turning off your computer (which is you)!

Join your cat if he's napping on your bed, or get under the covers or a favorite ultrasoft comforter. Don't try to sleep. Close your eyes and just rest. Make a deal with yourself that you will lie still for fifteen minutes.

Fighting afternoon slump
Afternoon Break

Stop. Right there. That candy bar won't make you feel good for long. An hour later you'll feel let down all over again and you'll still have the fat and calories to burn. Three o'clock in the afternoon is typically a low-energy time. To boost yours, take a break and walk around the office or the block, drink a cup of coffee or a caffeinated cola, and eat a light carbohydrate snack such as a Fig Newton, or peel an orange, then talk to a friend. A carbohydrate snack stimulates the brain to produce serotonin, the calming chemical that will help you to settle down and refocus. One or two cups of caffeinated coffee is linked with an improved ability to think clearly, make snap decisions, and you'll feel more energetic up to three hours after drinking it. More than that and caffeine will work against you, though, with possibly an acidic stomach and the jitters.

⁓

Close your eyes and say to yourself, "I am in control enough
to wipe my mind clear of stress for two minutes."
You may go back to your worrying—but for now, let it go.
You will be amazed with the feeling of success
and perspective it brings.

⁓

HOW TO STOP A HEADACHE WITHOUT MEDICATION

At the first sign of a headache, stop whatever you're doing for five minutes. Close your eyes and inhale and exhale deeply. Give yourself a scalp massage, moving your fingertips over your head, rubbing the blood vessels.

Find a point in the web of skin between your thumb and forefinger that is tender and squeeze it for a few minutes. This is an acupressure spot and may relieve your head pain. If not, try rubbing the top of your foot between your big toe and second toe or the inside of your shin, just below the knee.

Desk Drawer Healthy Munchables

Pack your briefcase, glove compartment, desk drawer, and office refrigerator with healthy munchables today!

Ready-to-eat cereals (pack it in small containers, or purchase them in small boxes).

Meal-in-a-bars such as Power Bars, Balance Bars, or lowfat granola bars.

Chocolate-covered espresso beans (a shot of sugar and caffeine).

Crystallized ginger (sweet-spicy, fat-free).

Lowfat cheese and whole grain crackers.

Fresh fruit.

Peanut butter.

Dried fruit such as apricots, prunes, figs, or raisins.

Animal crackers, vanilla wafers, gingersnaps, fig bars, and graham crackers.

Trail mix.

A small bag of chocolate (for emergencies!).

Nuts and seeds.

Rice cakes (try the flavored varieties).

Pretzels.

Air-popped popcorn (great for midafternoon snack to share).

Bread sticks.

Juice (in cans and paper cartons).

Bagels.

Herbal tea bags.

Vegetable sticks.

Bran muffins.

HOW TO STOP A HEADACHE MORE EFFECTIVELY WITH MEDICATION

To boost the power of aspirin or ibuprofen in relieving headaches, chase it with coffee or other caffeinated beverage.

Another tip is to put your head on ice. Cold eases pain by shrinking swollen blood vessels. Wrap a cold pack in a towel and place it on the painful area.

~

How to give popcorn more pizazz . . .

Cajun Popcorn

3 parts parmesan cheese
1 part chile powder
1 part garlic salt

Combine above ingredients and sprinkle over butter-flavored or lightly buttered popcorn.

Cinnamon Popcorn

3 parts cinnamon
2 parts sugar

Combine and toss with butter-flavored or lightly buttered popcorn.

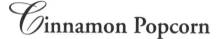

Sixty-Second Stress Relievers

Try to draw a nearby object—a cup, a plant, your filing cabinet.

Close your eyes and take slow, deep breaths. Fill every corner of your lungs, hold, then slowly exhale until you've squeezed it all out. Repeat. All that oxygen will charge you with energy.

Touch up your makeup. But first splash cold water on your face (so long as you use waterproof mascara.) Run cold water over your wrists, too, for a quick refresher.

Call Dial-a-Joke (or for a horoscope, the weather, a prayer).

Do a neck roll. Repeat five times, alternating directions.

Peel an orange. Breathe in the delicious aroma as you tear away the skin.

Progressive Muscle Relaxation

This head-to-toe relaxation will do you good any time of day. The entire relaxing procedure takes between five and ten minutes. If you're weary and really anxious to conquer the strains and tensions of life, do it daily or up to two or three times a day until you have learned to prevent tightness and tension.

First start with your feet. First, turn each foot a few times to loosen it up; then think of your feet as being very loose, dangling like two tassels. Now relax the calves and thighs. You might flex them a couple of times, or shake each leg a bit, then let your legs lie heavy—heavy as lead. Think of your legs and your feet as utterly relaxed—no tension, no tightness anywhere.

Now take a few breaths, as deep as possible. Breathe gently and make your exhalations longer than your inhalations. Feel your body sink into your seat. Banish every thought of tension and tautness. Next, tense your arms; stretch them as long as you can. Tense your fingers, spread them apart, make them as rigid as you can. Now make tight and hard fists, as though you were boxing.

Relax the muscles of your hands and arms and let them drop heavily by your sides. Your hands and arms should now be as relaxed as sleeping kittens. Now comes the neck, the part of the body that shows so much tension and is so susceptible to it. Roll your head from side to side a few times, as though you were saying no. Make believe your head is unbearably heavy, and then let it sink deep into the chair—assume that the neck has no power to move it.

The eyes are next, and it's very important that you learn how to relax them. First of all, squeeze the eyes a few times by just closing them tightly. Now open and close them a few more times, but lightly, delicately, loosely. If you are still tense and nervous, the eyelids will quiver. So keep on letting go and breathing calmly until your eyes no longer quiver and flutter. With the eyes closed, make believe that the muscles that control the eyeballs are loose, very loose, and completely relaxed—let go of all tightness and tension here, too.

〜

How to Get a Handle On Tomorrow's Work

As five o'clock draws near, list all of the tasks you need to do the next day. Are there any that can be delegated or handled later in the week? Assign a priority to each task and a preferred time of day to work on it.

Deliberately go over each task on your list. Close your eyes and see yourself completing it. Not only will you feel more calm about your progress tomorrow, you should feel a sense of control immediately. Do this every day for a week. Assess your progress. Note how, combined with your usual thorough preparation, much more easily your projects were completed and how much more calmly the days unfold. Your power of visualization will increase the more you use it.

The Perfect Antidote to Commuter Blues

How you handle life's little problems—such as what other people do on the freeways—will determine how much energy you have for things you love to do. Of course you've thought of avoiding peak commuting hours or taking a less-traveled route. After you've done that—make the best of it! Don't give others the power to control your mood. Don't let anybody take away your energy to play tonight. Use your head! Use it and relax—to classical music, motivational tapes, or how about the Bible or books on tape? (Did you know that three to five years of audio tape learning with a twenty-minute average commute can give you the equivalent of a college education?) Exercise your imagination and imagine where the guy in the car next to you is going. Or think that it's God in the car in front of you—thus there's a good reason for your automotive imprisonment. Listen to Laura Schlessinger or some other talk show host—use the time and use your (and their) energy. Plan, daydream, sing, imagine your next Hawaiian vacation. Smile at inconsiderate drivers. Imagine your crazy deceased uncle laughing with you in the front seat. And during this entire time, relax your body completely. Do this all day long and you will need less sleep and be able to physically accomplish much more—not to mention feel a heck of a lot better.

Did you know that three to five years of audio tape learning with a twenty-minute average commute can give you the equivalent of a college education?

Better yet, don't drive. Carpool. Take the bus. Then you may plan, make notes or a "to-do" list, or sit back and consciously think about what you want or wish to accomplish, both personally and at work, thereby giving energy to and increasing the chances of manifesting what you want. Time is life. Use it as mental and spiritual preparation for the day.

Going Home: Transition Time

Make the last hour of work a winding-down time. Complete the least-demanding tasks, return calls, pick up your work area, and clean your desk to get in the mood for going home.

Choose a vehicle that psychologically crosses over the two different areas of your life and do it at the end of every work day—no matter what. Your routine will clue your body to relax or to change and soon it will be doing that automatically.

To shift gears quickly, visualize yourself scooping up the day and throwing it into the river, where it floats away. Or see yourself flying to the moon and looking down to see your life differently.

Change into your gym clothes before leaving work. It's a concrete reminder that you're not working anymore. Automatically, your body will relax and want to do what it does in those clothes! Work out at the gym or run, walk, or swim at a park, in a beautiful neighborhood, or at a municipal pool.

Think of transition time as a time to restock our warehouse so that we can give—to ourselves and our loved ones. Shop for a small gift for your significant other—if only a candy bar, his favorite magazine, or rent a movie he would like. Write or type into your computer a relevant poem and wrap the gift in it.

The first five minutes after coming home are the most critical. Most of us tend to overlook those who are closest to us, treating strangers better than our own families. Give him a smile and a kiss even if you don't quite feel like it. Give each other time to detox. Save business talk for later.

ENERGY FOLLOWS PLEASURE

Plan something you love to do after work for instant regeneration. Your energy and happiness will inspire others, too!

◠

I've enjoyed a ritual every Friday afternoon of stopping by a bridge and throwing in a few coins, simultaneously making a wish (or ten). Actually I make as many wishes as the number of coins I pick up to throw, and I notice how some of the wishes change in just a week's time. Listening to myself, I feel appreciation for what I do have as well as get a better idea of what I want.

After You Get Home . . .

I heard of a young married woman who arranged to get home an hour before her husband so that she could throw off her masculine side before he came home. Making a clear transition will not only improve your evening, it may well recharge your relationship. Develop a routine for the first half hour immediately after walking in the door. Take a long, hot shower with a pulsating shower head. Make use of all your shower equipment: Loofah and moisturizing body wash. Change into loose-fitting clothes, work at a hobby, engage in an activity to come down, perhaps one that is quiet or lower key. Kick off your shoes, pet the cat, put on a CD or a meditation tape, walk the dog, water the plants, do the dishes, read the mail or a chapter from the book you're reading. Or you may need to simply nap.

Apart from making love, lifting weights is the most direct and quick route to smoothing away stress at the end of a long day or a difficult situation. Begin with three or five-pound weights and lift them to music or in conjunction with your regular exercise routine. Lifting weights produces endorphins, trims the body, and can give you a feeling of being in control because lifting weights is an activity that's governed by you alone— achievement, reward, and regularity is within your control (and your physical strength will grow as well).

DON'T EAT FOR ENERGY

Don't confuse being mentally tired with the need to eat, for the two are not necessarily connected.

The next time you're feeling groggy, get a glass of water or take a walk.

∽

Have quiet time for the first half-hour after getting home.
Tell the kids that they can be with and talk to mommy
when quiet time is up.

∽

Stress Relievers

Keep a snow globe on your desk. Turn it over at random to help keep things light!

Wear a brand-new shirt.

Keep an alcohol-based hair spray in your desk drawer. Use it to remove ink stains by spraying it on a cotton swab, then rub it away.

Keep an extra pair of nylons and a blazer, a sewing kit, safety pins, a toothbrush, and toothpaste at work.

Redefine a challenging situation in a less stress-provoking way by thinking "ain't it funny" or "ain't it grand" instead of "ain't it awful."

Hey, you can't afford not to exercise!
Exercise Dissolves Tensions Built Up During the Day

When we work hard, we need to play hard to balance ourselves. The best way to unwind for some of us is to switch to something else that is also stressful. It should require full concentration but must involve using a different part of the brain and body. Choose an activity that requires others and you've got your social needs involved, such as team sports, racquetball, tennis, badminton, working out at the gym, walking, or bicycling with a friend.

What benefits! Exercise gives us private time, a diversion to make you stop thinking about work, and it provides a truer perspective, reminding us that work isn't everything. And your relationships may improve because you won't be taking your stress out on your loved ones.

With every physical act, use your whole body—to wash your car, reach for something on a high shelf, or pick up papers off the floor.

Does your workplace have a built-in gym? If not, try out a few months' membership to a local gym. Exercise for twenty minutes during lunch or after work.

GETTING OUT YOUR FEELINGS ON THE WAY HOME (OR IN THE BATHTUB)

Dr. Barbara Mackoff, in her book *Leaving the Office Behind,* suggests identifying and connecting with your feelings at the end of the day before you get home.

She suggests telling the people off who upset you on the way home. She claims Nancy Reagan would do this in the bathtub. She would confront each person and spew off her anger with her choice of any derogatory comments she wished to make to that person. When we do this, we will be aware of our upset feelings and, by acting it out, we will not be a victim of our own unconscious reactions, nor will our loved ones.

Walk, walk, walk: During the morning or afternoon break or whenever you feel your energy lagging. (It will give you twice as much energy as a candy bar.) Walk to a neighborhood park. Swing on the swings, hang upside down from the jungle gym. Under no circumstances act your age!

Public pools, high schools, the YMCA, even some hotels offer lap swimming around noontime. Buy a swimming cap, a good pair of goggles and swim away stress. The world will look and be new.

Planning Maximizes Your Weekends

Ideally, one third of your life should be spent playing (in other words, re-creating yourself), one third sleep, and one third work. Balance it out: If you work hard, play hard!

In leisure, as in work, to benefit from your time you have to invest some energy and planning into it, or you may end up in front of the TV or working around the house all weekend. Make the most of your weekend by planning at least two relaxing activities you don't engage in during the week. Be sure they are opposite in nature. For instance, if you sit at your job, do something physical like ride a bicycle, plant a garden, or go dancing. If you have a physically taxing job, sit in the hot tub or go to a lecture.

I've made the goal of my weekends to completely let go of the work week by allowing myself to be completely absorbed in another reality. "Lose" yourself by getting totally involved in something you don't do during the week. (You'll always find yourself again!) Get away to a change of scenery—get out of the house! Here are some ideas: Take a walk on the beach and listen to the ocean roar; go out and have an interesting conversation with a stranger; take in some gorgeous scenery or a stirring play; get lost in an illusion by dressing up and going to a Renaissance festival; plan a romantic midnight swim or a hot-air balloon ride; learn a new dance step; or help out a friend. You owe it to yourself. These experiences are what wonderful weekends are made of.

～

*Do the birds chirping outside your window
sound like your beeper going off?
You're due for time off!*

～

Take Personal Days Off

Instead of a ten-day vacation, take one, two, or three days at a time, when you need it most. Declare your own personal holiday (I like to do it secretly). Call it a "(your name) Day"—a Judy Day, or a Carol Day—and play should not be an afterthought!

Schedule this day on the calendar when life isn't so festive and you need a break. Every now and then, I like to go through an ordinary day as if it were my last on Earth. It gives me a perspective I never get otherwise. I heartily recommend it. What will you do? (After this day has passed, look at what you chose. It may be an indicator of what you ought to be doing.)

Would you stay at home and take the time to just be—to just breathe? Strive to make all of your choices today based on your feelings. Pretend you're off a whole week (to trick yourself into really relaxing). Eat ice cream sundaes. Loll around in your pajamas and read a good book. Paint that old dresser or plant carnations. Rent *Casablanca*; paint your toenails. Get rid of what you hate—give or throw away shoes that pinch, skirts that don't fit right, unfinished projects, and books you haven't read that make you feel guilty. Your happiness is your most important product.

Or would you go on an adventure? Since this is a "working" day, you may well have to spend it by yourself, since everyone else is doing that. Make the most of being with yourself: Do something outrageous. Lose your watch. Watch your cat if you need to know what time it is. She will remind you that the only important times are nap time, meal time, and play time. Go skinny dipping. Visit your mother.

Other Suggestions

Start thinking about places you want to visit. Buy or borrow guidebooks, travel magazines, or visit the Internet. Drive to your place of power: Bring a sketch pad, a book, or camera. Window-shop; be a sightseer; take in a matinee or art exhibit; play pool in a honky-tonk bar; fly to Tahoe. Call up your significant other and have him meet you in a hot tub (at least he'd love the idea). If you want to take a trip and none of your friends has the time or money, take a trip on a women-only tour, such as Wild Women Adventures (800-992-1322). Let your hair down. Take a risk. Make memories and buy something to remember it by so that each time you see it your wonderful memories are relived.

ON YOUR FEET ALL DAY?

A quick fix for tired, swollen feet:

Soak feet first in hot water (a little warmer than a bath), then in ice water. Three minutes for the hot and one minute for the cold works best. Repeat three times, beginning and ending with hot water. This increases circulation, flushing out lactic acid that can build up and create pain.

To feel more pampered, some of us may like to soak while reading a trashy novel.

⁓

Pull on your most comfortable clothing, get in your car, and drive to a country town. Play your favorite tape—some emotional, soul-stirring music—and sing your feeling out enroute. Stop for breakfast at a restaurant where several cars are parked (it's a sign that something is good there). Ask the locals where the action is; read the paper; play the jukebox if they have one.

Feeling at Home When You Travel

Planning ahead will make you feel at ease and more secure. Travel is full of seemingly empty moments, so plan ahead to take advantage of time. Remember a pad and pencil in your glove box and purse or attaché to note bus schedules and museum hours. When riding on public transportation, your might bring a book to read, letters to answer, lists to make, or have your own brainstorming session. Other tips:

Life is an adventure or nothing.
—Helen Keller

Set up a home base near your hotel. Have breakfast at the same place every morning, where they'll treat you like a regular. Also, the routine will make you feel more secure.

Invest in a swimsuit and gym clothes you enjoy wearing. Most hotels have fitness facilities. Pack them!

Keep in touch by phone with your family and friends. It will make you feel more connected. Use your calling card if you don't want these calls to show up on the hotel bill.

Work out in your hotel room. Most motels have a VCR available to use. Bring an exercise video, pop it into the VCR, and go to town.

Sticking to a low-fat, high-fiber diet will keep you feeling well, alert, and keep your system regular. When traveling, especially on flights less than four hours, take along food that will travel well, taste okay cold, and not spill, such as bagels with packets of cream cheese, meals in a bar, fruit, and bottled water. Remember the water. Many times we think we want something to eat and we're just thirsty.

Instead of purchasing on-the-run food when traveling by car, brown bag your own. Don't skip breakfast, select a salad bar for lunch, and eat sensibly at dinner. The trick is to prevent hunger, because if you get too hungry you don't care what you eat.

Now don't get carried away with this take-your-own idea. A fun part of traveling is eating at places you don't often have the opportunity to visit, and when we're stressed, fat tastes extra good. And you deserve it, but be sensible about it. If you have a burger and fries for lunch, eat a nice salad for dinner.

If you travel and live out of your car or your suitcase, you can have a small case full of personal necessities. Or how about a small beautiful pillow in your car?

How to Get a Good Deal on a Hotel Room

Anyone can get a hotel room for less than the regular rate if you simply ask. Start by asking for the lowest rate. Then inquire about weekend promotions or special rates for members of large organizations, such as AAA. Corporate rates are often available if you have a business card, even if you are not traveling on business. Ask for a frequent-flier rate if you fly on an airline with which the hotel has a partnership. Family package rates, often available at resorts, include breakfast or recreational discounts. Emergency-situation rates are also given to people traveling because of family illness or stranded by natural disasters.

Make Air Travel More Enjoyable

Just because you can, it doesn't mean you should carry heavy luggage too far a distance. You will save possible extreme shoulder and back strain if you invest in a quality carry-on rollercase. Pack it with travel-size products and mix-and-match clothing. Choose garments that resist wrinkles, have personal-care products prepacked, and tuck a master list of things you want to take in your luggage so you don't forget anything important.

Dehydration can easily occur on a plane trip, so drink a lot of water. Avoid alcohol, caffeine, and salty snacks if you want to feel your best. Pack your own bottled water. Drink at least one eight-ounce glass of water per hour in flight.

Because there is no moisture in an airplane's pressurized cabin to plump up the skin, you'll need to prepare skin before you get on the plane to look fresh when you get off. Instead of washing your face and body with plain soap, try a two-in-one cleanser and moisturizer, a light moisturizer, eye cream, and Chapstick. And again, drink lots of water to moisturize from the inside out.

When you book a flight with an airline, order a special meal even if you don't need one for medical reasons. Why? They are prepared to order, so they're fresher than standard meals. You might try their special meals for dietary restrictions including lowfat, vegetarian, and low sodium. These need to be ordered twenty-four hours ahead.

There is less carbon dioxide toward the front of the plane. Cabin air, which is partly fresh and partly recirculated, has been blamed for headaches, congestion, dizziness, and drowsiness on long flights.

Plane take-off: I like to use every airplane take-off to visualize empowering myself or a project. This is how it works. As the plane accelerates, feel its power all around you. Now take it in. As the plane ascends, allow your imagination to draw in its power to yourself. See it become yours.

Counteracting Loss of Sleep

Almost half of the 1,600 business travelers surveyed by the National Sleep Foundation and Hilton Hotels reported having difficulty sleeping away from home.

The main culprit: Noise. Here are some suggestions to nip this one in the bud.

If the room is noisy, turn on the room ventilation system to block out other sounds. Pack earplugs.

Follow the same bedtime rituals you would at home (reading or watching TV, for example) and bring your pillow and alarm clock along.

Before bedtime, notice if the heater or air conditioner works, if you need more blankets, and so on, and call the front desk to get the information or supplies you need.

Set your watch to your destination's time zone as soon as you realize the time change and match your eating and sleeping schedule to it.

Forget that drink and coffee, opting maybe for herbal tea. You'll feel so much better in the morning that it will be worth it.

Making Yourself at Home in Your Hotel Room

Bring with you whatever makes you feel at home, perhaps . . .

A framed photograph of someone special in your life.

A small travel pillow or lap quilt.

Travel alarm.

A plug-in water heater to make instant coffee, cocoa, or instant soups.

A journal, a drawing pad, a book to read, or a portfolio filled with stationery for writing letters and letters to answer.

Your favorite cologne and scented bath oil.

Your coffee pot and coffee (country singer Lacy J. Dalton won't leave home without hers).

Healthy snacks, such as fresh fruit, fig bars, or rice cakes.

Consider having a massage, or at least try the sauna or jacuzzi.

If you have a kitchenette, a Crock-Pot can make cooking easy on ski trips, extended business trips, or any trip where you have kitchen facilities. Try the recipe "Roasted Chicken à la Crock-Pot" (page 53), adding a few sprigs of fresh rosemary or other herb from the market. Then you can return to your accommodations after a long day to a piping hot dinner. Pick up some French bread and a bottle of wine for a homey and romantic dinner for one or more!

Get Moving

Check out the hotel's facilities: The weight room, tennis and racquetball courts, jacuzzi, sauna, the pool. Did you pack your swimsuit?

If safe, take a walk or jog around the neighborhood—you'll also discover some interesting sites or learn something!

Pack a jump rope in your suitcase; great for rainy days.

Take the stairs instead of the elevator.

Oxygenate your bloodstream by doing deep breathing exercises (a good use of time while waiting in line): Inhale slowly and deeply over five seconds. Hold your breath for another five seconds, then exhale on the count of five; wait five seconds, then start at the beginning again. Focus on counting and feeling your breath move through your body. Repeat the entire exercise for the duration of your wait.

Homey Things to Do While Away from Home

Locate the city's renovated "old" part of town and walk through antique, second-hand, dollar, or local specialty gift shops.

Yard sales and estate sales, particularly in affluent areas, can yield sentimental and valuable antique treasures, such as old-fashioned linens, doilies, depression glass, vases, or picture postcards from the early 1900s (great for framing, or send them now).

Look through the travel brochures displayed at the hotel desk for ideas such as a day tour to a local specialty, such as a winery. These can be as laid back as a steamboat ride or as exciting as a swamp tour through the bayous of Louisiana to the pink jeep tours in Sedona, Arizona.

Explore available transportation options: Get on a bus, trolley, or subway and see the sites. Rent a horse, boat, jet ski, bicycle, or roller blades and make getting around part of the fun.

Go ahead and do what you really love to do! Do nothing else! You have so little time. How can you think of wasting a moment doing something for a living you don't like to do? What kind of a living is that? That is not a living, that is a dying!

—Neale Donald Walsch, "Conversations with God, Book I"

The local newspaper and tabloids will tell you of up-to-the-minute entertainment. If you are still undecided, ask a local about what to do in your area of interest or directions to specific nightclubs.

How To Find a Cozy, Down-Home Restaurant

Ask a local or a cab driver.

Look for the words "home cooking" or "old fashioned."

Smaller towns may have an airport that supports an in-house restaurant (some of these restaurants will land a plane and serve food at the same time). Entertaining and a real find!

Restaurants in old houses will tell you the ambience is likely to be homey and the food home style.

Let your first impression of a restaurant tell you what you need to know. Does the place look well tended? Does someone acknowledge your presence right away? Ask to look at a menu first. As a rule, the shorter the menu, the more likely it is that the food is fresher, made from scratch. If what they're serving doesn't suit you—don't hesitate to walk.

～

The Bigger Picture
Stop the world and let me off . . .

So you've worked too many hours? Get your perspective—you know, your life. Exercise helps reduce stress; so does having a social life. The more you've got going on outside the office, the less time you'll obsess about what's going on inside.

Rethink your priorities. What is really important to you? What is it you loved doing as a child? What were your hobbies, what games did you play? How did you spend your time? What people, places, and things gave you energy? We tend to continue to enjoy the same kinds of things all our lives. If you love to sew, be a full-time or a part-time dressmaker. If photography was your hobby, find a niche in the industry, work for a lab, or assist in a photo school where you can learn and allow you passion to move you through your day. This is what I did. I learned skills on the job while being paid for it. Do you love cooking? Cater cookies, cook meals for the elderly or homebound, market your grandmother's peanut brittle locally. Find passion in a hobby, then turn your hobby into work. The energy gained from working with what motivates you brings tremendous satisfaction. Life is so much more when you love what you're doing!

If You Need It More Basic

FOR EXTRA SECURITY

You can obtain a copy of the social security benefits paid in by having your employer call 800-772-1213.

Then compare it to your W-2s. An uncorrected mistake could reduce your lifetime benefits.

To find passion, first look for people, places, or things to appreciate. The act of appreciating establishes energy circuits from you to these things where your energy can flow to you—through you, and from you—to an object. We need an object of attention to establish a flow of passion!

It All Starts with What We Think About

It is a spiritual law that we attract to us what we think about. This is simply how we create our lives, whether we are conscious of it or not. If we are not conscious of it, we live our lives by default, by what others want, by what they create, or by the same thoughts that we think over and over (so we get the same things in different form, over and over). To get what we want we must first identify it, then think about why we want it and why we should have it. In short, give what you want your full attention and refuse to worry about the cost or how or when it will become yours.

Go the distance to determine what it is you really want to do, then set up the plan and take the risk. Life and time is too precious. This isn't a dress rehearsal, you know!

∼

Chapter 8

♥

Getting Back Control

To alleviate stress, get back in control

Are you a perfectionist? Most of us are. This belief is the cornerstone of most neurotic women who are no fun to be around—because when you're with a perfectionist, you subtly get the message that you also ought to be living up to their standards. What pressure on both of you! And how boring!

It is said that the first enlightenment is to be true to ourselves and be who we are, doing everything as well as we can is doing just that. Is perfection worth the effort? Who is more important than us that we need to impress? We can do just what we can do and no more. So relax and enjoy who you are. Now we can get onto enlightenment number two, which is we cannot control anyone but ourselves.

The primary cause of stress is the perception that we can control something or someone. We can only control ourselves, not anyone else; however, taking control of ourselves is actually taking control of situations, thus we *do* have control. What normally happens is that most of us view someone or something as threatening, or believe that everyone must like you or take care of you, or that you must perform without error. We tend to stress in the form of obsessing, fearing, and criticizing ourselves, becoming depressed,

Let go of blaming others because that leads to being a victim. There are no victims because we all have choices. We always have control over how we act. When we stop thinking we have choices, we have stress. Never say "I didn't have a choice"— instead, say "It was the best choice I had."

311

getting hysterical, overanalyzing, and so on, instead of rationally figuring this out.

Our Thoughts Determine Our Feelings

Our thoughts mean nothing in themselves. Words represent people, places, or things that have no meaning in themselves until we color them with meaning through our own experience. We determine a situation to be "good" or "bad" by the ages of five to seven. When we touched a hot stove, we learned it hurt us to touch it. If our mother got hysterical when we made a mistake, we may well have felt inadequate and are still hard on ourselves to this day. Our ideas and attitudes, or the way we see life, are usually the reflection of our early caregiver (usually mom or dad).

I had this demonstrated rather dramatically when I was in a seminar several years ago. The instructor was trying to get this message across to the audience and he called on a girl who volunteered. She said that she had been raped by three men and, of course, that incident had traumatized her to this day. The instructor told her to repeat the following sentence: "I was raped by three men," which she repeated. Then he said, "Add the following words: 'And the color blue looks good on me.'" She repeated the two phrases out loud and the sting of the first dissolved almost visibly from the second phrase. The instructor went on, "Now add: 'Especially in summertime.'" She repeated the entire sentence, "I was raped by three men and the color blue looks good on me especially in summertime." The words actually changed the meaning of the event by counterbalancing the words that described the event. The sentence was true, but it was seen from a different, all-encompassing viewpoint for the purpose of neutralizing her thoughts and feelings. If it is possible to change the meaning of a rape by using words, think what you can do with your stressors.

Picture your mind as a blue sky and your thoughts as clouds. Clouds (or thoughts) can drift by but we usually read them. Automatically we determine their meaning or how we feel about them, which directly determines our behavior and how we act or react. Our thoughts, therefore, are powerful because whatever our thoughts are, that is where we are going.

There is only one question of any relevance regarding any thought. Does it serve you to hold it? In terms of Who You Are and Who You seek to Be, does that thought serve you?

—NEALE DONALD WALSCH, "CONVERSATIONS WITH GOD, BOOK 2"

Most of us think habitually about our problems. Because they usually cause us to be emotional, we worry and obsess instead of seeing logically that our thoughts are kicking up emotional responses that may not be completely true.

Let's try to be more like Spock: Logical. What is the most stressful situation in your life? Write it down. Now, write as many as possible of the thoughts that instantly come up about it. Now, next to the automatic response, write down what would be a rational response. For example, if you're trying to leave an addictive relationship, when you think that you miss him, then feel that you want to be with him, a rational response might be "Well, so do all his other girlfriends." Or if you are stressed out about what a friend or co-worker has said to you, you may give the rational response that he may be having a bad day, perhaps he doesn't feel well, or he has a lot of pressure, so give him the benefit of the doubt and tell yourself he must have a good reason for saying what he did—and leave it like that for now. The goal is to remove the stress by becoming less attached. If the problem persists, respond at an appropriate time.

Now when these thoughts of your stressor keep coming up, you may choose to stop them. You might use a single word to obliterate your present thought, such as "cancel," "not now," or "delete." Your goal is peace. Bring yourself peace by choosing your thoughts, your emotions, your life.

TEST

Questions:
What can you control?

What can't you control?

Answers:
Yourself.

Anything and everything else.

～

If it has to do with anything or anyone other than yourself, you cannot control it.

～

Hidden Sources of Stress

Because it may seem "natural," many women may not even outwardly recognize their feelings of a loss of control over aging, a demanding job, or the stress from a family problem. Many of us push ourselves to be perfect (which is actually a fear of failure instead of a desire to succeed). Or we are unassertive and afraid to say no. Still others may have values that are out of sync with their lifestyles and they're not walking the walk, just talking the talk.

GUIDELINES FOR TAKING CONTROL OF A PARTICULAR SITUATION

Describe and analyze what is bothering you.

List what you want or need more (or less) of. (Ask yourself, "What results do I want?") For big problems, break it down into smaller results ("What can I do right now?")

List your options.

Formulate another plan of action.

～

Stress Weakens the Immune System

Whatever the reason, we no longer feel in control and the stress can have a negative impact on every body organ, including those that support the immune system. Stress is like electricity entering a fuse box. Too much overload, too many appliances, and the fuse blows. Physiologically, this can mean an overheating and resultant breakdown of the body's weakest system. In our society, the heart and blood vessels are the system most often attacked and weakened.

Your brain releases two powerful chemicals, cortisol and adrenaline. Cortisol raises blood pressure slowly and steadily. Adrenaline raises your blood pressure in a more violent fashion. Both chemicals also release high-energy fats and blood-clotting agents that etch chinks in the walls of your blood vessels, setting the stage for a variety of health complications. Stress can also impair the respiratory or immune system or your gastrointestinal tract. Besides heart disease, high blood pressure and strokes can also be related directly to stress levels and responses.

Early Signs of Stress

The most common signs of stress are an increase in sleeplessness and an inability to control anger. If you fall asleep easily but wake after a few hours, you are probably anxious or unable to control some unfinished mental or emotional business. Other early signs of stress are an increase in physical problems and illness, exhaustion, more problems with relationships, an increase in bad habits such as smoking and poor eating, and an increase in pessimistic thinking.

～

Worrying Doesn't Solve Anything

Worrying takes precious energy from us, uses up our time on Earth and causes us to age. I spent almost two years denying the fact that I had to leave my boyfriend and it wasn't until a friend told me I could have finished this book plus another one that I looked the truth in the eye. My time is my life. Your time is your life. Facing the truth is often the hardest part. Do not be critical with yourself—do be good to yourself, but look your problem in the eye. Determine where the control lies to give yourself peace or, if you are not ready to change it, give yourself a set time to worry—say fifteen minutes a day, if that helps—then let it go. If it is a situation that you can control, take charge, make a decision, and go from there. If not, decide to give it up. Give it to your higher power if that works for you and trust that the best outcome will happen, or trust that God is working through you and that you will become your own power. Chronic worriers spend as much as half of their lives worrying about things or whether they are going to do something about it. Ninety-nine percent of what we worry about never actually happens anyway. Rather than focusing on what you want freedom from, focus on what you have the freedom to do.

Ninety-nine percent of what we worry about never actually happens anyway. Rather than focusing on what you want freedom from, focus on what you have the freedom to do.

Take Charge

When we take charge of our life, we feel safer and reduce our fears, uncertainties, and doubts. Start by pinpointing the major things that bother you, or simply determining what it is that you need more of in your life. Then decide that you are going to have it over the next three months.

Take charge at home and at work by:

Setting boundaries and limits.

Delegating.

Not worrying about what others do or don't do.

Getting rid of as many details as possible.

Expecting less.

What Is Your Idea of Success?

If you don't have time for what matters, it is time to acknowledge just what is important to you. When you're on your deathbed and have lived what you would call the "perfect" life, what will you have attained? Picture it. Feel it. Now define your priorities to make that happen and restructure your life, if necessary, to give attention to those priorities. Keeping your "perfect" life in mind, make three sets of goals: Lifestyle, Action, and Morality. Lifestyle goals are long-term, to keep you motivated. They reflect basic needs and wants such as maintaining physical and mental health, having a good relationship with family, obtaining financial security, and so on. Action goals are short-term goals to keep you focused, such as what you would like to accomplish (buy a home, learn French, or climb a mountain) and what you'd like to be (a computer wiz, a dancer, or a gourmet chef). Morality goals enable you to live according to your deepest values. What would you be doing this minute if you knew you had just six months to live? Write it down. Taking this into consideration, contract a list of two to five goals for the next year (they may be the same or similar to the other two sets of goals). Together, these three sets of goals will help to define who you are and direct your everyday life through prioritizing your time.

Now write these goals on a three by five-inch card and keep it in your purse to remind you of what is most meaningful to you. When you are aware of what is meaningful, everything will have its own priority and value—and saying "no" becomes easier.

Give yourself permission to stick to what's important to you. Realize that your day is a success when you've stuck with your priorities—and that may mean the house isn't clean.

A balanced life, composed of work, friends, family, and activities that make you feel good, is the best preventive medicine for stress overload. Here are some suggestions for gaining control in specific areas:

Invest Your Money

Open a brand-new savings account somewhere and add a small stipend to it each and every payday.

A year later, surprise your husband with the knowledge of it. (Whether you do or not, it sure feels empowering!)

A good tip is AARP mutual funds. With an excellent track record, no front or back load fees, you can invest a minimum of $500 and watch it grow many times over (6–12%) a regular savings account of 2–3% interest. Call AARP at 800-253-2277.

Your Overall Life

Be aware that, on some level, you have chosen where you are and what you are doing. We co-create our lives: We're not victims. If you're not happy with it, get clear about your personal aspirations. Determine your priorities with the previous exercise. Make definite goals. Have a Plan B. Remember your options. Keep it simple.

Lifestyle

Be aware of your appearance. Stay fit and maintain your weight: Exercise vigorously for twenty to thirty minutes at least three times a week. Find time to relax. Take regular vacations. Treat yourself occasionally, whether it be a new dress or an evening out; cultivate hobbies; don't bring the office home with you. Avoid bad habits like smoking, drinking too much alcohol, taking drugs, and eating a lot of junk food. Develop as many talents as possible, which can prepare you for change and opportunity. Laugh more; life's too short to take it too seriously!

We learn to grow by letting go.

Give Up Guilt

When we feel guilty, we are punishing ourselves before anyone else gets a chance. Guilt inhibits self-love, self-esteem, and self-accomplishment—and is quite stressful! Eliminate this form of self-punishment and you will have much more emotional energy to spend on love and joy. Use it, also, to get to know your own soul.

Finances

Unless you are in control of your money, you will never feel as though you are in control of your life. You don't need to make a lot of money to feel in charge. Make a budget for yourself and/or your family and stick to it. Money is a major source of stress, so prevent problems before they get out of hand. Take a course on financial investing, or put your money in the hands of a knowledgeable stockbroker or friend that you feel good about. Know where your money is going.

Finances for Singles: The only real way to deal with money is to get a firm grip on your values, goals, and priorities. Once you get a true picture of where you want to be financially, you can begin to determine how to use the funds you have available to you to move toward that lifestyle. Get expert help if you need it, but do develop a long-term plan. Working toward that plan actually reduces stress in the long run.

Home and Security

If you're a morning person, go to bed earlier, then get up earlier. Share chores among the children and your mate. Plan out a week's meals. Keep a family calendar in view so you can keep track of school activities, everyone's doctor appointments, birthdays, events, and so on. Get an answering machine so that you may screen calls and not feel pressed to answer it. Keep in touch with your extended family.

Maintenance: Keep on top of car maintenance; make duplicate keys; copy important papers; put safety first; make repairs; get help with jobs you dislike.

Get control.
～

Personal Habits

Always tell the truth. Lies are hard to remember and to track. Develop routines. Avoid foods and chemicals that add to stress! If you're on an anxiety high, break the cycle by eating a balanced meal and avoiding excess coffee, chocolate, alcohol, food, and high-sugar indulgences such as Danishes and doughnuts on your coffee breaks.

Your Mate

Communicate. Know where you stand with each other and what level of commitment exists; give the benefit of the doubt; trust; assert yourself; to thine own self be true.

Strengthen your identity as a couple. Learn about each other's work so that you may lend support and understanding. Go out on a date with your mate at least once a month, or take more three-day weekends together. Remain friends: Discuss your day with your mate and encourage him to do the same with you every single evening.

At Work

Work up a strategic plan for your professional career. Know just what is expected of you; don't let paperwork pile up. Catch up over your morning coffee. Avoid rush hour. Commute a half hour earlier or later than peak time.

Friends

Put the effort into building a support network of friends by sharing more experiences and hobbies. It usually pays off when everything else doesn't.

Studies show that people who are satisfied with their marriages, friendships, and spiritual feelings live more fulfilling lives. When they are able to connect with people, they have a sense of belonging.

We learn to grow by letting go.

It's not easy to do but it works. Peace equals letting go of the past and living in the present (it is a present), making each moment, each day fresh and new. Another word for it is forgiveness and it releases tremendous energy that was stored in past problems—and best of all, it brings with it peace.

FAVORITE BILLBOARD:

Need Directions?
—GOD

Let God do what she's supposed to do, or . . .
We Can't Always Control

There is no pain greater than trying to hold onto something that is beyond our control. Yes, learning when not to control is as important as knowing when to control. Life is an ebb and flow and there is a season for everything. Many times we may not recognize what is best for us and at these times we need to learn to get out of our own way. We must pry off our ego's hold and learn to let go of people, places, things, or our own attitudes, trusting that everything really is working out for the best. Control what you can, detach from preconceived ideas and, sometimes, even your dreams, and let God do the rest. Oftentimes, that is just when we receive what we wanted in the first place. At least we get peace—and ourselves—back.

∽

*If you want a wild sense of inner peace,
love yourself ingeniously. If you want crazy wisdom
that fuels overflowing creativity, dare to be
your most generous self. If you want educational love
that keeps you guessing in the most pleasurable way,
lose some of your self-importance.
If you want the whole nutritious cocktail,
forget about being greedy for money, power, or sex.*

—ROB BREZSNY,
AUTHOR OF THE
SYNDICATED COLUMN
"REAL ASTROLOGY"

~

Bibliography

Allen, Pat. Tapes from her series "Woman to Man" and "Woman to Woman" from Pat Allen & Associates, 3355 Via Lido, Suite 205, Newport Beach, CA 92663.

Allende, Isabel. *Aphrodite*. New York: Harper Flamingo, 1998.

Bach, Richard. *Illusions*. New York: Delacorte Press, 1977.

Campbell, Jeff, and the Clean Team. *Speed Cleaning*. New York: Dell Publishing Co., Inc., 1991.

Chopra, Deepak, M.D. *Creating Health; How to Wake Up the Body's Intelligence*. Boston, Mass.: Houghton Mifflin Company, 1991.

Claremont de Castillejo, Irene. *Knowing Woman: A Feminine Psychology*. New York: G. P. Putnam's Sons, 1973.

Crenshaw, Theresa L., M. D. *The Alchemy of Love and Lust: How Our Sex Hormones Influence Our Relationships*. New York: Pocket Books, 1996.

Cunningham, Donna. *Moon Signs*. New York: Ballantine Books, 1988.

Duerk, Judith. *Circle of Stones: Women's Journey To Herself*. San Diego, Calif.: Lua Media (now InnsFree Press, Philadelphia), 1999.

Duerk, Judith. *I Sit Listening To The Wind*. San Diego, Calif.: Luna Media (now InnsFree Press, Philadelphia), 1990.

Eliot, Robert S., M.D. *From Stress to Strength: How to Lighten Your Load and Save Your Life*. New York: Bantam Books, 1994.

Emmanuel. *Emmanuel's Book* and *Emanuel's Book II*. New York: Bantam Books, 1989.

Estes, Clarissa Pinkola, Ph.D. *Women Who Run with the Wolves*. New York: Ballantine Books, 1992.

Family Circle Magazine; 9/21/93, "Coping Style," pages 88-90.

Fast, Julius. *The Pleasure Book*. New York: Stein and Day, 1975.

Glamour Magazine, December 1993. "Stress: You don't have to live with it anymore," page 230.

Hanson, Peter G., M.D. *The Joy of Stress.* Kansas City: Andrews, McMeel & Parker, 1986.

Helmstetter, Shad. *Finding The Fountain of Youth Inside Yourself.* Thorndike, Maine: Thorndike Press, 1990.

Hirschman, Jane R., Carol H. Munter, Janae R. Hirschmann, and C. Peter Herman. *Overcoming Overeating.* New York: Fawcett Books, 1998.

Hochschild, Arlie. *The Second Shift.* New York: Avon, 1997.

Holland, Barbara. *Endangered Pleasures.* New York: Little Brown and Company, 1995.

Johnson, Robert A. *She.* New York: Religious Publishing Company (now HarperCollins), 1976.

Keen, Sam. *The Passionate Life: Stages of Loving.* New York: HarperCollins Publishers, 1983.

Leatz, Christine A. *Career Stress/Personal Stress: How to Stay Healthy in a High-Stress Environment.* New York: McGraw-Hill, 1992.

Lerner, Rokelle. *Living in the Comfort Zones.* Deerfield Beach, Florida: Health Communications, Inc., 1995.

————. *Affirmations For The Inner Child.* Deerfield Beach, Florida: Health Communications, Inc., 1990.

Mackoff, Barbara. *Leaving the Office Behind.* New York: Dell Publishing Co., 1984.

McGee-Cooper, Ann. *You Don't Have To Go Home From Work Exhausted!* New York: Bantam Books, 1962.

Ornstein, Robert, Ph.D., and David Sobel, M.D. *Healthy Pleasures.* Reading, Mass.: Addison-Wesley, 1989.

Robbins, Anthony. *Personal Power! How To Increase Your Energy* (tape).

Rodegast, Pat, and Judith Stanton, compilers. *The Choice for Love.* New York: Bantam Books, 1985

Rosenthal, Normal E., M.D. *Seasons Of The Mind: Why You Get the Winter Blues & What You Can Do About It.* New York: Bantam Books, 1989.

Roth, Geneen. *Why Weight? A Guide to Ending Compulsive Eating.* New York: Plume, 1993.

St. James, Elaine. *Simplify Your Life.* New York: Hyperion, 1994.

Sark. *Companion: How to Free Your Creative Spirit.* Berkeley, Calif.: Celestial Arts, 1991, 1998, 1999.

Venolia, Carol. *Healing Environments.* Berkeley, Calif.: Celestial Arts, 1988.

Wallace, Arnie, Ph.D. *Chocolate Ain't Enough . . . No More!* Solvang, Calif.: Challenger Press, 1991.

Walsch, Neale Donald. *Conversations with God, Books 1 and 2.* New York: G. P. Putnam's Sons, 1997.

Warshaw, Robin. "Make Time For What Matters." Cooking Light Magazine, Jan/Feb 1994, pages 40-44.

Wilson, Margery. *Double Your Energy and Live Without Fatigue.* Upper Saddle River, New Jersey: Prentice-Hall, Inc., 1967.

Woodman, Marion. *Addiction to Perfection.* Toronto: Inner City Books, 1982.

Wurtman, J., and M. Danbrot. *Managing Your Mind and Mood Through Food.* New York: Rawson Publishing Company, 1986.

ℐndex

Recipes are listed by main ingredients
(in bold type) and often by title.
When there is more than one page
number attributed to a recipe,
the actual page number of
the recipe is also in
bold type.

☽REACH FOR THE MOON

Llewellyn publishes hundreds of books on your favorite subjects!
To get these exciting books, including the ones on the following pages,
check your local bookstore or order them directly from Llewellyn.

Order by Phone
- Call toll-free within the U.S. and Canada, 1-800-THE MOON
- In Minnesota, call (651) 291-1970
- We accept VISA, MasterCard, and American Express

Order by Mail
- Send the full price of your order (MN residents add 7% sales tax) in U.S. funds, plus postage & handling to:

> **Llewellyn Worldwide**
> **P.O. Box 64383, Dept. K824-9**
> **St. Paul, MN 55164–0383, U.S.A.**

Postage & Handling
(For the U.S., Canada, and Mexico)
- $4.00 for orders $15.00 and under
- $5.00 for orders over $15.00
- No charge for orders over $100.00

We ship UPS in the continental United States. We ship standard mail to P. O. boxes. Orders shipped to Alaska, Hawaii, The Virgin Islands, and Puerto Rico are sent first-class mail. Orders shipped to Canada and Mexico are sent surface mail.

International orders: Airmail—add freight equal to price of each book to the total price of order, plus $5.00 for each non-book item (audio tapes, etc.).

Surface mail—Add $1.00 per item.

Allow 2 weeks for delivery on all orders.
Postage and handling rates subject to change.

Discounts
We offer a 20% discount to group leaders or agents. You must order a minimum of 5 copies of the same book to get our special quantity price.

Free Catalog
Get a free copy of our color catalog, *New Worlds of Mind and Spirit.* Subscribe for just $10.00 in the United States and Canada ($30.00 overseas, airmail). Many bookstores carry *New Worlds*—ask for it!

Visit our website at www.llewellyn.com for more information.

Mother Nature's Herbal
JUDY GRIFFIN, PH.D.

A Zuni American Indian swallows the juice of goldenrod flowers to ease his sore throat . . . an East Indian housewife uses the hot spices of curry to destroy parasites . . . an early American settler rubs fresh strawberry juice on her teeth to remove tartar. People throughout the centuries have enjoyed a special relationship with Nature and her many gifts. Now, with *Mother Nature's Herbal,* you can discover how to use a planet full of medicinal and culinary herbs through more than 200 recipes and tonics. Explore the cuisine, beauty secrets, and folk remedies of China, the Mediterranean, South America, India, Africa, and North America. The book will also teach you the specific uses of flower essences, chakra balancing, aromatherapy, essential oils, companion planting, organic gardening and theme garden designs.

ISBN 1-56718-340-9

7 x 10, 448 pp., 16-page color insert

$19.95

Sensuous Living
Expand Your Sensory Awareness

NANCY CONGER

*T*ake a wonderful journey into the most intense source of delight and pleasure humans can experience: the senses! Enjoying your sense of sight, sound, smell, taste, and touch is your birthright. Learn to treasure it with this guide to sensuous living.

Most of us revel in our senses unabashedly as children, but societal norms gradually train us to be too busy or disconnected from ourselves to savor them fully. By intentionally practicing sensuous ways of living, you can regain the art of finding beauty and holiness in simple things. This book provides activities to help you engage fully in life through your senses. Relish the touch of sun-dried sheets on your skin. Tantalize your palate with unusual foods and taste your favorites with a new awareness. Attune to tiny auditory pleasures that surround you, from the click of computer keys to raindrops hitting a window. Appreciate light, shadow, and color with an artist's eye.

Revel in the sensory symphony that surrounds you and live more fully. Practice the fun techniques in this book and heighten every moment of your life more—you're entitled!

ISBN 1-56718-160-0
6 x 9, 224 pp., illus.

$12.95

To order, call 1-800-THE MOON
Prices subject to change without notice

The Goddess Path
Myths, Invocations & Rituals

Patricia Monaghan

For some, the goddess is a private intellectual search, where they can speculate on her meaning in culture and myth. For others, she is an emotional construct, a way of understanding the varying voices of the emerging self. Then there are those for whom she is part of everyday ritual, honored in meditation and prayer. All are on the goddess path.

If you have never encountered the goddess outside your own heart, this book will introduce you to some of her manifestations. If you have long been on this path, it will provide prayers and rituals to stimulate your celebrations. *The Goddess Path* offers a creative approach to worship, one in which you can develop and ritualize your own distinctive connection to her many manifestations from around the world.

Includes invocations, myths, symbols, feasts and suggestions for invoking the following goddesses: Amaterasu (Self-Reflection); Aphrodite (Passion); Artemis (Protection); Athena (Strength); Brigid (Survival); the Cailleach (Power in Age); Demeter & Persephone (Initiation); Gaia (Abundance); Hathor (Affection); Hera (Dignity); Inanna (Inner Strength); Isis (Restorative Love); Kali (Freedom); Kuan-Yin (Mercy); the Maenads (Ecstasy); The Muses (Inspiration); Oshun (Healing); Paivatar (Release); Pomona (Joy); Saule & Saules Meita (Family Healing).

ISBN 1-56718-467-7
7½ x 9⅛, 288 pp., illus.

$14.95

To order, call 1-800-THE MOON
Prices subject to change without notice

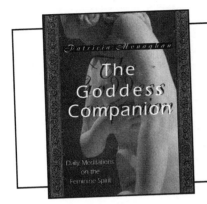

The Goddess Companion
Daily Meditations on the Feminine Spirit

Patricia Monaghan

Engage your feminine spirit each day of the year! Here are hundreds of authentic goddess prayers, invocations, chants and songs—one for each day of the year. They come from dozens of sources, ranging from the great classical European authors Ovid and Horace, to the marvelously passionate Hindu poets Ramprasad and Ramakrishna, to the anonymous gifted poets who first composed the folksongs of Lithuania, west Africa, and Alaska. In fresh, contemporary language that maintains the spirit of the originals, these prayers can be used for personal meditation, for private or public ritual, or for your own creative inspiration. They capture the depth of feeling, the philosophical complexity, and the ecological awareness of goddess cultures the world over. Organized as a daily meditation book, *The Goddess Companion* is also indexed by culture, goddess, and subject, so you can easily find prayers for specific purposes. Following each prayer is a thoughtfully written piece of prose by Patricia Monaghan which illustrates the aspects of the Goddess working in our everyday lives.

- A perpetual calendar with a daily reading on each page—366 in all
- Includes prayers from Greece, Rome, North and South America, Lithuania, Latvia, Japan, Finland, Scandinavia, India, and many others in translations that fully reveal their beauty, making them immediately accessible and emotionally powerful

ISBN 1-56718-463-4

7½ x 9⅛, 408 pp., bibliography, index

$17.95

To order, call 1-800-THE MOON

Prices subject to change without notice

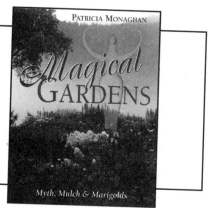

Magical Gardens
Myth, Mulch & Marigolds

PATRICIA MONAGHAN

*L*ike ancient alchemists, gardeners transform common materials—seed, soil, sun, and water—into the gold of beauty and nourishment. In the process, gardeners transform their own souls as well; time spent in the garden is a sacred time, a time of meditation and worship. For such gardeners, *Magical Gardens* offers insights in making a more conscious connection between soul and soil, between humus and the human spirit.

Plant an Angel Garden, which comes into its own in the moonlight, shining with its own secret radiance . . . or an Aphrodite's Bower, abundant with flowers and passion, crowded and dense with bloom . . . or a Sorcerer's Secret Garden, where in voluptuous privacy you can feel secure enough to envision utter freedom. Myths, meditations, and magical rituals are combined with garden plans that honor the old divinities and the old ways.

ISBN 1-56718-466-9
8½ x 11, 208 pp.

$17.95